ABC SPORTS COLLEGE FOOTBALL ALL-TIME ALL-AMERICA TEAM

FOREWORD BY **KEITH JACKSON** EDITED BY **MARK VANCIL**

HYPERION

NEW YORK

ABC SPORTS COLLEGE FOOTBALL ALL-TIME ALL-AMERICA TEAM

Edited by Mark Vancil

Copyright © 2000 by ABC Sports, Inc.

All rights reserved. No part of this book may be used or reproduced in any manner whatsoever without the written permission of the Publisher. Printed in the United States of America. For information address: Hyperion, 77 West 66th Street, New York, New York 10023-6298.

Library of Congress Cataloging-in-Publication Data

ISBN: 0-7868-6710-8

FIRST EDITION

10 9 8 7 6 5 4 3 2 1

PHOTOGRAPHY CREDITS

ABC SPORTS	7, 15, 25, 58, 63-65, 121
ALLSPORT	72, 73, 111
AP WORLDWIDE PHOTOS	54, 58, 72, 73, 105, 127, 137-139, 160
ARCHIVE PHOTOS	58, 75, 77, 80, 84
JAMIE BAHR / ALLSPORT	152
ROBERT BECK / ICON SPORTS MEDIA INC.	101
AL BELLO / ALLSPORT	59, 89, 96
JOHN BIEVER / SPORTS ILLUSTRATED	34, 170, 173
JOHN BREYER / SPORTS ILLUSTRATED	57
CHANCE BROCKWAY	46, 50, 59, 98, 102, 144, 145, 147-149, 154, 156, 166, 172-175
RICHARD CLARKSON / SPORTS ILLUSTRATED	34
STEVE COLE	58, 59
CORBIS/BETTMAN	6, 8-14, 16-30, 32, 33, 35, 36, 40, 42, 44, 45, 48, 53, 58, 59, 67, 69, 77, 91, 103, 107, 123, 124, 126, 127, 137, 143, 144, 165
COTTON BOWL ARCHIVE	41, 83
J. D. CUBAN / ALLSPORT	111
SCOTT CUNNINGHAM	58, 123, 128, 129
JONATHON DANIEL / ALLSPORT	59, 149, 153, 175
TIM DEFRISCO / ALLSPORT	25, 71
JAMES DRAKE / SPORTS ILLUSTRATED	43
TONY DUFFY / ALLSPORT	71
STEPHEN DUNN / ALLSPORT	48, 97, 111
DAVID DUROCHIK / SPORTPICS	49, 91
RIC FOGEL / SPORTFOLIO	90, 142
BILL FRAKES / SPORTS ILLUSTRATED	57
SCOTT HALLERAN / ALLSPORT	74, 114
ANDY HAYT / SPORTS ILLUSTRATED	58, 137, 140
JOHN IACONO / SPORTS ILLUSTRATED	123, 166
ICON SPORTS MEDIA INC.	158, 159
WALTER IOOSS, JR.	4, 59-62
WALTER IOOSS, JR. / SPORTS ILLUSTRATED	34, 49, 57, 59, 89, 93, 161, 174
JED JACOBSON / ALLSPORT	111
MARK KAUFMAN / SPORTS ILLUSTRATED	1
HEINZ KLUETMEIER / SPORTS ILLUSTRATED	113
DAVID KLUTHO / SPORTS ILLUSTRATED	34
MARK LANGELLO / SPORTFOLIO	171
NEIL LEIFER	47, 54, 55, 59, 106, 107, 124, 125, 167-169, 176
NEIL LEIFER / SPORTS ILLUSTRATED	76, 169
CARYN LEVY / ALLSPORT	157
BILL LUSTER / SPORTS ILLUSTRATED	135
ANDY LYONS / ALLSPORT	114
RICHARD MACKSON / SPORTS ILLUSTRATED	65, 86, 87
JOHN MCDONOUGH / SPORTS ILLUSTRATED	12, 37
RICHARD MEEK / SPORTS ILLUSTRATED	38
AL MESSERSCHMIDT	136
PETER READ MILLER / SPORTS ILLUSTRATED	142
ANTHONY NESTE / SPORTS ILLUSTRATED	12
NOTRE DAME UNIVERSITY	118, 132, 134
PENN STATE UNIVERSITY	143
MICKEY PFLEGER / SPORTS ILLUSTRATED	63, 64
MIKE POWELL / ALLSPORT	71, 72
BOB ROSATO / SPORTS ILLUSTRATED	119, 120
ROSE BOWL ARCHIVE	39
MANNY RUBIO / SPORTS ILLUSTRATED	58, 75, 79
BILL SMITH / SPORTS ILLUSTRATED	102
SPORTFOLIO	58, 89, 90, 91
SPORTING NEWS	117
SPORTS ILLUSTRATED	31, 36, 37, 43, 52, 56, 58, 59, 66, 76-78, 81, 82, 85, 89, 94, 95, 100, 103, 108, 109, 111-113, 123, 132, 133, 136, 141, 162-164
ALLEN STEELE / ALLSPORT	146, 150
DAMIAN STROHMEYER	12, 46, 59, 149, 151, 153
AL TIELEMANS / SPORTS ILLUSTRATED	109, 114, 162
TONY TOMSIC / SPORTSCHROME	70
UNIVERSITY OF COLORADO	158
UNIVERSITY OF GEORGIA	122, 159
UNIVERSITY OF MARYLAND	126
UNIVERSITY OF PITTSBURGH	99
UNIVERSITY OF SOUTHERN CALIFORNIA	58, 59, 89, 92, 96, 97, 110, 149, 155
UNIVERSITY OF WASHINGTON	130, 131
KEN WHITE / ALLSPORT	170
JOHN WILLIAMSON / ALLSPORT	59, 68, 69, 88, 103, 115, 116, 117
JOHN ZIMMERMAN / SPORTS ILLUSTRATED	2, 3

For my grandparents, Sam and Mary Kathryn Mabel
No life has been so blessed as that which they have touched

MV 2000

For all the lists, teams and all-time bests spawned by the new millennium virtually none of them could escape the one flaw common to such arrangements: Context. In the case of college football, the inability to connect players from one era to another is born from the evolution of the game itself and the fact its roots extend to the 19th century.

No one knows that better than ABC Sports which in 1966 became the first network to televise a full slate of national games. The year is significant because the game played then is essentially the same game played in 2000. The two-platoon system, which came into vogue with the abolition of complicated and sometimes comical substitution rules, created the platform for specialists, more complicated offensive and defensive systems and ultimately a game that in its complexity and sophistication mirrors the professional version.

The ABC Sports All-Time All-America Team is comprised of players from 1966 through the 1999 seasons selected by a 29-member Blue Ribbon Panel of ABC Sports experts. In an attempt to reflect the changes in defenses, offenses and special teams, we added an additional player to the defense and offense at the expense of a kick return specialist which did not become a position on the NCAA consensus All-America teams until 1993.

But the team is unique for another very important reason: Not only were all the panelists alive during this 33-season era, but most of them saw these players compete — usually in person. Some of them such as Pepper Rodgers and Frank Broyles were among the greatest coaches of the last half-century. Others such as Keith Jackson, Chris Schenkel and Bill Flemming lent a presence to the college game that in turn grew its popularity coast-to-coast. Still others such as Tim Brandt, Gary Danielson, Dean Blevins, Dan Fouts, Bob Griese and Lynn Swann played college football during the period.

Their selections will no doubt invite scrutiny and debate, the interaction around which sport has always revolved. In the case of college football, it's only fitting ABC Sports would lead the discussion.

××××××

For a generation, Keith Jackson has been among the most beloved voices of sport in America. Long before he became recognized as the voice of college football, Jackson covered virtually every major event around the globe. And like the best of his fraternity, the warmth, character and passion that define his work are fundamental to the man.

As with the interaction with Chris Schenkel, Bill Flemming and others, our time with Keith smoothed an otherwise impossible schedule. He looked out for us when he had no obligation to do so and lent his time when we had no right to request it. These are people whose presence will forever be a part of the collective memory, not just because of how they plied their craft but because of the men they have always been when the camera went dark. They are from a generation, the greatest of all some say, which stamped a sense of duty, honor and integrity on an entire country. Our experience mirrored those thoughts.

For someone who grew up listening to them and watching the games they described, their kindness throughout this project was beyond expectation and never to be forgotten.

××××××

For more than seven consecutive weeks at Rare Air Media, the nights turned into days and the days back into nights with little notice. John Vieceli, whose brilliance is matched only by his passion, coordinated a project that virtually everyone — including our clients at Hyperion and ABC Sports — considered impossible. Along with Steve Polacek, who never once backed down, Liz Fulton and everyone else at Rare Air Media, specifically Shereen Boury, Mark Alper, Melinda Fry, Dennis Carlson, Carol Scatorchio and Jim Forni, John led a race to produce excellence against a clock with very little available time.

They found thousands of images from dozens of sources all over North America. In the case of John and Steve, they worked around the clock for more than 30 straight days. They caught naps in sleeping bags on the wood floors beneath the hum of computers. Liz contacted more than 40 schools, ran down notes, facts and photographs and coordinated contact with virtually everyone. Melinda and Dennis worked to manipulate a deadline that defied reason while Jim kept the entire company rolling amid a steady stream of flights, meetings and presentations.

Meanwhile, Steve Richardson and his group conducted more than 40 interviews and pieced together a brief on college football's elaborate history. Without Steve's unique combination of reputation and work ethic, this book would not have happened. Not even the most unreasonable request at the most unreasonable hour elicited anything more than a simple response, 'I'm on it.'

At Hyperion, Bob Miller, Martha Levin and Gretchen Young managed to steer the project through the storm of doubts and deadlines. Gretchen's guidance, help and support were critical given the demands of not just this project, but all the others she balanced simultaneously. I also want to thank David Lott and Natalie Kaire for their important work behind the scenes.

At ABC Sports, the input and assistance came from the top down. Howard Katz, Bob Apter, Cynthia Vannoy, Kelly Drinkwine, Mark Mandel and Ben Keeperman disrupted their schedules to respond with little advance warning. Also, special thanks to those who helped to keep the promotion and programming initiatives alive — Teri Wagner at ABC Sports, Andy Sippel at ESPN The Magazine, Larry Fried and Sean Hanrahan at ESPN ABC Sports Customer Marketing and Sales. Given the day-to-day business of running a network, the input and consideration spoke to their commitment.

SPECIAL THANKS

Ken Leiker, Mike McKenzie, Ron Higgins, Bud Withers, Cody Monk, Kevin Rettig, Prem Kalliat, Chance Brockway, Walter Iooss, Jr., David Durochik, Neil and Howie Leifer

At the SBC Cotton Bowl: Charlie Fiss

At the Tostitos Fiesta Bowl: Shawn Schoeffler

At Central Florida Press: Larry Liotta, Nicole Carrington

At Professional Graphics: Pat, Steve, and David Goley, Vince Llamzon

At Rare Air Media: Andrew Pipitone, John Arthurs, Paul Sheridan, Esq.

At Home: Laurita, Alexandra and Samantha

CONTENTS

KEITH JACKSON

It was 1966 and the leadership of the American Broadcasting Company made the decision to spend the money necessary to acquire exclusive television broadcast rights for Division I college football games.

The amount of money was miniscule compared to the fiscal madness that exists in the 21st century. But the point to be made is that one network had the nerve in the middle 1960s to go get the game and do something with it.

In the 34 seasons leading to 2000, ABC Sports televised 1,790 college football games nationally and/or regionally, including the post-season. That means ABC has invested more money, time and energy in college football than any other media. The return on that investment has not been all that great financially, but there is more involved with this game than just money. The game and all the ancillary activities add up to something that defies dollar value. There is the vitality of regeneration every time people of all ages return to the campus for the weekly festival. It's continuity, pride, a sense of belonging. It's roots. And ABC Sports has done considerable work on this game that reaches into every crevice of our society.

Growing up on that reluctant farmland along the Alabama—Georgia state line, professional football and basketball were not a part of my world. Surviving was a prime concern because a couple years after I arrived the Great Depression hit the nation. A decade later, it was World War II.

But despite those trying times, sport persisted in the pastures, on the prairies, in the parks and up and down streets all over America. Back in those days, Major League Baseball was played in just 10 northern and midwestern cities, if you count Brooklyn part of New York City.

Everywhere else, college football was king!

Which very well may explain why the game carries such deep feelings and traditions. Football provided momentary relief in the hard times. People used to enduring had no trouble understanding the basics of the game. Football consists of having the strength and will to endure while exercising opportunity. Failing your opportunity just meant hunkering down and waiting for another one. Sometimes it got dark before the next chance presented itself and you lost the contest.

Years later I heard a city fella on the radio call the game simple — merely the act of acquiring real estate and then protecting your acquisition. Well, basically he was right, but when some of us were growing up we couldn't spell acquisition, never thought about it and if somebody mentioned it, Gramma probably would have offered 'em a mustard poultice.

I know all us "old timers" like to carry on about the old days, but if our taxes are paid, we're allowed. Every time I blow the dust off the history books and wander across those pages of the past, I am astounded at the people from those early years, the coaches and the players. The people who really laid the foundation and poured the cement for the future.

You want the names? Stagg, Yost, Bryant, Wilkinson, Robinson, Royal, Neyland, Wade, Warner, Crisler, Rockne, Blaik, Broyles, Thomas, Hayes, Schembechler, Bierman, Jones, Alexander, Leahy, Parseghian, Little and on and on.

Down in the coal country of West Virginia there is one small region that gave us three fine coaches: John McKay, ex-Southern California, Frank Kush, ex-Arizona State and Don Nehlen, coaching into 2000 at West Virginia University.

Some little tidbits you might find interesting: Gus Dorais, who was the quarterback who threw the ball to Knute Rockne and led Notre Dame out of anonymity in 1914 with a huge victory over the mighty Black Knights of Army at West Point, coached for a time at Gonzaga. He actually took 'em to a bowl game on Christmas Day, 1922. Gonzaga lost to West Virginia 21-13 in the San Diego Christmas Classic. Dorais also had a fine coaching career at the University of Detroit. Funny thing, neither school plays football anymore. Gonzaga quit in 1941 and never went back to it after the war. Detroit quit in 1964. Rockne you must know about. If you don't, then you probably should go on to another subject. Incidentally, Rockne wanted the Notre Dame football team to be called the Ramblers. And Rockne, who was a native son of Norway, always had the name his mother gave him mispronounced. The correct pronunciation is Kuh-Nute, not Noot. So much for that old show-biz line about just spelling the name right.

One of the best locker-room speeches ever might have come from Paul Bryant when he needed something profound before his "Lil ole boys"

stomach. That probably contributed to ostrich becoming an entrée.

In 1916, the Tournament of Roses organizers fully realized they had a chance to make their festival into an extravaganza and they brought back a college football matchup featuring Brown from the East and Washington State from the West. Washington State won 14-0, though it was still a college back then coached by Bill "Lone Star" Dietz, who had graduated from Carlisle in 1912. The use of the game as the finale to a civic celebration worked and as more and more tourists came and left money, soon the Tournament of Roses was on its way to becoming one of the world's greatest annual celebrations.

To be sure, other cities were watching and learning.

Miami had the Palm Festival and while it was fine it needed a bigger finish. Up stepped a fella named Ernie Seiler from Selma, Alabama, who had been a collegiate athlete at Oklahoma A&M. Ernie was plenty quick and he came prepared with all the information of the success out West. The University of Miami had good teams then, which meant the host team would be at home with no travel expenses.

went out to play a bigger, faster and highly regarded Tennessee team. Bear walked in, looked at 'em as he walked through and just as he was leaving said, "Boys, be brave." They won the game.

Obviously many things had impact on the evolution of college football, but at the core of every turn there is and always has been the old greenback. The years following World War II were particularly dramatic for growth and expanded the horizons for an entire nation. It was the birthing time for the phenomenon we simply call sport.

At the turn of the 20th century, the city of Pasadena, California, started a civic celebration which eventually became world-famous as the Tournament of Roses. The organizers thought they needed more than a concert in the park to finish their party, so they dared to bring coach Fielding Yost and his "Point-a-Minute" Michigan Wolverines out for a game against Stanford, judged the best of the West at the time.

Bad matchup. Michigan whupped 'em 49-0 and the Pasadena folks decided to try something else. There was a horse show finishing with chariot racing but with all the dust that night there was no repeat performance. Then somebody sold ostrich racing and that was kinda fun until one of the cranky birds kicked the festival chairman's wife in the

When you talked tourists in those days in Florida the first thought had to be New York, and sure enough Manhattan College had a powerhouse team called the Jaspers. Now keep in mind, the committee proposing this bold experiment didn't have deep pockets. And coach Chick Meehan made it very clear in the initial conversation he wanted $1,500 in hand before his team left Grand Central Station. Up steps sharp ol' Ernie again, suggesting that maybe we oughta invited the sheriff of Dade County to join the Festival Committee. The sheriff, as the legend goes, then invites any number of shadowy citizens to make civic contributions for the cause and, in short order, Coach Meehan had his money and was on his way to Miami.

Miami won the game 7-0 and the folks in Miami knew they had found their finale. On January 1, 1935, the first Orange Bowl game was played. Bucknell beat Miami 26-0.

The first Sugar Bowl game was played in New Orleans in 1935. Tulane, in its own stadium, beat Temple 20-14. The Sugar Bowl game was played in Tulane Stadium through 1974 when Nebraska beat Florida 13-10. I covered that game with Barry Switzer, Oklahoma's coach at the time, as my color commentator.

The Cotton Bowl came into being in 1937 on the Texas State Fairgrounds in Dallas with TCU beating Marquette 16-6. For years those games were the Big Four and vital elements in substantial civic celebrations. We should note that the folks of El Paso actually held the Sun Bowl a year before the Cotton started in Dallas. Hardin-Simmons and New Mexico State played to a 14-14 tie. Point to be made here, these post-season events added mightily to the image and growth of college football as a marketable product and fertilized the eternal argument for a national playoff.

As part of this evolution of college athletics, the All-America team rose in stature. It was started by Walter Camp, the man who is considered the father of the game. His first All-America team was chosen in 1889 and included five Tigers from Princeton, three Elis from Yale and three lads in Crimson from Harvard. One of the ends on that team was A. Alonzo Stagg and the quarterback from Princeton was named Edgar Allan Poe. A guard, William W. Heffelfinger, alias "Pudge," became the first three-time All-American.

The first non—Ivy League player chosen by Camp was C. B. Herschberger

All-America team. Chosen by all the announcers and commentators who have worked televised games since 1966, you now have a panel consisting of people picking players who actually have seen them play the game!

No panel can pick a team upon which everybody will agree. That's not possible anytime, but especially now. And there are rules changes that affect the play of certain types of athletes. For example, if offensive linemen still had to keep their hands tucked into their bodies you wouldn't have so many 300-pounders playing up front. Freeing their arms helped the passing game. Being allowed to push helps protect quarterbacks. The specialization that exists today where there are players for certain circumstances has dramatically changed the game and in some instances a truly gifted athlete can play both ways. The scholarship limit of 85 players has been a factor in some players playing both offense and defense. Few teams actually have 85 players unless their conference rules allows them to "over recruit" assuming a certain amount of attrition will occur annually.

As you read and debate our choices on these pages, you should know there are some of us who don't feel it is essential that an All-America

in 1898 out of the University of Chicago. Walter Camp had been a halfback at Yale (1876-1881), which probably explains some of the Ivy League dominance in the early days. The second non—Ivy League player was Isaac Seneca of Carlisle in 1899. The first "western" player was William Heston, a Michigan halfback (1903-04). The first "southern" player Camp chose was a center from Georgia Tech, Ashel Day, in 1918.

Walter Camp died in 1925, but his name lives on through the Walter Camp Foundation in New Haven, Connecticut. The Walter Camp award is given annually in recognition of the top offensive back in the country at a very festive awards dinner on the Yale campus.

By the time of Camp's death, sportswriter Grantland Rice was prominent enough to succeed Camp as the national writer picking the All-America team. Right off, Rice chose two players from the real West — Ernie Nevers of Stanford and George Wilson of Washington. All-America teams haven't been the same since.

The Associated Press joined in 1936 with its own team and numerous others followed. The American Football Coaches Association picked its first team in 1946. There must be 900 different All-America teams chosen these days and, frankly, we felt it might be a fair time for ABC Sports to have its

college football player ever played in the NFL.

For a life well lived, what you are doing when you are 40 years of age is obviously more important than what you were doing at 20. But when you are an All-America college football player, your mountain may not be as high as the ones other people face later in life.

Being chosen All-America is important, but being remembered as an All-American. . . that is really special.

Enjoy the book.

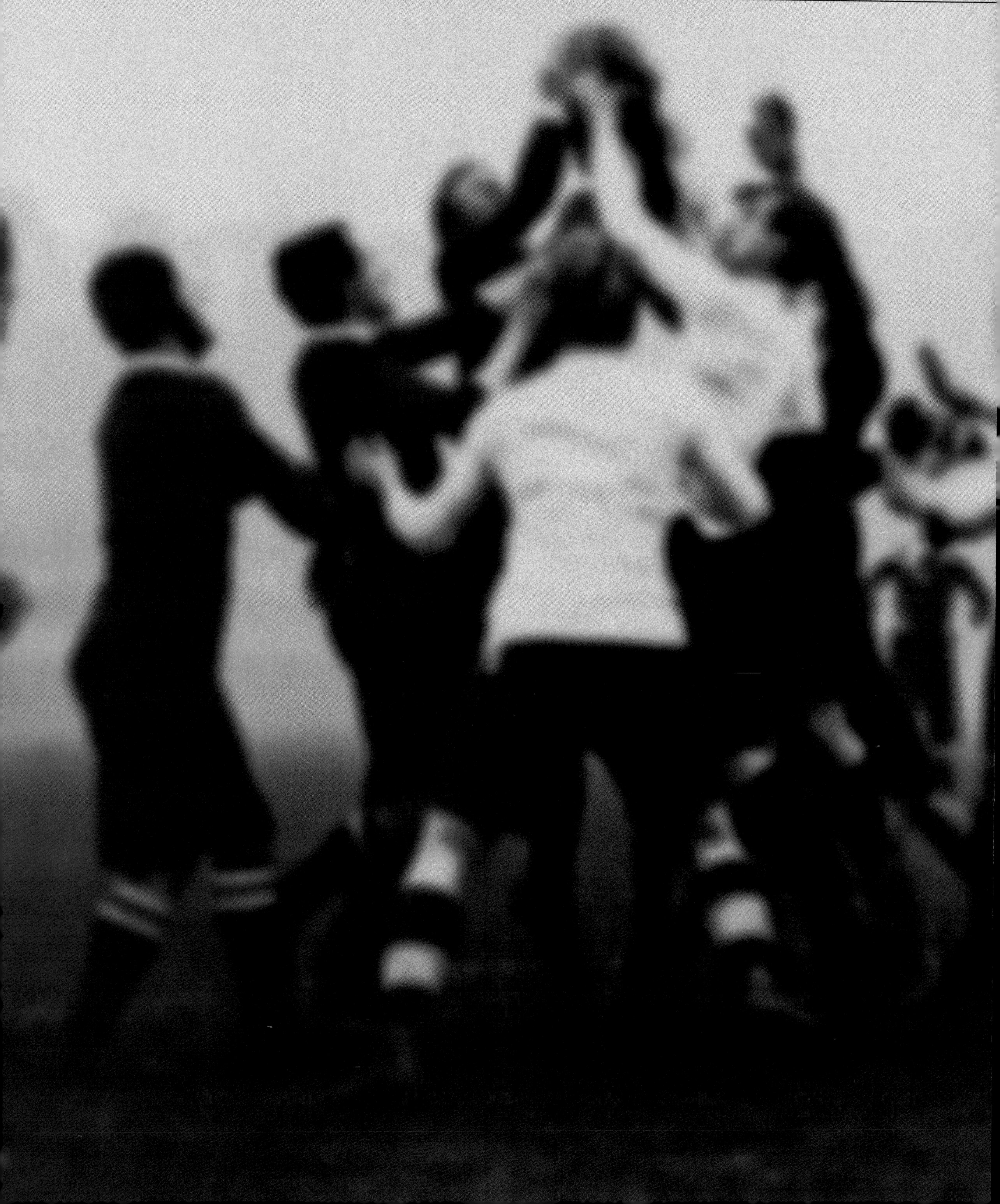

CHAPTER ONE

O N A COOL AFTERNOON IN THE SHADOW OF FALLING LEAVES, A GROUP OF YOUNG MEN GATHERED AT THE COMMONS ON THE CAMPUS OF RUTGERS UNIVERSITY. THE GAME THEY WOULD PLAY THAT DAY HAD 25 MEN TO A SIDE AND WOULD RESEMBLE SOCCER MORE THAN FOOTBALL. THAT MUCH, AND NOT A WHOLE LOT MORE, HAD BEEN DECIDED BY THE STUDENTS FROM RUTGERS AND PRINCETON, ALL OF THEM IN STREET CLOTHES AND LITTLE ELSE SAVE FOR A FEW FASHION FORWARD RUTGERS PLAYERS SPORTING SCARLET STOCKING CAPS. THEY HAD CONVENED TO PLAY A GAME THEY CALLED FOOTBALL. THOUGH LITTLE ELSE IN THE WAY OF PROCEDURE WOULD CARRY THE CENTURY, THE TEAMS AGREED THAT A COIN FLIP WOULD DECIDE WHO RECEIVED THE BALL FIRST. THE LOSER WOULD BE FORCED TO DELIVER THE BALL BY KICKING IT OFF A TEE, ANOTHER SURVIVOR IN THE GAME'S ENSUING EVOLUTION. ALL ELSE BORE ONLY PASSING RESEMBLANCE TO A GAME THAT DOMINATES THE FALL

"FOOTBALL IS A GAME OF CONTROLLED ANGER. IT IS A GAME OF RETRIBUTION. IT'S ABOUT WILL. THAT'S WHY THE WORK ETHIC OF FOOTBALL IS SO IMPORTANT. THAT'S WHY THE STRUCTURE OF THE GAME IS SO IMPORTANT. EVERYBODY ADMITS THAT THE GAME HAS SOME THUGGERY, NO QUESTION. IT'S A GAME OF CONTROLLED ANGER THAT INVITES RETALIATION, INVITES BULLIES. BUT IT'S ALSO A GAME THAT HUMBLES BULLIES. IT IS A GAME IN WHICH A LITTLE GUY 5-FEET-7-INCHES, 150 POUNDS CAN CAST THE WINNING STONE. WILL, DESIRE

TIMELINE ▶

THE FIRST "FOOTBALL" GAME IS PLAYED	THE FIRST HARVARD–YALE GAME	NEW RULES: LINE OF SCRIMMAGE AND 11 MEN TO A SIDE
18 69	18 76	18 80

CHAPTER I   **13**

On Nov. 6, 1869, the game commenced with each side's captain monitoring the scoring area. There were no touchdowns, field goals or defensive safeties. They counted goals, which accumulated at a point apiece. Offense, or what passed for offense, had no passing or running. The ball advanced — such as it was — with a kicker being led down field by Bulldogs, forerunners to offensive linemen. Fielders, or defensive players, essentially guarded specific parts of the field. All scoring came via a kick through what resembled goal posts. If the game looked like soccer, then the scoring looked more like tennis. Rutgers was declared the victor by scoring six goals first. Princeton finished with four. Though birth would follow at its own pace, college football had been conceived.

From this basic structure evolved one of the most sophisticated team sports ever devised and a uniquely American one at that. Pass offenses with five-inch-thick play books, defenses that move players according to the slightest offensive set, blocking schemes that resemble hieroglyphics when diagrammed on paper and specialists who do everything from snap the ball from center to holding for field goals now define the

WALTER CAMP
THE FATHER OF AMERICAN FOOTBALL

who played until they dropped on afternoons between classes at Ivy League schools. The game was born in the Northeast among the upper crust. Princeton, Yale, Harvard and Penn helped transform college football from a soccer-like contest into something more in line with traditional rugby. Testing one's manhood seemed to be as much the point as winning the contest. Indeed, there were few rules mandating violence.

Slowly, the college game moved from a rugged, run-oriented contest to one that included the forward pass and, eventually, thanks to rules changes and unlimited substitution, an age of specialists.

College football's giant in the early days was Walter Camp, whose nickname "The Father of American Football" is secure even today. A captain at Yale from 1878-81, Camp played in the first Harvard–Yale game in 1876 and later coached the school's football team. An accomplished swimmer and baseball player, Camp was credited with establishing the first All-America team in 1889 and, after the turn of the century, helped create the forerunner of the National Collegiate Athletic Association, which would initially establish playing rules.

PERHAPS THE ONLY ELEMENT OF COLLEGE FOOTBALL THAT HASN'T CHANGED IS THE SHEER

BRUTALITY

game at even the high school level.

Perhaps the only element of college football that hasn't changed from those early days is the sheer brutality born of large men slamming into one another. For all the changes in the speed, size, physical condition and strength of modern-day players, the college football game of the late 20th century is something less than its dangerous predecessor. Rules changes, highly engineered light-weight padding, shock-absorbent helmets and a constant shuttle of players in and out of the game has mitigated the depth of physical toll players experienced in the early years.

What is now a highly detailed game of chess once amounted to hand-to-hand combat. College football was a game of survival for gentlemen turned weekend warriors

Camp's passion and knowledge put him in the middle of the game's development on and off the field. For nearly 45 years until his death in 1925, Camp defined the parameters of the game we see today. In 1880, the Rules Committee, under Camp's direction, established a line of scrimmage and 11 men to each side. Two years later, he encouraged rules stipulating three downs and a distance of five yards to retain possession of the ball. An umpire was added in 1887, a head linesman in 1894 to go with a referee. And in 1896, at the urging of doctors, coaches and players alike, soft leather helmets were added, though not mandatory. With the two-platoon system still decades away, college football was moving forward on the brute force of its players.

| UMPIRE ADDED | WALTER CAMP ESTABLISHED THE FIRST ALL-AMERICA TEAM | HEAD LINESMAN ADDED TO GO WITH A REFEREE | SOFT LEATHER HELMETS ARE ADDED |

18|87   18|89   18|94   18|96

"COLLEGE FOOTBALL HAS TO BE THE GREATEST GAME.

RUTGERS AND PRINCETON WERE PLAYING WHEN U.S. GRANT WAS IN THE WHITE HOUSE. OTHER TEAMS HAVE BEEN PLAYING EACH OTHER SINCE GROVER CLEVELAND WAS PRESIDENT. AT THE MICHIGAN–OHIO STATE GAME IF YOU EXCHANGED UNIFORMS AT HALF TIME, THE FANS WOULD STILL ROOT FOR THE UNIFORMS. PEOPLE WHO FOLLOW COLLEGE FOOTBALL ARE LIKE WALTER MITTY. THEY LOOK BACK AND WISH THEY HAD BEEN THE SATURDAY HERO, WHICH TO ME ALWAYS HAS BEEN MORE GLAMOROUS THAN BEING THE SUNDAY HERO. COLLEGE FOOTBALL HAS TO BE THE GREATEST GAME."

— BEANO COOK former ABC Sports announcer

"In the old games, it was a matter of will and how tough you were," recounts R. C. Slocum, Texas A&M coach. "You would slug it out until the end. It was not a high-speed contest. It was who could hang in there the longest. Now, the speed of the game is greater at the end because you have fresher players."

The "Flying Wedge" defined the brutality of the early college game. The biggest and strongest offensive players would form a moving "wedge" to shield a ballcarrier. They would attack the defense as quickly as possible, large men slamming into one another with elbows, knees and fists flying. With little protective gear, the sight of blood, broken bones and unconscious players was typical.

The Harvard–Yale game in 1894 epitomized the violence. Nicknamed the "Hampden Park Blood Bath," four regular players on each side suffered serious injuries in Yale's 12-4 victory over the Crimson. Yale tackle Fred Murphy was knocked unconscious for five hours. One player had a broken back, another lost an eye and still another would end up having a leg removed because of an

"FLYING WEDGE"

injury sustained that day. The horror of those injuries led to the brief termination of that series and others in the 1890s. Yale and Harvard didn't play football again until 1897. Meanwhile, the Army–Navy series, every bit as dangerous as the Harvard–Yale rivalry, suspended play from 1894 through 1898 because of the injuries reported in the 1893 game between the two academies.

Not surprisingly, most rules common to the order of today's game didn't exist. There were no limits on college eligibility, which allowed Camp to play six seasons for Yale. Schools and coaches determined when, where and how many games they wished to play. And despite the lack of protective equipment in a game built on man-to-man combat, back-to-back games were common.

On April 20 and 21 in 1888, Michigan and Notre Dame played consecutive days on the Notre Dame campus with the Fighting Irish winning both. In 1899, Sewanee, a small Episcopal school located in the Tennessee mountains, played 12 teams and shut out 11 of them, including a five-game, six-day stretch through three states. Sewanee traveled 2,500 miles via Pullman Special for a five-game swing that took the team through Texas, Louisiana and back to Tennessee. Sewanee shut out five schools—Texas, Texas A&M, Tulane, LSU and Ole Miss (University of Mississippi) — by a combined score of 91-0. Even more amazing was the fact that just 15 of the team's 21 players played in the games.

"That remains one of the most staggering achievements in the history of sport," says Joe Paterno, Penn State coach.

Sewanee, now the University of the South and a Division III school, became a charter member of the Southeastern Conference in 1933. In 1940, after compiling an 0-37 record in league games, the school withdrew.

But it was Camp's Yale team, along with Princeton and the University of Pennsylvania, that formed the first dynasties in college football. From 1876-1909, Yale won 93.4 percent of its games. Princeton won 90 percent of its games from 1877-1903, while Penn claimed an 87.5 winning percentage from 1894-1908.

"I think it's the spirit of college football that makes the game so great," says Chris Schenkel, former ABC Sports announcer. "It started in the Ivy League and it was great because it brought young people and their families together. In 1946, I did the first television game with Harvard. So I always had a great sense of the Ivy League. Years later, Frank Broyles and I did a Dartmouth–Princeton game for ABC. He never had done an Ivy League game and I think he resented going. It turned out to be a great game

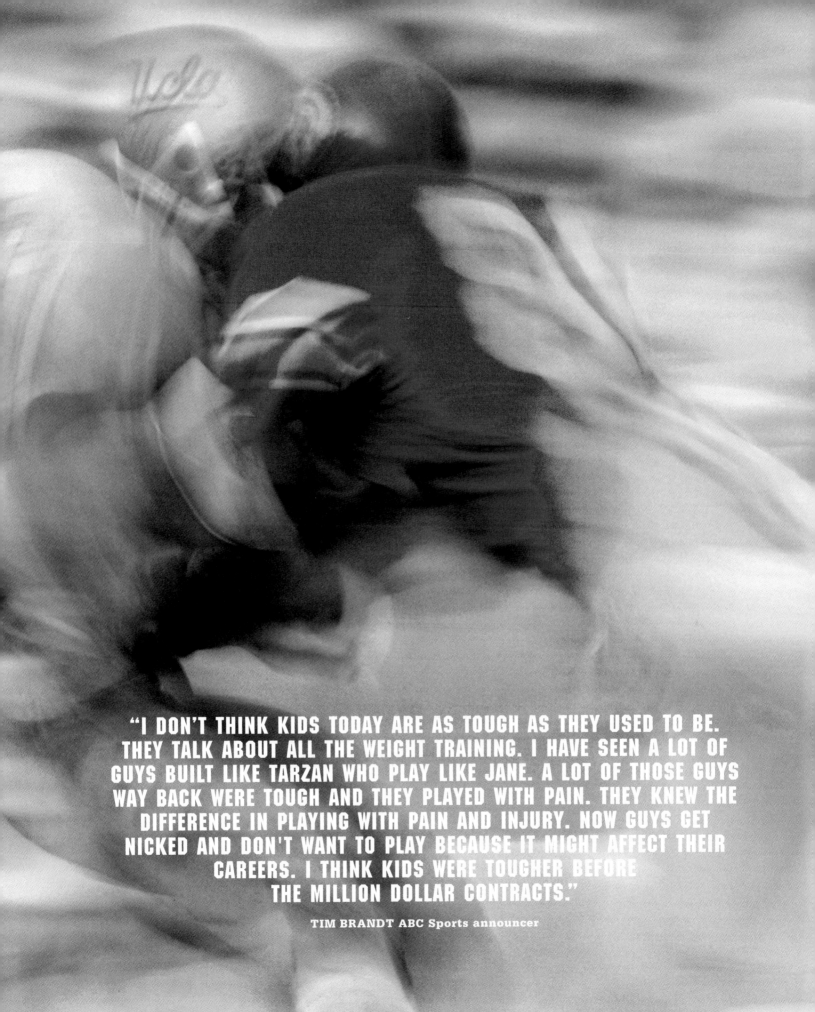

"I DON'T THINK KIDS TODAY ARE AS TOUGH AS THEY USED TO BE. THEY TALK ABOUT ALL THE WEIGHT TRAINING. I HAVE SEEN A LOT OF GUYS BUILT LIKE TARZAN WHO PLAY LIKE JANE. A LOT OF THOSE GUYS WAY BACK WERE TOUGH AND THEY PLAYED WITH PAIN. THEY KNEW THE DIFFERENCE IN PLAYING WITH PAIN AND INJURY. NOW GUYS GET NICKED AND DON'T WANT TO PLAY BECAUSE IT MIGHT AFFECT THEIR CAREERS. I THINK KIDS WERE TOUGHER BEFORE THE MILLION DOLLAR CONTRACTS."

TIM BRANDT ABC Sports announcer

and after it was over fans moved down onto the field in an orderly fashion. The whole field was covered with friends and family and players. Don Shula's son was down there, Jack Kemp's son was in the game. Frank never had seen anything like that before and he asked me what was going on. I told him that's the way it is in the Ivy League."

The greatest of the early players might have been Yale's 6-foot-3-inch, 205-pound guard William "Pudge" Heffelfinger (1888-91), the first three-time All-America as chosen by Camp. David Nelson, in his book *Anatomy of a Game*, described the Yale giant this way: "At the beginning of the decade (1890s), a new strategy developed wherein a blocker would lead the ballcarrier through the line and around the ends. One hundred years later this technique is still a major part of offensive football. . . Heffelfinger would push, pull and block his way through the line and around the end, while reaching back to grab the runner by the rings of the belt and pull him through the hole."

"PUDGE" HEFFELFINGER
YALE FOOTBALL

In Heffelfinger's first season, Yale scored 694 points and shut out all 13 opponents. A player named Amos Alonzo Stagg, later the great coach and innovator at the University of Chicago, was an end on that Yale team.

In those days, Michigan became the leader among the so-called "Western" teams as the game's popularity in the East began to migrate West. In 1879, Michigan became the first college football team west of the Allegheny Mountains to play football. Two years later, Michigan played the first intersectional schedule when it headed East and lost to Harvard, Yale and Princeton during a period of five days. It took another 13 years, but Michigan became the first "Western" team to defeat an Eastern power when the Wolverines knocked off Cornell 12-4 in 1894.

That was only the beginning of Michigan's compelling football heritage. From 1901 to 1905, Michigan established itself as a national power by going undefeated 56 straight games under the guidance of coach Fielding H. Yost. The Wolverines went 55-0-1 during the streak and outscored opponents by a staggering 2,831-40 margin. Not only did Michigan average more than 50 points, but its opponents averaged less than a point per contest.

Michigan's streak was interrupted in 1903 against Minnesota in a game that ended in a 6-6 tie. Still, the streak continued for nearly two full years until Stagg's University of Chicago team knocked off Michigan 2-0 on a safety before a crowd of 25,791 at Marshall Field, at the time the largest audience for a college football game outside of the East.

"At the heights in the '50s and '60s, schools would have nearly unlimited scholarships and stockpile players," said Merle Harmon, former ABC Sports announcer. "That was before the NCAA stepped in and put in scholarship and coaching staff limitations. But teams in the early days sometimes had only 10 to 15 players, who played all the time. How many guys did Stagg and all of those older coaches have appear on the field?"

★ MICHIGAN TRADITION ★

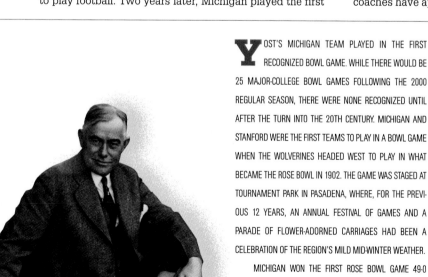

YOST'S MICHIGAN TEAM PLAYED IN THE FIRST RECOGNIZED BOWL GAME. WHILE THERE WOULD BE 25 MAJOR-COLLEGE BOWL GAMES FOLLOWING THE 2000 REGULAR SEASON, THERE WERE NONE RECOGNIZED UNTIL AFTER THE TURN INTO THE 20TH CENTURY. MICHIGAN AND STANFORD WERE THE FIRST TEAMS TO PLAY IN A BOWL GAME WHEN THE WOLVERINES HEADED WEST TO PLAY IN WHAT BECAME THE ROSE BOWL IN 1902. THE GAME WAS STAGED AT TOURNAMENT PARK IN PASADENA, WHERE, FOR THE PREVIOUS 12 YEARS, AN ANNUAL FESTIVAL OF GAMES AND A PARADE OF FLOWER-ADORNED CARRIAGES HAD BEEN A CELEBRATION OF THE REGION'S MILD MID-WINTER WEATHER.

MICHIGAN WON THE FIRST ROSE BOWL GAME 49-0 AGAINST A STANFORD TEAM THAT INCLUDED GUARD WILLIAM ROOSEVELT, SECOND COUSIN OF PRESIDENT TEDDY ROOSEVELT. LIKE OTHERS DURING THAT TIME, WILLIAM ROOSEVELT PLAYED PART OF THE GAME WITH INJURIES THAT WOULD SIDELINE EVEN THE TOUGHEST FOOTBALL PLAYERS TODAY – A FRACTURED LEG AND THREE BROKEN RIBS.

WILLIE HESTON GAINED 170 YARDS ON 18 CARRIES, A ROSE BOWL RUSHING RECORD THAT STOOD FOR 57 YEARS. AND AN OVERFLOW CROWD OF MORE THAN 8,000 OCCUPIED AN AREA WITH ONLY 1,000 SEATS. THE ENSUING TRAFFIC JAMS AND STAMPEDE, PLUS THE FACT MICHIGAN SO DOMINATED THE GAME, CAUSED ORGANIZERS TO REVERT TO POLO THE FOLLOWING SEASON AND LATER CHARIOT RACES. THE FOOTBALL GAME EVENTUALLY RETURNED IN 1916 AND GAVE WAY TO THE NOTION OF DECIDING A TRUE NATIONAL CHAMPION WITH A SEASON-ENDING GAME – AN ARGUMENT THAT CONTINUES TO THIS DAY – PITTING TOP TEAMS FROM DIFFERENT PARTS OF THE COUNTRY.

INCIDENTALLY, MICHIGAN NEARLY BALKED AT PLAYING THE FIRST ROSE BOWL BECAUSE IT HAD BEEN PROVIDED ONLY $2 A DAY IN MEAL MONEY. WHEN THE ORGANIZERS INCREASED THE FEE TO $3, MICHIGAN RELENTED.

AMOS ALONZO STAGG BECAME THE ARCHITECT OF A GAME FOR WHICH WALTER CAMP HAD SUPPLIED THE ORIGINAL DRAWINGS. PERHAPS THE MOST CREATIVE AND INNOVATIVE COACH OF ANY ERA, STAGG TURNED THE UNIVERSITY OF CHICAGO INTO A NATIONAL POWER.

STAGG COACHED CHICAGO FOR 41 SEASONS STARTING IN 1892 AND WAS THE MOST INFLUENTIAL AND FORWARD THINKING MEMBER OF THE RULES COMMITTEE FOR 54 YEARS. WHILE COACHING AT THE SPRINGFIELD (MASS.) INTERNATIONAL YMCA COLLEGE IN 1891, STAGG IS CREDITED WITH PLAYING THE FIRST INDOOR FOOTBALL GAME AGAINST YALE, WHICH DEFEATED HIS TEAM 16-10. AND IN 1896, HE WAS THE FIRST TO INTRODUCE THE HUDDLE INDOORS AT CHICAGO STADIUM, LONG BEFORE IT WAS USED OUTDOORS. HE WAS AMONG THE FIRST TO UTILIZE THE TACKLING DUMMY. AND LEGENDARY NOTRE DAME COACH AND PLAYER KNUTE ROCKNE LATER GAVE STAGG CREDIT AS THE FIRST COACH TO USE THE SHIFT.

HE WAS THE FIRST TO INSTALL PRIORITY SEATING AT GAMES. HE DEVELOPED THE MAN IN MOTION. AND WHEN THEY CHANGED THE RULES ALLOWING PASSING IN 1906, HE STARTED ACCENTUATING SPEED AND QUICKNESS RATHER THAN BRUTE FORCE. HE ALSO REVOLUTIONIZED RECRUITING AND ESTABLISHED THE ATHLETIC DORM ON CAMPUS.

"Stagg had greater fluidity of conversation, a greater ability to express himself compared to Camp. Stagg studied for the ministry and if he hadn't been a football player, he would have been a preacher. The ministry had a profound influence on Amos. The reason he didn't become a preacher was because of the stress he felt in delivering a sermon. I'll never forget the famous parable Fritz Crisler gave me and which Stagg had given Fritz: 'Leave me no compromise on things half done, keep me with a stern and stubborn pride and when at last the fight is won God keep me still unsatisfied.' That was Stagg's. There's no way in the world anybody could have said it any better than Stagg. Camp may have been a writer good enough to be published by *Collier's*, but in my opinion, he was second best to Stagg when it came to expressing himself. Stagg could tower over a room. He could fill a room with rhetoric. All coaches try to fill a locker room. Stagg could do it." — KEITH JACKSON

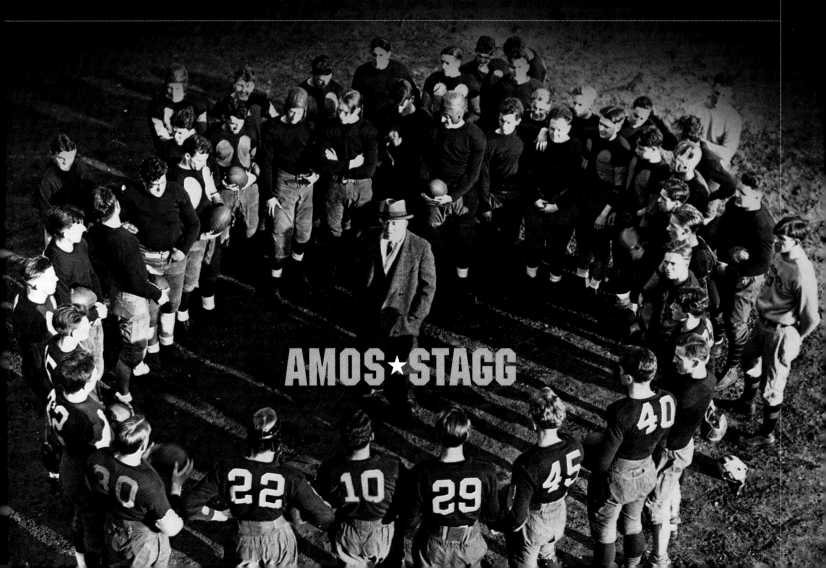

AMOS ★ STAGG

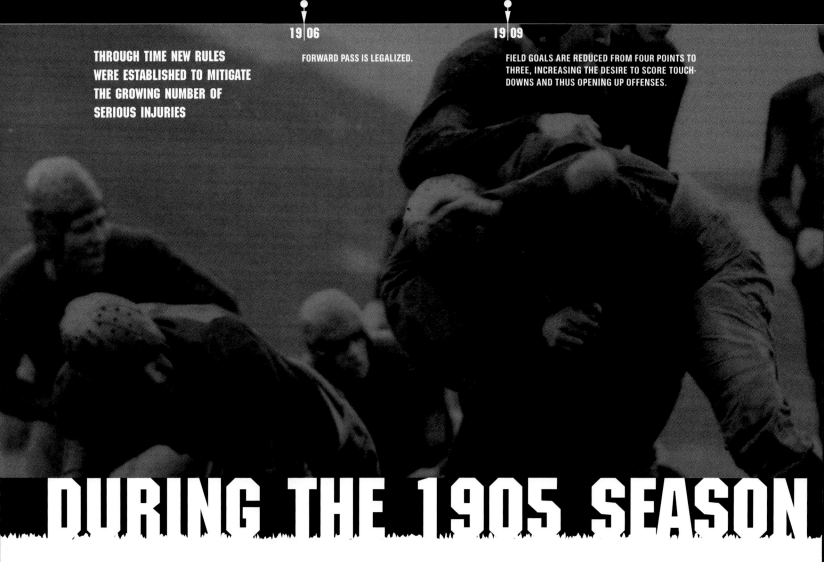

THROUGH TIME NEW RULES WERE ESTABLISHED TO MITIGATE THE GROWING NUMBER OF SERIOUS INJURIES

19|06

FORWARD PASS IS LEGALIZED.

19|09

FIELD GOALS ARE REDUCED FROM FOUR POINTS TO THREE, INCREASING THE DESIRE TO SCORE TOUCH-DOWNS AND THUS OPENING UP OFFENSES.

DURING THE 1905 SEASON

Led by 5-foot-8-inch, 190-pound back Willie Heston, the Wolverines' first two-time All-American, Michigan was known as the "Point-A-Minute" team. In the first century of college football — 1869 to 1969 — Heston held the record for touchdowns scored with 72 despite the fact there were no forward passes in the era in which he played.

"I think that Heston, had he played in the days of the forward pass, would have been one of the greatest receivers of all time," said Yost, "because he had the quickest break of any football player who ever lived."

Stagg quickly became a leader in the development of pass plays after the forward pass was legalized following the 1905 season. Incidentally, the pass was introduced by the rules committee as a way to mitigate the growing number of serious injuries. In fact, the sport had become so dangerous that it wasn't uncommon for a player to be killed on the field.

"During the 1905 season, there were 19 fatalities," said John Adams, modern-day NCAA secretary and rules editor. "In 1906, President Roosevelt stepped in. He was either going to clean up the game or abolish it. There was a big crisis in football at that time. And there were things done to clean it up."

Although there was hardly a rush to passing on a national scale, the passing game Eddie Cochems employed at Saint Louis University opened up the game and reduced the number of deaths.

"College football was coached more brutally in the 1920s, '30s and '40s," said Pepper Rodgers, former ABC Sports announcer and former player and head coach. "Someone asked me the other day why discipline isn't the same as it was under Notre Dame's Frank Leahy and Georgia's Wally Butts. And I told them the Marine Corps is not as tough as it was because you can't beat people upside the head. Everything has changed compared to the early years. Go back to Bear Bryant when he was at Texas A&M. He would start camp with 100 players and end up with 30. It was survival of the fittest. Coaches today are a lot more forgiving. Whoever heard of water breaks in those days? I don't know why more players didn't die."

Still, the rules at that time made it difficult to rely strictly on the pass. A team could pass from behind the line of scrimmage, but the pass had to be caught five or more yards right or left of center. The ball went to the other team if the pass failed to touch a player of either team before hitting the ground. If, however, the ball was touched by

19|10

GAME STANDARDIZED TO 60 MINUTES WITH FOUR
15-MINUTE QUARTERS AND A HALFTIME BREAK.

FLYING WEDGE EFFECTIVELY ELIMINATED WITH SEVEN
MEN REQUIRED ON THE LINE OF SCRIMMAGE.

19|12

FIELD REGULATION DEFINED AS 100 YARDS LONG
WITH TWO 10-YARD END ZONES.

OFFENSIVE TEAMS ALLOWED FOUR DOWNS TO
GAIN 10 YARDS FOR A FIRST DOWN.

PLAYERS REQUIRED TO WEAR NUMBERS ON
THEIR UNIFORMS.

THERE WERE 19 FATALITIES

either team and hit the ground, it could be recovered by either team.

"So it took courage to pass the ball," said Adams.

Even decades later, the forward pass remained a tough sell to some coaches, specifically Ohio State's legendary Woody Hayes. According to Hayes, of the four things that could happen on a pass play — quarterback sack, successful reception, incomplete pass and interception — three of them were bad and Hayes didn't like the odds.

Still of all the changes, the introduction of the forward pass might have had the most long-term impact. And it was one of Stagg's former players, Jess Harper, who initiated the first real passing assault in a major game. Harper, head coach of Notre Dame in 1913, took the Fighting Irish to West Point to battle the powerful Black Knights of Army.

Notre Dame quarterback Gus Dorais and end Knute Rockne, who later would become one of the game's legendary coaches, set the stage for a monumental upset of the bigger, stronger Knights. Army had built its reputation on a powerful running game and considered the small Catholic school from Indiana a minor factor on its 1913 schedule.

All that changed when Dorais and Rockne combined to pick Army apart. Not only did Notre Dame establish itself as a budding power with the 35-13 victory, but Army helped make sure the forward pass was here to stay by using it later in the season to defeat Navy.

Years later, in a 1930 article in *Collier's Weekly*, Rockne wrote about Dorais and the Army game: "We spent a whole summer vacation in 1913 at Cedar Point on Lake Erie. We worked our way as restaurant checkers, but played our way on the beach with a football, practicing the forward pass. There was nothing much else for two young fellows without much pocket money to do and it made us familiar with the innovation that was to change the entire character of football."

Notre Dame made a national statement with the victory over Army. But at Carlisle, the tiny school in south central Pennsylvania, Jim Thorpe was establishing an era all his own thanks in part to coach Pop Warner. A master innovator, Warner found the perfect player in Thorpe to leverage his system. Warner is credited with creating the single wing and double wing formations. With little depth or size, the Indians under Warner used their quickness to execute highly deceptive plays that led to victories over a number

NOTRE DAME BECAME COLLEGE FOOTBALL'S MOST PUBLICIZED SCHOOL OF THE 20TH CENTURY, AND CARLISLE'S JIM THORPE BECAME THE MOST FAMOUS PLAYER. THE 6-FOOT-1-INCH, 190-POUND THORPE WAS AN AMERICAN INDIAN WHO ARRIVED AT CARLISLE IN 1907 AT THE BEGINNING OF COACH GLENN "POP" WARNER'S SECOND TENURE AS COACH OF THE INDIANS, WHO PLAYED AN INTERSECTIONAL SCHEDULE AND EVEN TRAVELED BY RAIL TO THE WEST COAST. THORPE, FROM OKLAHOMA, WAS A GREAT PASSER, KICKER AND DEFENSIVE BACK. CHICAGO BEARS COACH GEORGE HALAS ONCE SAID OF THORPE, WHO WAS ALSO AN OLYMPIC TRACK STAR, "GETTING TACKLED BY THORPE WAS LIKE GETTING HIT WITH A 4 BY 4."

THORPE WAS A THREE-TIME ALL-AMERICA

HIS GREATEST SEASON WAS IN 1912 WHEN CARLISLE COMPILED A 12-1-1 RECORD AND THORPE SCORED 198 POINTS. THORPE'S MOST MEMORABLE GAME CAME AGAINST ARMY. HE RETURNED A KICKOFF 95 YARDS FOR A TOUCHDOWN ONLY TO HAVE THE PLAY NULLIFIED BY A PENALTY. ON THE ENSUING KICKOFF, THORPE WENT 100 YARDS FOR A TOUCHDOWN. IN A SURVEY CONDUCTED BY ABC'S WIDE WORLD OF SPORTS AT THE END OF THE 20TH CENTURY, THORPE WAS NAMED ATHLETE OF THE CENTURY.

JIM THORPE IN ACTION

GLENN "POP" WARNER
CARLISLE COACH

"Thorpe was voted the greatest athlete of the first 50 years. I don't see how he wasn't voted the greatest athlete of the century by ESPN. What he did in the 1912 Olympics is what sets him apart. He was a great football player."

— BEANO COOK

ROUGHING THE PASSER RULE IS ADDED AND THE MIDDLE OF THE BALL IS MADE SMALLER   ENDS AND BACKS BECOME ELIGIBLE FOR THE FORWARD PASS   CHAPTER I   **21**

19|14   19|16

of more powerful opponents despite never having a team that averaged more than 170 pounds a man.

If Thorpe represented the dominant individual of the era, the 1909 Yale team coached by Howard Jones, who would become better known as head coach at Southern California, represented the most dominant team of any era. Yale had six first-team All-Americans and put on a display of power unlikely ever to be matched. Not only was Yale unscored upon, but no team penetrated its 28-yard line.

The passing game continued to evolve thanks in part to the roughing the passer rule instituted in 1914. The ball also became smaller in the middle, which made it easier to throw. And in 1918, ends and backs became eligible for the forward pass.

With the resumption of the Rose Bowl in 1916, West Coast teams finally earned respect when Washington State beat Brown 14-0. A year later, Oregon stopped Penn by the same score, another notch in the belt for Western football.

But Notre Dame quickly became the major national story.

With Rockne taking over in 1918, Notre Dame compiled a 105-12-5 record in the 13 seasons until his death in an airplane crash in Kansas in 1931. Much of the Notre Dame folklore was spawned from the Rockne era thanks to Grantland Rice, who wrote one of the most famous phrases in football history, and Rockne's creation of the legend of George Gipp. Together with Notre Dame's success on the field, the Fighting Irish became college football's only truly national team.

"The old padre running the university understood marketing," said Keith Jackson. "He realized that up the road in Chicago there was a newspaper or two he could use. They were in the perfect position to capitalize because they were a private university. You have to remember, they were called the Catholics for a while. The circumstances were just right. They had a coach and an athletic director in Jess Harper who could deliver.

"Then Knute Rockne came along. He was a chemistry teacher and he might have gone to Alaska and sold refrigerators if he hadn't gone into football. He was a salesman and he could have sold anything. Notre Dame had Chicago and New York. Columbia never captured New York City. Notre Dame has always been the dominant college football team in New York City because there are all kinds of Catholics there, not just the Irish."

Like Warner, Rockne was a strategic genius. His famous shifts and cunning plays only served to make the Notre Dame talent even

THE FOUR HORSEMEN & THE GIPPER

1924 NOTRE DAME BACKFIELD: STUHLDREHER, CROWLEY, MILLER AND LAYDEN

THE 1920 SEASON, KNUTE ROCKNE'S THIRD AT NOTRE DAME, WAS THE LAST ONE FOR GEORGE GIPP, AN ALL-AROUND STAR FOR THE IRISH WHO CONTRACTED STREP THROAT DURING A NOVEMBER VICTORY OVER NORTHWESTERN. GIPP DIED IN DECEMBER AT THE AGE OF 25.

ON HIS DEATHBED, ACCORDING TO LEGEND, GIPP TOLD ROCKNE THAT WHEN MATTERS SEEMED HOPELESS, TO GO OUT AND "WIN JUST ONE FOR THE GIPPER." EIGHT YEARS LATER, ROCKNE USED THAT LINE DURING A PRE-GAME SPEECH BEFORE HIS BRUISED AND BATTERED IRISH FACED AN UNBEATEN ARMY TEAM AT YANKEE STADIUM.

THE IRISH PULLED OUT THE GAME 12-6 WITH TWO SECOND-HALF TOUCHDOWNS IN AN INSPIRATIONAL COMEBACK. YEARS LATER RONALD REAGAN PORTRAYED GIPP IN THE FILM, *KNUTE ROCKNE: ALL-AMERICAN*, WHICH PREMIERED OCT. 4, 1940, IN SOUTH BEND, FURTHER ENHANCING THE LEGEND.

NATIONALLY RENOWNED SPORTSWRITER GRANTLAND RICE, WITH A LITTLE HELP FROM THE NOTRE DAME PUBLICITY DEPARTMENT, ONLY ADDED TO THE GLOW AROUND NOTRE DAME FOOTBALL IN 1924.

WHILE COVERING NOTRE DAME'S STIRRING 13-7 VICTORY OVER ARMY FOR *THE NEW YORK*

GEORGE GIPP

HERALD TRIBUNE, RICE USED THE NOTRE DAME BACKFIELD OF STUHLDREHER, CROWLEY, MILLER AND LAYDEN, WHICH PLAYED 30 GAMES AND LOST ONLY TO NEBRASKA TWICE, TO CREATE ONE OF THE MOST FAMOUS LEADS TO A NEWS STORY EVER WRITTEN.

ACTUALLY, RICE OVERHEARD GEORGE STRICKLER, THE YOUNG PUBLICITY MAN FOR THE IRISH, SAY THE NOTRE DAME BACKFIELD REMINDED HIM OF *THE FOUR HORSEMEN OF THE APOCALYPSE*. RICE'S LEAD THE NEXT DAY READ, "OUTLINED AGAINST THE BLUE-GRAY OCTOBER SKY, THE FOUR HORSEMEN RODE AGAIN..."

STRICKLER, WHO LATER BECAME SPORTS EDITOR OF THE *CHICAGO TRIBUNE*, HAD WATCHED *THE FOUR HORSEMEN OF THE APOCALYPSE* STARRING RUDOLPH VALENTINO THE NIGHT BEFORE THE GAME. STRICKLER, EVER THE EYE FOR A GIMMICK, NOT ONLY DROPPED THE LINE IN THE PRESS BOX, HE ALSO ARRANGED FOR THE FOUR PLAYERS TO MOUNT HORSES WHEN THEY RETURNED TO THE NOTRE DAME CAMPUS FOR A PICTURE THAT WAS DISTRIBUTED ALL OVER THE COUNTRY BY THE WIRE SERVICES.

WITH THE FOUR HORSEMEN PLAYING THEIR FINAL GAME TOGETHER IN 1925, NOTRE DAME CAPPED AN UNBEATEN SEASON (10-0) AND A NATIONAL CHAMPIONSHIP WITH A 27-10 VICTORY IN THE ROSE BOWL OVER POP WARNER'S STANFORD TEAM.

★ GEORGE GIPP AND THE FOUR HORSEMEN ★

"ROCKNE

IS THE GREATEST COLLEGE FOOTBALL FIGURE OF THE 20TH CENTURY, NO IFS, ANDS, BUTS ABOUT IT. PEOPLE RECOGNIZE HIS PICTURE NOW. THEY KNOW IT'S ROCKNE. WHEN HE DIED, IF I RECALL, IT WAS THE FIRST FUNERAL EVER BROADCAST NATIONALLY ON RADIO. THAT'S THE KIND OF IMPACT HE HAD. FOR ME, IT WAS EASY TO PICK ROCKNE AS THE NO. 1 COACH. HE HAS BEEN DEAD 70 YEARS AND EVERYBODY STILL KNOWS HIS NAME."

— BEANO COOK

KNUTE ROCKNE

more imposing. His philosophy also was unique. He drilled his players on fundamentals relentlessly, but he would not scrimmage his regulars after the first game of every season.

But the Notre Dame success was not without controversy. Rockne's shifts were on the fly, which meant the players were in motion when the ball was snapped. Stagg, the baron of the Rules Committee, claimed the Irish were violating the spirit of the rules by not coming to a complete stop. In 1927, a new rule requiring a one-second stop on shifts was instituted.

Rockne's most compelling innovation, however, was the idea of moving the Irish around the country for games. By scheduling intersectional games with teams such as Southern California, Navy, Georgia Tech, SMU, Baylor and retaining the Army series, Rockne set the Irish apart. Whether a part of his plan or not, Rockne successfully created a national following for his team among Catholics and others. Notre Dame became recognized as the national Catholic school. Other big time Catholic schools of the time – Fordham, Duquesne, St. Mary's and Holy Cross — became lost in the Irish shadow.

While Notre Dame was college football's most glamorous team of the 1920s, Illinois' Red Grange became the most glamorous player of the era. The Midwest produced some of the most heralded players of the 1930s as the Big Ten Conference came to the forefront of college football.

Although Michigan had been the pioneer of football west of the Alleghenies, other schools were catching up. Ohio State, Illinois and Minnesota had powerhouse teams with star players. And they built big stadiums to showcase them. As the United States' population grew, the great land-grant universities in the Midwest became the beneficiaries of the growing need for education on a large scale, needs not able to be met by private schools in the East.

Indeed, many of those schools were either near or over capacity, some with as many as 4,000 undergraduates. With the rapid growth of schools in the Midwest came an equally fast growth rate for major college sports.

And the "Galloping Ghost" provided the impetus.

During a three-year period from 1923-25, Grange gained 3,647 total yards running essentially the same play and without benefit of the forward pass to keep defenses guessing.

"One time somebody asked (former Clemson coach) Frank Howard about Red Grange and how many yards Red might gain today," said Pepper Rodgers, former head coach at Kansas, UCLA, and Georgia Tech. "Howard said, 'About 800.' The other person said, 'Hell, some of these

RED GRANGE: A LEGEND IS MADE

WITH GOOD REASON, THE LEGEND OF RED GRANGE EVOLVED FROM A SINGLE GAME AGAINST MICHIGAN IN 1924.

IN THE GAME'S FIRST 12 MINUTES, GRANGE TOUCHED THE BALL FOUR TIMES AND SCORED FOUR TOUCHDOWNS. THERE WERE TWO KICKOFF RETURNS — ONE 95 YARDS, THE OTHER 67 YARDS — AND TWO SPRINTS FROM SCRIMMAGE FOR 56 YARDS AND 44 YARDS.

ILLINOIS COACH BOB ZUPPKE THEN REMOVED GRANGE FROM THE GAME UNTIL THE SECOND HALF WHEN GRANGE SCORED A FIFTH TOUCHDOWN ON A 12-YARD RECEPTION AND PASSED 18 YARDS FOR A SIXTH. IN ALL, GRANGE ACCOUNTED FOR 262 YARDS IN THE FIRST 12 MINUTES AND 402 TOTAL YARDS IN A 39-14 VICTORY ON THE DAY CHAMPAIGN'S MEMORIAL STADIUM WAS DEDICATED.

TWELVE YEARS LATER, ZUPPKE, WRITING IN *ESQUIRE* MAGAZINE, SAID "RED HAD THAT INDEFINABLE SOMETHING THAT A HUNTED WILD ANIMAL HAS - UNCANNY TIMING AND THE BIG BROWN EYES OF A ROYAL BUCK. I SKETCHED A TEAM AROUND HIM LIKE THE COMPLEMENTARY BACKGROUND OF A PAINTING."

☆ 1924 **ILLINOIS** VS **MICHIGAN** 1924 ☆

IN THE FIRST 12 MINUTES, GRANGE TOUCHED THE BALL 4 TIMES AND SCORED 4 TOUCHDOWNS

HE SCORED A 5TH IN THE SECOND HALF ON A 12 YARD RECEPTION FOLLOWED BY A TOUCHDOWN PASS OF HIS OWN.

95 YARD KICKOFF RETURN	67 YARD KICKOFF RETURN	56 YARD TD FROM SCRIMMAGE	44 YARD TD FROM SCRIMMAGE	12 YARD TD RECEPTION	18 YARD TD PASS
1ST TD	**2ND TD**	**3RD TD**	**4TH TD**	**5TH TD**	**6TH TD**

402
TOTAL YARDS

guys are getting 2,000 yards.' Howard replied, `Well, Red is 65 years old.'"

Michigan gained a measure of redemption in 1925 when another Big Ten legend, sophomore end Bernie Oosterbaan, helped hold Grange without a yard in a 3-0 Wolverines victory.

Said Michigan coach Fielding Yost, "Grange didn't gain enough yards to bury him in, even if they had buried him head down."

The 6-foot, 185-pound Oosterbaan accumulated nine letters at Michigan starring in baseball, basketball and football. His eight touchdown receptions led the Big Ten in 1925. In 1926, Oosterbaan ran 60 yards with a Minnesota fumble for a touchdown in a 7-6 Michigan victory that produced a tie for the Big Ten title. And in 1927, he threw three touchdown passes in a 21-0 victory over Ohio State.

"Running into him was like getting an electric shock," Red Grange said of practicing against Nagurski as a professional. "If you tried to tackle him anywhere above the ankles, you were liable to get killed."

"Football in those days was a man-to-man fight on the field," Yost said in a 1935 article by Grantland Rice. "Almost anything went. Today the rules have changed most of this. There are penalties for clipping, for piling up, for roughing the kicker, for striking with the palm of the hand, for anything that looks like intentional roughness. That's one big difference."

With college football firmly established in the Midwest, the sport moved across the Mississippi. In 1921, California won a share of the national title with a victory over Ohio State in the Rose Bowl. And with the death of Walter Camp in 1925, Grantland Rice took over creating the All-America

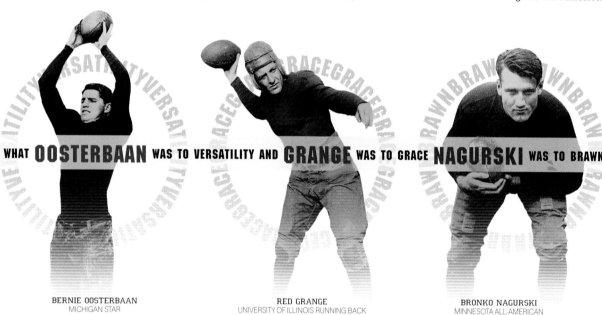

WHAT **OOSTERBAAN** WAS TO VERSATILITY AND **GRANGE** WAS TO GRACE **NAGURSKI** WAS TO BRAWN

BERNIE OOSTERBAAN
MICHIGAN STAR

RED GRANGE
UNIVERSITY OF ILLINOIS RUNNING BACK

BRONKO NAGURSKI
MINNESOTA ALL-AMERICAN

Wrote *Detroit News* reporter H. G. Salsinger: "He is an end, a lineman, a quarterback and a halfback—what more can you ask?"

What Oosterbaan was to versatility and Grange was to grace, Minnesota's massive Bronko Nagurski was to brawn. Nagurski, who grew up in the ice-cold iron region of International Falls, Minnesota, mirrored the conditions of his hometown. Tough, strong and fearless, the 6-foot-2-inch, 235-pound Nagurski had a size 19 neck and size 19 ring finger to match. He was named All-America in 1929 at defensive tackle, but he was just as good as a battering-ram fullback.

According to legend, there's still a crack in the wall at Wrigley Field, compliments of Nagurski, who played on the Chicago Bears.

team for *Collier's Magazine* through 1947. It was Rice who helped the rest of the country find out what was happening with college football in the West when he named Stanford fullback Ernie Nevers and Washington back George Wilson to the 1925 team, the first players ever selected from the West.

At the same time, Howard Jones's USC teams had become the toast of Los Angeles. After coaching at Ohio State, Yale, Iowa and Duke, Jones established the first football dynasty out West. In his 16 seasons at USC, the Trojans won three national titles and five Rose Bowls before Jones died of a heart attack at the age of 56.

One of the keys to Jones's success was getting Notre Dame on the USC schedule.

During the fall of his first year, Jones dispatched 26-

THE LARGEST PAID CROWD EVER [112,912] WATCHES NOTRE DAME DEFEAT USC IN CHICAGO'S SOLDIER FIELD   KNUTE ROCKNE IS KILLED IN A PLANE CRASH   CHAPTER I   25

19|29   19|31

year-old graduate manager Gwynn Wilson to Lincoln, Nebraska, to talk to Rockne about starting a series with USC. Jones knew the Notre Dame–Nebraska series was coming to an end and the Irish would have an opening on their schedule. It was Wilson's job to convince Rockne to play the series. But Rockne was hesi-tant. He told Wilson, who had brought his new bride on the trip, he would talk to his wife on the train back to Chicago. Wilson's wife helped close the deal when she con-vinced Mrs. Rockne how hospitable the people in southern California were. There also was some talk about Mrs. Wilson suggesting that Mrs. Rockne would have an opportunity to meet movie star Rudolph Valentino in

scrimmaged — every day. He also was known to forget the names of even his own players.

"I'd been sitting on the bench and he would say, 'Hey, you get in there.' I got in and went 65 yards for a touch-down," recalls Nick Pappas, a USC tailback from 1935-37. "We won the game. After all that, the players wouldn't call me Nick. They'd say, 'Hey, you, what's doing?'"

Even into the 1930s, traveling to the Midwest by train sometimes could take a week. Said Pappas: "We'd leave on Tuesday. House up in Chicago and then train down to South Bend for the game. Then we'd get back on the train Monday. We saw the country. These kids today don't see what we saw. We went through the Grand Canyon by

Hollywood. The deal was closed.

In 1926, Notre Dame and USC filled the Los Angeles Coliseum with the Irish winning 13-12. In 1927, before a paid audience of 99,573 at Chicago's Soldier Field, Notre Dame won again, this time 7-6. Two years later, the two teams set a record by playing in front of 112,912 at Soldier Field, the largest paid crowd to see a college football game.

Under Jones, the Trojans were known as the "Thundering Herd," thanks to the predictable, but powerful USC offense. Jones's favorite play was off tackle, with the wingback blocking the end, the tackles blocking the defensive tack-les and the tailback cutting up the hole. USC used only a few plays but executed them flawlessly.

USC also came prepared. Jones had his players run 10 100-yard sprints before practice every day. Then they

rail and that sort of thing."

Not until 1940, when Fritz Crisler's Michigan team beat California in Berkeley 41-0, did a team fly cross-country for a game on the West Coast. The first team actually to fly to a foot-ball game is believed to be the University of New Mexico in 1929, which was coached by Roy Johnson. New Mexico had a game scheduled against Occidental College. Johnson, unsure of the safety of flight, had only his second stringers and a manager fly to Los Angeles on a Ford Tri-Motor. Occidental won the game at the Rose Bowl 26-0. The first team returned to Albuquerque by plane, the second team by train.

Schools in the South were the last to embrace the game. But what they lacked in early history, they made up for with passion. Southern football gained its first major notice when Alabama defeated Washington 20-19 in the 1926 Rose Bowl, winning the region's first national title under Alabama coach Wallace Wade. After that game, six southern teams, including Tulane, Georgia Tech and SMU, played in the next 11 Rose Bowls. Until then, southern football had been considered minor league.

Virginia had one of the early teams in the South and in 1890 lost at Princeton 115-0. Only occasionally did southern teams raise their level of play to compete with the teams in the East, Midwest or West during the early years of the 20th century.

But in the mid-1920s, college football became part of the fabric of day-to-day life in the South to a greater degree than any other place in the country. With less than a dozen professional baseball teams in the North and East in the post–World War I years and professional football and basketball years away from taking hold of the country's imagination, southern fans' only identification with a sport other than college football came by scratchy radio broadcasts and press dispatches of professional baseball games.

"Well, I grew up in Atlanta and Georgia Tech and Georgia were the teams," said Frank Broyles, former ABC Sports announcer and legendary head coach. "The baseball team then was the Class A Atlanta Crackers. But college football was the biggest thing in the state by far. Tech and Georgia football games were the dominant subjects in the discussion of sports. That was who and what people identified with, Georgia or Georgia Tech and college football. There weren't any major sports except those. College football was very big across Georgia, Alabama and Tennessee. In those days, the Tennessee–Alabama game was the game of the year. It had more prestige than any game except Army–Navy."

Indeed, Southerners flocked to stadiums in Birmingham, Tuscaloosa, Auburn, Athens, Knoxville, Atlanta and Baton Rouge to see college football. And that passion only deep-

NOTRE DAME AND USC PLAYED AGAIN IN 1929, BEFORE A

ened. Of the top 20 largest stadiums in college football entering the 2000 season, 11 were in the South, headed by 104,000-seat Neyland Stadium at Tennessee, second nationally in capacity only to Michigan Stadium (107,501 seats). In 1999, the football-crazy Southeastern Conference played to 98.7 percent capacity in home stadiums, averaging an all-time high for any conference of 70,521 per game.

Alabama compiled a 61-13-3 record under Wade from 1923 to 1930, winning three national championships and two Rose Bowls. A native of Tennessee, Wade had played guard for Brown. After an Army stint during World War I, Wade became a captain in the cavalry and spent his time training in the United States. He later won a Bronze Star in World War II and came home with a sense of discipline he translated to the football field.

Mild-mannered, Wade normally sat on the bench during games and seldom yelled at officials. Though he requested his players not date during the season, Wade also had a soft side. Bruce Bell, an Alabama student, hitchhiked home to see the 1931 Rose Bowl, Wade's last game as coach of Alabama, without a ticket. Bell had participated in scrimmages at Alabama, but never had played in a game. Wade couldn't get him a ticket, so he gave him an extra uniform. Bell got into the only college game of his career, a 24-0 Alabama victory over Washington State.

Wade's teams were big and brooding, but they set the tone for a regimented, organized program, which emphasized strong line play. Hence, Alabama's linemen acquired the nickname of "Red Elephants" 70 years ago.

Wrote Everett Strupper of the *Atlanta Journal* in October, 1930, a few days after covering an Ole Miss–Alabama game: "That Alabama team of 1930 is a typical Wade machine, powerful, big, tough, fast, aggressive, well-schooled in the fundamentals, and the best blocking

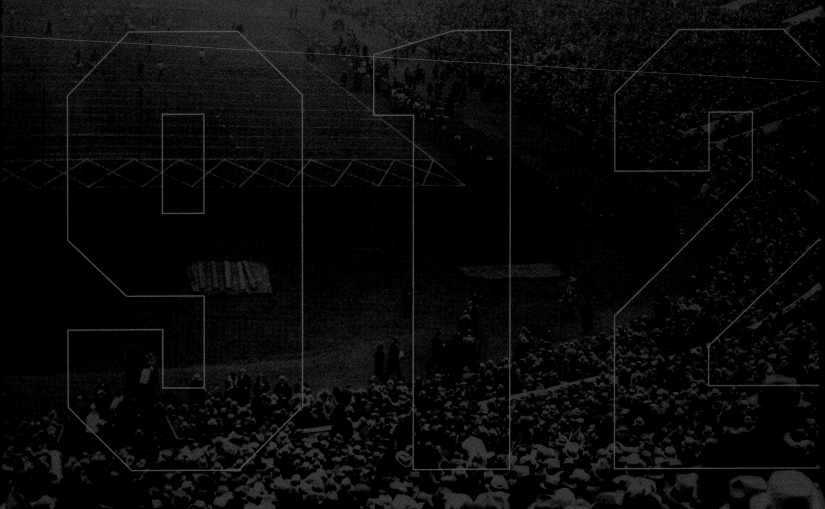

RECORD CROWD OF 112,912 AT CHICAGO'S SOLDIER FIELD

28   CHAPTER I   THE SIZE OF THE FOOTBALL IS FURTHER DECREASED   TEAMS NO LONGER PENALIZED FOR MORE THAN ONE INCOMPLETE PASS IN A SERIES OF DOWNS

19|34   19|34

team for this early in the season that I have ever seen. When those big brutes hit you, I mean you go down and stay down, often for an additional two minutes."

Wade's biggest Southern rivalry during that era was with Tennessee and General Robert Neyland, who was building a powerhouse at the doorstep of the Great Smoky Mountains. Neyland used many of the same principles as Wade, teaching repetition and discipline and utilizing a conservative offense that would pound the ball into opposing defenses.

In 1928, Neyland's Volunteers handed Alabama a 15-13 loss in Tuscaloosa, signaling the beginning of a border war that still sizzles today. The night before Neyland

ALABAMA COMPILED A 61-13-3 RECORD UNDER WADE FROM 1923 TO 1930 WINNING THREE NATIONAL CHAMPIONSHIPS AND TWO ROSE BOWLS. HE WON A BRONZE STAR IN WORLD WAR II AND CAME HOME WITH A SENSE OF DISCIPLINE HE TRANSLATED TO THE FOOTBALL FIELD.

shutouts.

"He was a great believer in the kicking game," said current Tennessee professor Andrew Kozar, who was a running back on Neyland's 1950-52 teams. "He was a great believer in field position. He would give the opposition the ball if he had bad field position. He wanted them to make the mistakes so he could turn his offense loose on the other side of the 50. He would punt on first and second down quite a bit. If a team would punt and he didn't like the field position, he would kick it back. He would put his best players on defense."

Neyland was regarded as the first coach in the South to use telephone hookups

NEYLAND'S SIX AXIOMS

★ DON'T SAVE YOURSELF, GO THE LIMIT. THERE ARE GOOD MEN ON THE SIDELINE WHEN YOU ARE EXHAUSTED. ★

★ IF THE GAME OR BREAKS GO AGAINST YOU, DON'T LIE DOWN, PUT ON MORE STEAM. ★

★ IF THE LINE GOES FORWARD, THE TEAM WINS. IF THE LINE COMES BACKWARD, IT LOSES. ★

★ A MAN'S VALUE TO HIS TEAM VARIES INVERSELY TO HIS DISTANCE FROM THE BALL. ★

★ FOOTBALL IS A BATTLE. GO OUT AND FIGHT AND KEEP IT UP ALL AFTERNOON. ★

★ PLAY FOR THE BREAKS, WHEN ONE COMES YOUR WAY, SCORE. ★

ROBERT NEYLAND TENNESSEE COACH

★ GENERAL ROBERT NEYLAND ★

had locked up the team in a motel, unheard of in those days.

"He told us to think football, to think about beating Alabama," McEver said. "He let us out for dinner, then locked us in our rooms again. When it was time to play, he let us out. That's how you beat Alabama."

That victory put the Volunteers on the map. And Neyland became the most storied Southern coach outside of Alabama's Paul "Bear" Bryant. Neyland, who played at Army, built a program based on defense and the kicking game. Among his many sayings were:

*One good blocker is worth three ballcarriers.

*75 percent of football is above the neck.

*No offensive play should be used in a game until it has been rehearsed 500 times.

Of Neyland's 173 victories at Tennessee, 107 were

WALLACE WADE
HEAD COACH ALABAMA

from the sideline to the press box. He was among the first coaches to time punters and passers with a stopwatch and the first coach to film practices and games. Neyland was an innovator in the equipment area as well, introducing tear-away jerseys, low-top shoes and lightweight hip pads. He also was among the first to cover a field with a tarpaulin during bad weather and to have his team stay in motels, even for home games.

Frank Broyles graduated from Georgia Tech in 1947 and turned down professional football and baseball offers to become backfield coach at Baylor. And when he did, Broyles brought the memory of General Neyland with him.

"When I went to work for Bob Woodruff at Baylor in 1947, he handed me Neyland's quarterback play book," said Broyles. "I took Neyland's principles of the game right from that 1927 play book. He had six of them. I put them up

THE FIRST PASS INTO THE END ZONE DURING A SERIES OF DOWNS, OTHER THAN 4TH, COULD BE INCOMPLETE WITHOUT A LOSS OF POSSESSION   CHAPTER I   29

19|34

on the blackboard before every game I ever coached. Johnny Majors did the same thing. They were the axioms of winning football."

Given his tendency for conservatism, Neyland's teams seldom passed. When Neyland recruited John (Tex) Davis out of Texas in the early 1950s, Neyland told him Tennessee will throw the ball "20-30 times." Quipped Davis when he got to Tennessee, "I didn't know he meant the whole season."

In 1934, the Rules Committee made it even easier to pass, an option even the most conservative teams were forced to reconsider.

1. The size of the middle of the football was reduced even more, allowing quarterbacks to grip the ball easily with one hand.

2. Until 1934, teams were penalized five yards for more than one incomplete pass in a series of downs. That rule was eliminated.

3. The first pass into the end zone during a series of downs, except on fourth down, could be incomplete without loss of possession.

Alabama head coach Frank Thomas, who succeeded Wade, took advantage of the new rules and a brilliant receiver to loosen things up for the Crimson Tide. Don Hutson caught six passes for 165 yards and two touchdowns in a 29-13 victory over Stanford in the 1935 Rose Bowl. Because Thomas was a disciple of Knute Rockne, Alabama halfback Dixie Howell passed from the old Notre Dame box alignment.

Future Alabama coaching legend Paul "Bear" Bryant was a teammate of Hutson's on that Alabama team.

"Don had the most fluid motion you've ever seen when he was running," said Bryant. "It looked like he was going just as fast as possible, when all of a sudden he would put on an extra burst of speed and be gone. Don had great hands and excellent moves, but the thing about him that

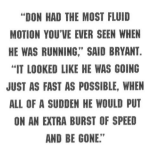

"DON HAD THE MOST FLUID MOTION YOU'VE EVER SEEN WHEN HE WAS RUNNING," SAID BRYANT. "IT LOOKED LIKE HE WAS GOING JUST AS FAST AS POSSIBLE, WHEN ALL OF A SUDDEN HE WOULD PUT ON AN EXTRA BURST OF SPEED AND BE GONE."

BEAR BRYANT
ALABAMA HEAD COACH

DON HUTSON
ALABAMA RECEIVER

was most dangerous was his ability to run in an open field. He could really move, with an excellent change of pace."

The passing game also dipped into the Southwest, which didn't become a major player in college football until the mid-1930s when TCU, SMU and Rice became national teams and started going to major bowls. The University of Texas, the most popular team in the state years later, didn't go to its first bowl until after the 1942 season. But football flourished at the state's private schools, which were located in the large, metropolitan areas of Houston and Dallas–Fort Worth without any competition from professional football.

The passing trend found its way to Texas Christian University in Fort Worth in the mid-1930s. Slingin' Sammy Baugh and Davey O'Brien became two of the most noted passers of the era. Baugh was named the Football Writers Association of America starting quarterback on its All-Time team from 1920-68. Baugh also was a back who passed out of the old single-wing.

"Baugh's passes were usually short, but what precision!" said Clark Shaughnessy, the Stanford and Chicago Bears coach who later helped popularize the T-formation.

During an era when the national norm was to complete less than 38 percent of one's passes, Baugh completed nearly 50 percent and TCU won 28 of its 38 games.

"Back in those days most teams, even in the pros, would only throw on third down and then they always tried a deep pass," Baugh said in *The Greatest Moments in TCU Football History*. "Dutch (Meyer, the TCU football coach) taught us the short passing game, and early on he told me, 'You can throw from your own 1-yard line if you see an opening.' We were doing a lot of things nobody else had thought of."

In 1935, Grantland Rice and nearly a dozen of the other noted newspapermen of the day covered the biggest game in Southwest Conference history up until that point, SMU's 20-14 victory over TCU, a battle of two 10-0 teams. Baugh's team lost the game and had to settle for a trip to the Sugar Bowl; SMU went to the Rose Bowl. The Southwest Conference had arrived on the national scene with a flair and offensive unpredictability never before seen.

The 5-foot-7-inch, 150-pound O'Brien, the Southwest Conference's first Heisman Trophy winner in 1938, was even more accurate than Baugh. During his career, O'Brien completed 56 percent of his passes and led the nation in passing in 1937 and 1938 when TCU compiled an 11-0 record.

Said Jim Crowley, one of Notre Dame's Four Horsemen and Fordham's coach at the time, "When you see him in the first period, he looks like just another ballplayer. In the second, he sort of warms up and you have to notice him.

"It was the first time I ever heard *Victors*, the Michigan fight song. It was 85-0 in favor of Michigan that day and I heard it after every touchdown and after every point. It was a significant game. Fritz Crisler, the Michigan coach, had tried to hold the score down. At that time, Chicago was more concerned with academia. And after the season, Chicago resigned from the Big Ten. That game was one of the determining factors. Fritz felt bad. He had graduated from Chicago and played for Stagg.

"But every time Tom touched the ball he could have gone for a touchdown. Probably subconsciously, that game was one of reasons I wanted to go to Michigan, which I eventually did. I subsequently worked with Tom a number of times at ABC and we became good friends."

But the evolution of college football had just started when World War II shut down a number of programs

THE HEISMAN TROPHY ★

★

WHEN DAVEY O'BRIEN WON THE HEISMAN TROPHY IN 1938 IT SIGNALED THE END TO EASTERN FOOTBALL DOMINANCE. CHICAGO QUARTERBACK JAY BERWANGER WON THE FIRST AWARD IN 1935 WHEN ONLY PLAYERS EAST OF THE MISSISSIPPI WERE ELIGIBLE AND THE TROPHY WAS KNOWN AS THE DAC (DOWNTOWN ATHLETIC CLUB) TROPHY.

THE FOLLOWING YEAR, THE AWARD WAS OPENED UP TO ALL PLAYERS AND RE-NAMED FOR JOHN HEISMAN, THE FIRST ATHLETIC DIRECTOR OF THE DOWNTOWN ATHLETIC CLUB IN NEW YORK CITY. YALE PLAYERS WON THE FIRST TWO HEISMAN

TROPHIES AFTER BERWANGER WON THE INITIAL DAC AWARD. BUT O'BRIEN WAS THE FIRST OF SEVEN STRAIGHT NON-EASTERN PLAYERS TO WIN THE AWARD.

THE HEISMAN TROPHY'S STRIKING FEATURE ALWAYS HAS BEEN "THE POSE." ODDLY, IT BEARS NO RESEMBLENCE TO HEISMAN, A FORMER BROWN AND YALE PLAYER WHO HAD A 36-YEAR COACHING CAREER. SCULPTOR FRANK ELISCU ENLISTED PLAYERS FROM NEW YORK UNIVERSITY AND FORDHAM TO POSE FOR THE CLAY MODEL OF WHAT WAS TO BE A BRONZED TROPHY OF A FOOTBALL PLAYER DRIVING FOR YARDS, WITH A SIDESTEP, AND A THRUST OF THE RIGHT ARM.

You are fond of him by the third quarter. And by the time the fourth quarter ends, you love him."

By the mid-1930s, college football was booming. Four more bowl games were added between 1935 and 1937 including the Orange, Sugar, Cotton and Sun. In 1936, the Associated Press established the first national poll of sportswriters, ranking teams from all regions. And radio, as it had done for baseball, was helping college football gain notoriety across the country.

The 1927 Rose Bowl already had become the first sporting event to be broadcast nationally on radio and all the major radio networks were vying for bowl game rights.

"My first memory of college football was 1939 when I was living in Gary, Indiana," said Bill Flemming former ABC announcer. "Tom Harmon had gone to the same high school, Horace Mann High, a few years earlier. Michigan played Chicago at Stagg Field in 1939. For Tom, it was his junior year, and they were touting him as one of great backs of all-time.

around the country. Though the passing game had arrived, it remained unsophisticated at best. The quarterback still didn't receive the ball from under center and the option game was years off. It wasn't until 1939 that helmets became mandatory after too many players were carried off the field unconscious.

"You didn't get a water break unless they threw it on your face when you fainted," says Merle Harmon. "You had to go, go, go. Then, after practice, you had to run two laps around the track. That was conditioning in those days."

If World War II provided a breather, it would be the war's end that fueled college football into a new age. The return of thousands of bigger, stronger and more mature men heading to college campuses, along with a suddenly booming economy, drove college football into the modern era.

1999	RON DAYNE	WISCONSIN [TB]
1998	RICKY WILLIAMS	TEXAS [TB]
1997	CHARLES WOODSON	MICHIGAN [DB/WR]
1996	DANNY WUERFFEL	FLORIDA [QB]
1995	EDDIE GEORGE	OHIO STATE [RB]
1994	RASHAAN SALAAM	COLORADO [RB]
1993	CHARLIE WARD	FLORIDA STATE [QB]
1992	GINO TORRETTA	MIAMI [QB]
1991	DESMOND HOWARD	MICHIGAN [WR]
1990	TY DETMER	BRIGHAM YOUNG [QB]
1989	ANDRE WARE	HOUSTON [QB]
1988	BARRY SANDERS	OKLAHOMA STATE [RB]
1987	TIM BROWN	NOTRE DAME [WR]
1986	VINNY TESTAVERDE	MIAMI [QB]
1985	BO JACKSON	AUBURN [RB]
1984	DOUG FLUTIE	BOSTON COLLEGE [QB]
1983	MIKE ROZIER	NEBRASKA [RB]
1982	HERSCHEL WALKER	GEORGIA [RB]
1981	MARCUS ALLEN	SOUTHERN CAL [RB]
1980	GEORGE ROGERS	SOUTH CAROLINA [RB]
1979	CHARLES WHITE	SOUTHERN CAL [RB]
1978	BILLY SIMS	OKLAHOMA [RB]
1977	EARL CAMPBELL	TEXAS [RB]
1976	TONY DORSETT	PITTSBURGH [RB]
1975	ARCHIE GRIFFIN	OHIO STATE [RB]
1974	ARCHIE GRIFFIN	OHIO STATE [RB]
1973	JOHN CAPPELLETTI	PENN STATE [RB]
1972	JOHNNY RODGERS	NEBRASKA [WR]
1971	PAT SULLIVAN	AUBURN [QB]
1970	JIM PLUNKETT	STANFORD [QB]
1969	STEVE OWENS	OKLAHOMA [HB]
1968	O. J. SIMPSON	SOUTHERN CAL [HB]
1967	GARY BEBAN	UCLA [QB]
1966	STEVE SPURRIER	FLORIDA [QB]
1965	MIKE GARRETT	SOUTHERN CAL [HB]
1964	JOHN HUARTE	NOTRE DAME [QB]
1963	ROGER STAUBACH	NAVY [QB]
1962	TERRY BAKER	OREGON STATE [QB]
1961	ERNIE DAVIS	SYRACUSE [HB]
1960	JOE BELLINO	NAVY [HB]
1959	BILLY CANNON	LSU [HB]
1958	PETE DAWKINS	ARMY [HB]
1957	JOHN DAVID CROW	TEXAS A&M [HB]
1956	PAUL HORNUNG	NOTRE DAME [QB]
1955	HOWARD CASSADY	OHIO STATE [HB]
1954	ALAN AMECHE	WISCONSIN [FB]
1953	JOHNNY LATTNER	NOTRE DAME [HB]
1952	BILLY VESSELS	OKLAHOMA [HB]
1951	DICK KAZMAIER	PRINCETON [HB]
1950	VIC JANOWICZ	OHIO STATE [HB]
1949	LEON HART	NOTRE DAME [E]
1948	DOAK WALKER	SOUTHERN METHODIST [HB]
1947	JOHNNY LUJACK	NOTRE DAME [QB]
1946	GLENN DAVIS	ARMY [HB]
1945	DOC BLANCHARD	ARMY [FB]
1944	LES HORVATH	OHIO STATE [QB/HB]
1943	ANGELO BERTELLI	NOTRE DAME [QB]
1942	FRANK SINKWICH	GEORGIA [HB]
1941	BRUCE SMITH	MINNESOTA [HB]
1940	TOM HARMON	MICHIGAN [HB]
1939	NILE KINNICK	IOWA [HB]
1938	DAVEY O'BRIEN	TEXAS CHRISTIAN [QB]
1937	CLINT FRANK	YALE [HB]
1936	LARRY KELLEY	YALE [E]
1935	JAY BERWANGER	CHICAGO [HB]

CHAPTER TWO

AS ONE DECADE TRUDGED INTO THE NEXT AND THE 1930S GAVE WAY TO THE 1940S, COLLEGE FOOTBALL HAD BECOME A NATIONAL DISTRACTION FROM THE TWIN BEASTS OF DEPRESSION AND VIOLENCE. WHETHER ON THE FOOTBALL FIELD OR WORKING TO GRIND A LIVING OUT OF THE GREAT DEPRESSION, EVERY YOUNG MAN IN AMERICA WALKED IN THE SHADOW OF A WAR THAT HAD BEEN PUT INTO MOTION BY 1940.

IF THE WORLD WAS ABOUT TO CHANGE, THEN SO TOO WAS FOOTBALL. INSTEAD OF THE BALL BEING SNAPPED BACK TO A QUARTERBACK OR HALFBACK STANDING THREE-TO-FIVE YARDS BEHIND THE LINE, THE T-FORMATION PLACED THE QUARTERBACK IN A CROUCHED POSITION DIRECTLY BEHIND CENTER.

At home, America voiced its neutrality and football carried the country through the fall of 1940 on the buzz of an innovator named Clark Shaughnessy. The coach had moved from the University of Chicago to Stanford, which was coming off a 1-7-1 record. For Stanford officials, the lure was Shaughnessy's ideas about a new offensive system that worked off something called the "T-formation." They knew Shaughnessy had spent time communicating the new offense to George Halas and his Chicago Bears. They also knew just about anything was better than a single victory in nine games.

Indeed, Shaughnessy, who had replaced the legendary Amos Alonzo Stagg at Chicago, had been tinkering with the concept for more than four years while assisting Halas and the Bears on the side. A version of the T-formation existed, but Shaughnessy effectively re-engineered the initial concept. Scouting Bears' opponents for Halas, Shaughnessy developed the "man in motion." He split an end to one side, then put a back in motion to the other. The formation, more than 20 years ahead of its time, now had two wide receivers and a tight end. In the 1960s Shaughnessy's genius would be called the "pro set."

If the world was about to change, then so, too, was football. Instead of the ball being snapped back to a quarterback or halfback standing three-to-five yards behind the line, the T-formation placed the quarterback in a crouched position directly behind center. The approach allowed flankers, or wide receivers, to take defenders downfield on a pass play or simply act as a decoy on running plays.

Pedigree aside, Stanford's players were incredulous the first time Shaughnessy went to the chalk board.

"In walks this man, ramrod straight, well built with dark gray hair, dressed immaculately in a dark suit and fedora," recalls Milt Vucinich, a reserve fullback at Stanford during that era. "He wore that all the time. He was very serious-minded, all business. He said, 'We're going to bring in a new formation. It's going to be confusing to you for awhile. But I promise you we're going to win the (Pacific Coast Conference) championship.' The way he said it, we thought, 'By God, maybe there was something to it.'"

Though history would prove Shaughnessy correct, Pop Warner and practitioners of power football such as General Robert Neyland at Tennessee and Bernie Bierman at

Minnesota considered the "T" a passing fad. Though the power game would last into the 1980s at schools such as Oklahoma, Texas, Ohio State and others, no one could ignore the reality or viability of Shaughnessy's approach by the time the 1940 season — college and professional — ended.

He was named Coach of the Year in 1940 by "coiling up the defense in as small an area as possible, then running around or throwing over it." Shaughnessy did so by moving guards, ends and tackles from balanced to unbalanced lines. At the same time, Stanford's man in motion confused defenders before the play unfolded.

Indeed, no college defense was prepared for the kind of movement that preceded Stanford's offensive attack. But Shaughnessy also had the fuel that

THOUGH HISTORY WOULD PROVE SHAUGHNESSY CORRECT, POP WARNER AND PRACTITIONERS OF POWER FOOTBALL SUCH AS GENERAL ROBERT NEYLAND AT TENNESSEE AND BERNIE BIERMAN AT MINNESOTA CONSIDERED THE "T" A PASSING FAD.

"Only two teams used the T-formation, Stanford and the Chicago Bears" says Vucinich. "It was unique and really revolutionized football. Everything changed to the T-formation. It was as simple as that. By the time I was a senior, every school we played against had the T-formation."

As the world shook with war heading into the 1941 season, the college game continued to evolve. Germany had invaded Greece and Yugoslavia in April and then the Soviet Union in June. In October, the U.S.S. *Reuben James* was sunk and 116 sailors were killed.

Anticipating the inevitable, the Football Rules Committee instituted more liberal substitution rules starting with the 1941 season to help reduce

FORMATION

drives any innovation—talent. Halfback Frankie Albert moved to quarterback and the backfield was rounded out by 230-pound strongman Norm Standlee, accomplished sprinter Pete Kmetovic and all-around threat Hugh Gallarneau.

They became known as the "Wow Boys" and completed a perfect 10-0 season when they defeated Nebraska 21-13 in the Rose Bowl.

But the true measure of Shaughnessy's brilliance played out nearly a month earlier. Despite the addition of Sid Luckman before the 1940 season, the Bears offense lunged and stalled with Shaughnessy no longer on site to explain the nuances of his creation. Chicago did average a team record 27.1 points a game and it was the only team in the league utilizing the T.

But on November 17, the Redskins employed a 5-3-2-1 defense that throttled the Bears in a 7-3 victory. Though Chicago would score 78 points and win its next two games to set up a rematch in the championship game, Halas called on Shaughnessy. The coach took a few days off and headed for Chicago to help Luckman fine-tune the Bears offense. It worked.

Chicago destroyed Sammy Baugh and the Washington Redskins 73-0 for the 1940 championship and Shaughnessy's vision had been confirmed coast-to-coast.

CLARK SHAUGHNESSY
STANFORD FOOTBALL COACH

injuries and mitigate the player drain in the event of war. The policy proved critical to keeping the game alive during the coming war years.

Though college campuses anticipated America's eventual participation, the violence outside the country's borders remained a distant echo. On the football field, Missouri coach Don Faurot added another wrinkle to the T-formation, calling back on his days as captain of Missouri's basketball team.

Faurot called his innovation the "split T" and it worked off the principles of a basketball fast break. In other words, Faurot's offense, which turned out to be the forerunner to the Wishbone, was designed to attract defenders to the ball before the ball was flipped to an open man.

"Split-T plays had a far better average than our single-wing plays," said Paul Christman, a former Missouri quarterback. "The option play and split line enabled us to run inside or outside the defensive end without blocking him. Our basic plays included a handoff to the dive man, a keeper by the quarterback inside the defensive end, a pitchout to the halfback outside the end and a running pass by the halfback either way."

But successive events early in December of 1941 changed everything everywhere and college football was

no exception. After the December 7 attack on Pearl Harbor, The Selective Service Act was amended 12 days later and it required all men ages 18 to 64 to register for the armed forces with those 20 to 44 available for military service.

For most of the next four years, college football, like the rest of society, struggled to hold itself together. Rules prohibiting gatherings of more than 5,000 on the West Coast essentially shut down the game there. Stanford didn't even have a team from 1942 to 1945. Other schools throughout the country either suspended play or shut down programs completely.

Meanwhile, the 1942 Rose Bowl was moved to North Carolina and the annual Notre Dame–USC match was suspended from 1943 through 1945.

Still, football, particularly the college version, had become such a part of the larger culture that it continued on military bases around the country. When Faurot enlisted in the Navy, he was sent to coach football at Iowa Pre-Flight, a move that ultimately helped further the evolution of the college game in the post-war years.

DON FAUROT
MISSOURI FOOTBALL COACH

NOTRE DAME RUNNING
THE OPTION PLAY

His two assistants at Iowa Pre-Flight were Jim Tatum and Bud Wilkinson, both of whom would become coaches at Oklahoma.

"I remember going up to Iowa State in 1943 to see Iowa Pre-Flight play Iowa State," said Merle Harmon. "Iowa State had these poor little 17- and 18-year-olds playing while Iowa Pre-Flight had Bernie Bierman coaching the team with Jim Tatum and Bud Wilkinson as his assistants. They beat the living daylights out of Iowa State. They were ahead 30-something to nothing and this little Iowa State running back broke into the clear. I can remember this Iowa Pre-Flight defender patting that little ole Iowa State guy on the fanny. He could have tackled him at any time. But he just patted him on the fanny as the guy crossed the goal line. Iowa Pre-Flight won 33-13."

Unfortunately for Tatum and Faurot, Wilkinson turned Oklahoma into a national power at their expense. Wilkinson replaced Tatum at Oklahoma, who lasted a year, and proceeded to beat Faurot's Missouri teams 11 straight times.

Conveniently, commanders agreed football amounted to good exercise. The competition, they reasoned, kept the soldiers' spirits up and provided the people at home with positive entertainment.

For players, football offered a transitional respite from what lay ahead. Indeed, players and coaches often found themselves playing the game one year and shipped off to war the next.

On college campuses, freshmen became eligible and even former professionals, if they were military trainees, were allowed to play. Rationing of gas and numerous other commodities led to attendance drops and even coaches agreed to suspend scouting and divulge offensive formations the week before games. All rules governing practices also were waived which allowed for unlimited summer workouts.

The first major game to be affected was the 1942 Rose Bowl, which was moved to Durham, North Carolina. Wallace Wade's Blue Devils were undefeated and agreed to play in the game against Oregon State. But the home

OKLAHOMA RUNNING
THE OPTION PLAY

field proved no advantage and North Carolina lost 20-16 before a crowd of 56,000 in the only Rose Bowl played outside Pasadena.

"When I was 10 years old Clint Castleberry was No. 19 on the Georgia Tech team," said Pepper Rodgers. "He threw the jump pass left handed. I was right handed, but I learned how to throw it left-handed just like Castleberry. They were unbeaten in 1942 and played Georgia for the right to go to 1943 Rose Bowl. Tech got beat 34-0. I called Clint Castleberry at his house after that game and told him how sorry I was. He got killed in the war the next year."

By then, military teams were more than just a passing fancy. In the final 1942 Associated Press poll, 12 of the 20 ranked teams, including powerhouses Army and Navy, were service teams such as Randolph Field, Iowa Pre-Flight, Great Lakes and Fort Pierce. Needless to say, many of the country's best athletes had flocked to the military academies.

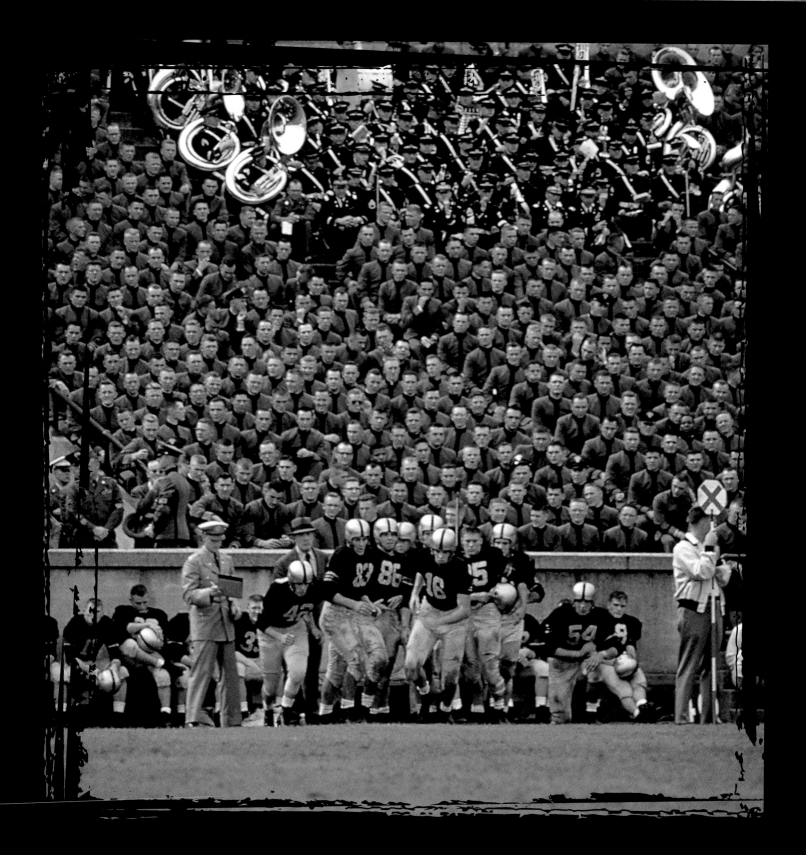

"The attitude of the military leadership at that time was to
keep up morale. They used athletics for that purpose."

— KEITH JACKSON

The one civilian team that stood the test of the war years was Notre Dame. Using the T-formation, the Fighting Irish won the national title in 1943 and quarterback Angelo Bertelli became the school's first Heisman Trophy winner despite playing only six games. Bertelli was called into military duty by the Marines halfway through the season.

After the 1943 season, Notre Dame Coach Frank Leahy also departed for military service. Army took advantage of the Irish losses to win back-to-back titles in 1944 and 1945, beating Notre Dame by a combined score of 91-13 those seasons.

War or no war, Army would have been a power in any season thanks to one of the most memorable backfields in college football. Glenn Davis and Doc Blanchard were consensus All-Americans from 1944-46, with Blanchard

Army was so powerful that when Michigan came to Yankee Stadium to play Army in October, 1945, Michigan's innovative coach, Fritz Crisler, who had 17- and 18-year-olds playing against the older Army players, decided to platoon eight players each on offense and defense. Crisler hoped to keep the score down by bringing in fresh teams on both sides of the ball.

It worked. The Wolverines lost by a respectable 28-7 margin after going into the fourth quarter even.

"Fritz Crisler was the originator of two-platoon system in football," said Bill Flemming. "It was during the War in 1945 and he had these young kids at Michigan. At the service academies they had these hardened athletes. So when Army and Navy played it was fine. But when Michigan played Army at Yankee Stadium, Crisler believed there was no reason he couldn't substitute an entire unit of defensive players.

31 PLAYERS TOOK THE OATH OF ENLISTMENT

1942

IMMEDIATELY FOLLOWING THE 1942 ROSE BOWL, NORTH CAROLINA COACH WALLACE WADE LEFT FOR THE ARMY. HE WAS COMMISSIONED AS A MAJOR IN THE ARMY FIELD ARTILLERY BATTALION AND EVENTUALLY WON THE BRONZE STAR.

THE SAME DAY, 31 PLAYERS TOOK THE OATH OF ENLISTMENT INTO THE NAVAL AIR CORPS DURING HALFTIME OF THE TEXAS A&M - ALABAMA COTTON BOWL IN DALLAS.

MARTIN RUBY TEXAS A & M TACKLE

MARTIN RUBY, A TACKLE, WAS ONE OF THE TEXAS A&M PLAYERS WHO STOOD TO TAKE THE OATH AFTER THE FIRST HALF. HE ALSO HELPED DEMONSTRATE THE TRANSIENT NATURE OF COLLEGE FOOTBALL IN THOSE DAYS. RUBY WAS NAMED ONE OF THE 1942 COTTON BOWL'S OUTSTANDING PLAYERS. TWO YEARS LATER, HE EARNED THE SAME HONOR PLAYING FOR THE RANDOLPH FIELD MILITARY TEAM IN A 7-7 TIE WITH TEXAS IN THE 1944 COTTON BOWL.

★ THE 1942 ROSE BOWL ★

INTO THE NAVAL AIR CORPS DURING HALFTIME

winning the 1945 Heisman Trophy and Davis taking the award in 1946.

With Mr. Outside (Davis) and Mr. Inside (Blanchard), Army had the most powerful offense in the nation. But Army also had a unique depth of talent and maturity, given the on-going war.

"(Vince) Lombardi was the offensive backfield coach," recalled Bill Yeoman, the Army center in those days. "It didn't make any difference what we practiced because we knew when we got in the game it was going to be a Short Trap, G Block Off Tackle, the Hook Pass and a draw play. That was it. We could run those blindfolded against any defense you put up there. Sid Gillman was my offensive line coach. Before practice even started, we would go through sled drills. Your legs were gone before you got to practice, but you were in pretty good shape."

He sprang it on Army and up until fourth quarter played them even, 7-7. That's where the two platoon game was born. I think it led to so much specialization that college football has lost its camaraderie. That's why I admired Charles Woodson and Deion Sanders, who could go both ways."

The war ended August 15, 1945, just in time for college football to join the greatest economic and social expansion of the century. Tens of thousands returned home from the war and headed for universities on the GI Bill. Those who had left as teenagers came home grown men. And many of them decided to strap on shoulder pads.

Chuck Bednarik, who would become one of professional football's greatest players, was one of those who came back bigger, stronger, older and more mature in every way after the war.

"Army had some great players," recalls Bednarik, who starred for the University of Pennsylvania from 1945

"I HAD BEEN A WAIST GUNNER OF A B-24 LIBERATOR. BY THE TIME I WAS 19, I HAD COMPLETED SIX BOMBING MISSIONS IN EUROPE. I WAS DISCHARGED ON OCTOBER 11, 1945 AND I WAS A 20-YEAR-OLD FRESHMAN IN NOVEMBER. I WAS ELIGIBLE FOR THE LAST FOUR GAMES OF THE YEAR.

I HAD NO PROBLEMS MAKING THE TEAM BECAUSE THOSE OTHER KIDS WERE 17 AND 18 YEARS OLD. I HAD JUST FINISHED 30 BOMBING MISSIONS OVER GERMANY. SO I SAID, 'GET OUT OF MY WAY.'"

— CHUCK BEDNARIK
University of Pennsylvania

CHUCK BEDNARIK
UNIVERSITY OF PENNSYLVANIA

through 1948. "But they were 19 and 20 years old. They were older than the kids just going to college. Then, after the war, the guys who were drafted when they were sophomores and juniors were 24, 25, 26.

"I had been a waist gunner of a B-24 Liberator. By the time I was 19, I had completed six bombing missions in Europe. I was discharged on October 11, 1945 and I was a 20-year-old freshman in November. I was eligible for the last four games of the year. I had no problems making the team because those kids were 17 and 18 years old. I had just finished 30 bombing missions over Germany. So I said, 'Get out of my way.'"

Fred Jacoby, later the commissioner of the Mid-American and Southwest conferences, was one of those kids at Ohio State when the older guys returned from the war.

"I was a 17-year-old freshman, but a lot of those guys came back to finish their degrees," said Jacoby, whose

college career ended because of injury. "In our dorm we had 10 double-decker beds, 20 guys living in the same room with standout lockers. We had guys who were 28, 29 and married who were coming back on the GI Bill."

"You had a lot more bulk when guys came back from the War," said Merle Harmon. "It was not so much that guys were playing in the service. I went into the Navy at 17 and I weighed 165 pounds. When I came back, I weighed 195. The guys coming back to school after the war were bigger. These guys coming back, especially the ones who were in combat, they weren't kids anymore. People had problems adjusting. I wasn't 19 anymore. Coaches had to adjust to guys coming out of the service. They really weren't freshmen. They might have been freshmen academically, but not mentally."

"The difference was age, experience and size," said Frank Broyles. "Those things had changed dramatically

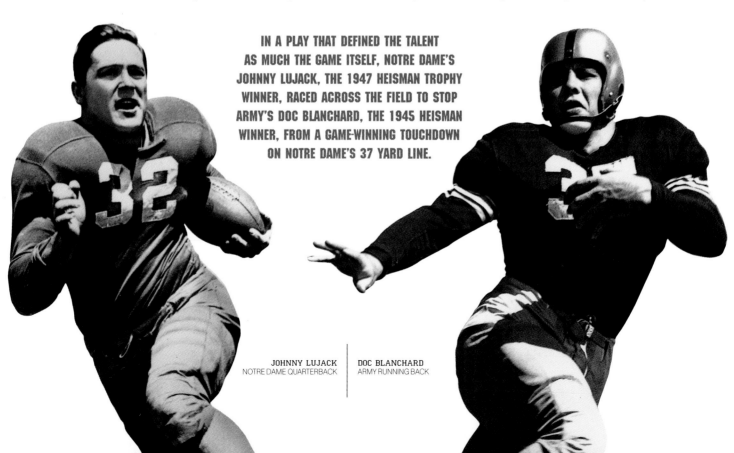

IN A PLAY THAT DEFINED THE TALENT AS MUCH THE GAME ITSELF, NOTRE DAME'S JOHNNY LUJACK, THE 1947 HEISMAN TROPHY WINNER, RACED ACROSS THE FIELD TO STOP ARMY'S DOC BLANCHARD, THE 1945 HEISMAN WINNER, FROM A GAME-WINNING TOUCHDOWN ON NOTRE DAME'S 37 YARD LINE.

JOHNNY LUJACK
NOTRE DAME QUARTERBACK

DOC BLANCHARD
ARMY RUNNING BACK

between 1941 and 1946. Every school had three or four older guys, 22, 23, 24. I was the backfield coach at Baylor when I was 22. They listed my age as 25 so I would be older than the players I was coaching."

The players were older, stronger and as a result the level of play increased dramatically. All of which was never more apparent than in the 1946 Army–Notre Dame game that ended in a scoreless tie. Fourteen future or current All-Americans played in the game with two College Football Hall of Fame coaches — Notre Dame's Frank Leahy and Army's Red Blaik — on the sidelines.

In a play that defined the talent as much as the game itself, Notre Dame's Johnny Lujack, the 1947 Heisman Trophy winner, raced across the field to stop Army's Doc Blanchard, the 1945 Heisman winner, from a game-winning touchdown on Notre Dame's 37 yard line.

"They said Blanchard couldn't be stopped one-on-one in the open field," Lujack said later. "Yet I did it. I really can't understand all the fuss. I simply pinned him against the sideline and dropped him with a routine tackle."

Notre Dame and Army finished one-two in the country, but neither ended up in the Rose Bowl. Notre Dame didn't play in any bowl from 1925 to 1970, but Army was forced out of the 1946 Rose Bowl when the Big Ten and Pacific Coast Conference (forerunner to the Pacific Eight and later the Pac-10) agreed to send their respective champions to the game every year.

DOAK WALKER SMU BACK

With Major League Baseball not yet on the West Coast and professional football still finding its way, the Rose Bowl was the country's marquee sporting event. By gaining access to that game on an annual basis, the Big Ten quickly became one of college football's most powerful conferences. Recruiting improved dramatically and Big Ten schools dominated the Rose Bowl for years until the West Coast teams caught up.

"Everybody was mad down in Southern California," remembers Wiles Hallock, former Pac-10 commissioner. "Glenn Davis (Army halfback) was from Southern California. They had a big banquet down in Los Angeles to announce the union and he was there. Everybody was disappointed that Army wasn't in the Rose Bowl. Illinois beat UCLA 45-14 and the Big Ten won 12 of the first 13 games."

One fact of college football the war didn't change was Notre Dame's dominance of the sport. The Fighting Irish won national titles in 1946, '47 and '49. After the tie with Army in 1946, Notre Dame didn't lose another game — its

14-14 tie with USC in 1948 notwithstanding — the rest of the decade.

The service academies eventually started to fade from the top of college football as other schools moved to fund the sport throughout the 1950s and '60s. But not every school looked at the sport the same after the war. Even at schools such as Nebraska, which would become a dominant player, officials questioned the idea of spending money on sports instead of directing those funds into academics.

"There was a feeling at that time on many campuses that college football shouldn't take away from the academics at the school and that it shouldn't be entertainment or big business," said Don Bryant, Nebraska's long-time sports information director. "There was a reluctance at a lot of schools, including Nebraska, to get in the modern way of running a football program and giving scholarships. We didn't have a true scholarship program until after 1953.

"The NCAA had rules to permit scholarships, but we didn't do it right from the start. Economics was a big reason. Some schools jumped right in. Others were reluctant because of what giving scholarships was going to cost."

By 1950, the college game was more popular in more places than the professional version, particularly in some of the larger cities of the South. In Texas, small private schools such as Rice, Texas Christian and Southern Methodist were drawing huge crowds in the state's two largest metropolitan areas, Dallas–Fort Worth and Houston, despite relatively small enrollments.

But what truly drove college football in the post-war years is what always has fueled sport in America: The search for heroes.

The war had produced enough of the military version to last decades, so when SMU's Doak Walker arrived with stunning ability and matinee idol looks, an entire nation took notice.

Walker made the covers of *Life, Collier's, Look* and *Sport* magazines and won the 1948 Heisman Trophy. But Walker did more than run and pass. Like most players of the era, Walker worked both sides of the ball and excelled at every part of the game.

"I coached against Doak Walker for three years," said Frank Broyles, former ABC Sports announcer and legendary head coach. "I remember that SMU had the Dallas market to itself. TCU was over there, but SMU owned the

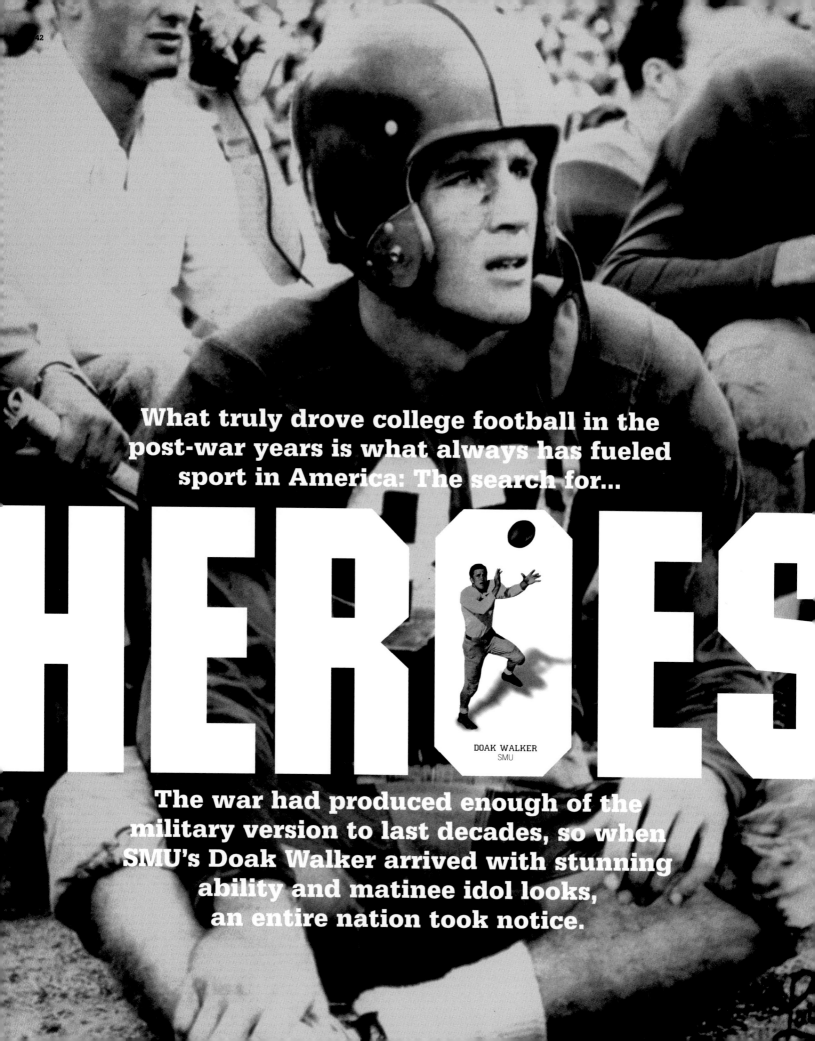

What truly drove college football in the post-war years is what always has fueled sport in America: The search for...

HEROES

DOAK WALKER
SMU

The war had produced enough of the military version to last decades, so when SMU's Doak Walker arrived with stunning ability and matinee idol looks, an entire nation took notice.

Dallas market. In 1949, Baylor moved a home game to the Cotton Bowl for money. We (Baylor) beat SMU 35-26 that day before more than 63,000 fans. But Doak Walker was a phenomenon. He could do it all, and he could play today just as effectively as anybody."

"You were a well-rounded All-American back then," said Bednarik, who finished third to Walker in the 1948 Heisman voting. "I snapped the ball on punts, extra points and field goals in college. I know I'm the last guy in pro football to play both ways at age 35. It was the same there as in college. I was in the game every play as linebacker and every play as a center, plus snapping the ball on punts, extra points and field goals. Guys get $500,000 a year for that alone today."

Walker's impact on the sport was surpassed only by his impact on the local economy. Because of Walker's popularity, SMU moved its home games from 23,000-seat Ownby Stadium to the Cotton Bowl midway through Walker's junior season. Twice during Walker's senior year, SMU played before crowds of more than 75,000 at the Cotton Bowl, which expanded to increase capacity by nearly 30,000 seats to meet the Walker ticket demand.

Nearby in Oklahoma, Wilkinson was building one of college football's greatest dynasties. Wilkinson's teams won 92.3 percent of their games and were so dominant

starters for two quarters or less, which affected the individual statistics of everyone.

"Bud always thought the second team was as good as the first, so we only got to play two quarters a game," said halfback Tommy McDonald, who finished third in the 1956 Heisman balloting. "Everybody else my senior year, Jim Brown, Paul Hornung, John Brodie and Lenny Dawson, got to play four quarters. But we acted like we had no superstars, and we really didn't."

Wilkinson was highly organized and he understood public relations, often inviting writers over to his house after games. He seldom raised his voice and motivated with a firm, but sometimes emotional detachment. He rarely criticized his players in public. And the only way players usually knew where they stood was when Wilkinson posted the first, second and third teams each Monday of game week. "If you had a bad game, he'd drop you down," McDonald said.

"Great leadership always has a degree of what I call mystique," says former Colorado athletic director and coach Eddie Crowder, who was a quarterback and later an assistant coach with Wilkinson. "Bud Wilkinson clearly had it. Bear Bryant had it. Bob Devaney had it."

"It was like taking a football lesson every day doing a game with Bud Wilkinson," said Chris Schenkel. "He was

ARCHIE GRIFFIN
OHIO STATE

MARCUS ALLEN
USC

HERSCHEL WALKER
GEORGIA

TONY DORSETT
PITTSBURGH

that the Big Eight became known as Oklahoma and Seven Dwarfs. At one point, the Sooners won 47 straight games, still an NCAA Division 1A record. They did it by turning Dan Faurot's manipulation of the T-formation into a full-time option offense.

"Don Faurot invented option football," says Darrell Royal, former Texas coach and ABC announcer who also played at Oklahoma. "Coach Wilkinson perfected it."

Despite the dominance, Oklahoma produced only one Heisman Trophy winner, Billy Vessels in 1952. But that only underscored the depth of talent at Oklahoma. Wilkinson had so many great players that he often used his

one of the great ones right there with Darrell Royal, Bear Bryant. He should have been president of the United States. He was bright enough and he was political enough. He ran for the Senate in Oklahoma and he would have won if he would have switched parties. But that wasn't something he would do. That's the way he was. I can't say enough about Bud Wilkinson."

As a starting quarterback, Crowder got to meet with Wilkinson one hour each day Monday through Friday of game weeks. And from those meetings, Crowder got a glimpse of Wilkinson's inside world. Wilkinson believed in being quicker and in better condition than the opposition.

He instituted the hurry-up huddle and would surprise teams with other "gadget" plays.

"In his office, he had something like a chess board, except that it was football field," Crowder said. "And he actually had little plastic players. He would align them in different defenses and start you at your own 20-yard line and have you call plays. He would change the time and score on the board and move the plastic players as the session went on. By the time you did that drill for a year or two, you were thinking along the same vein as he was."

If Wilkinson led with a soft shoe, Woody Hayes perfected the boot. A former naval lieutenant commander during the war, Hayes had a different view of leadership and it had nothing to do with public relations. First at Denison and then Ohio State, Hayes was a dictator whose demand for military-like discipline and procedure turned

the Buckeyes into a national power. Hayes also produced some of the greatest coaches the college game ever has known, including his eventual nemesis, Bo Schembechler, who played for Hayes at Miami of Ohio, Carmen Cozza, the legendary Yale coach, and Ara Parseghian, who was an assistant under Hayes at Miami of Ohio.

"ABC Sports assigned me to handle the play-by-play on the telecast of an Ohio State game in 1968," said Merle Harmon. "I had never met coach Woody Hayes but understood he could be rather tough on the media. The day before the game in Columbus, I met the coach in his office. He was pleasant but pressed for time and it was obvious I wasn't going to be there long.

"He gave me the basic stuff on the game and then said, 'Is there anything else I can do for you?' Stammering, I replied, 'Well, you could show me your game plan for tomorrow.' I immediately wanted to bite my tongue for making such a stupid request.

"I waited for his explosion but it never came. 'Oh,' said Woody, 'I couldn't do that but there won't be any surprises. We're pretty basic. I will share a little deal we played around with yesterday — a fake field goal. But we would have to have the perfect situation to use it.'

BUD WILKINSON
OKLAHOMA HEAD COACH

"Then he told me what the perfect situation would have to be. Sure enough, that 'situation' came up in the game and I alerted the producer to look for a fake field goal and a forward pass. And that's exactly what happened. It almost went for a touchdown. And I thought Woody Hayes was a 'three yards a cloud of dust' coach.

"Several years later I met coach Hayes and asked him if he had ever used the fake field goal again. 'Nope,' he said. 'It was a once-in-a-lifetime play for me. The next time we line up for a fake field goal, we'll run the ball.'"

"It was a good time to be there," said Cozza, who played for Hayes at Miami of Ohio and later coached at Yale for 41 seasons. "Woody and Ara both had a big influence on all of us. Woody was tough. You knew when he was around because he screamed at you. But he also had a good side to him. And you better not cut class. Everybody graduated.

"No matter where we traveled, we always got a little pamphlet called, 'Where You're Going' from Woody. It gave you information like the history of a place. Woody was big on that."

Hayes's devotion to the running game, at least in the early years, might have had something to do with the way the winds were blowing on the Football Rules Committee. The abolition of platoon football in 1953 affected offenses the rest of the decade. With players required to play both ways, wide receivers became a luxury fewer teams chose to employ.

In 1951, major college teams averaged 18.9 passes a game. Four years later, the figure dropped to 13.6 and never topped 16.5 the rest of the decade. Conversely, teams were running the ball an average of nearly 50 times a game. Of the 10 Heisman Trophy winners in the 1950s, nine of them were running backs.

The only school to buck the trend? Notre Dame, of course. Quarterback Paul Hornung won the 1956 Heisman, beating out some of the greatest running backs of any era including Johnny Majors of Tennessee, Tommy McDonald of Oklahoma and Jim Brown of Syracuse. All of which was far more a testament to the Irish public relations machine than Hornung's ability, something even Hornung recognized.

"I can't believe it," Hornung said upon being told he won the award. "I didn't think I was even up for consideration."

A little more than a decade later, it would be a Notre Dame–Michigan State game on ABC Sports College Football Game of the Week that would propel college football and the network's coverage of the game.

"We were lucky to get a marquee game like that the first year," said Chris Schenkel, who teamed with Bud Wilkinson on ABC's Sports first full schedule of college football broadcasts in 1966.

If Hornung had played for any other school there is a good chance all consideration would have centered on Brown, Majors and McDonald. Though Hornung was a great player, Notre Dame finished 2-8 that season and he remains the only Heisman winner to come from a losing team.

But that experience confirmed a reality no one understood as well as Notre Dame. Hornung's victory centered on the fact writers from all over the country paid attention to Notre Dame. The Irish tried to take advantage of that by putting together its own television network in the early 1950s.

By then, television quickly was surpassing radio for ad dollars and America's attention. In January of 1950, national sponsors were moving from radio to television at such a rate that *Variety* described the exodus as "the greatest exhibition of mass hysteria in biz annals." In 1951, *I Love Lucy* made its debut and by the end of 1952, 20 million households had television, a 33 percent increase from the previous year.

None of this was lost on Notre Dame, but the school wasn't alone. The NCAA seized control of television rights in 1952 precisely because of the Irish business interests.

"One of my first memories of college football was during my high school playing days," said Jack Arute, ABC Sports announcer. "Our entire football team watched the Michigan State–Notre Dame game in 1966. I remember the intensity of that game. We all marveled at how hard they played. The game ended in a tie. And I think it was the only tie I have ever witnessed, in person or on television, that I thought a tie was fitting."

NCAA executive director Walter Byers voided the Notre Dame deal because the association said it would give the Irish an insurmountable recruiting advantage. If Notre Dame persisted, said Byers, the NCAA would boycott Irish opponents by keeping them off television. The independent Irish fell in line, albeit for the time being.

"Television played a tremendous part in all of the things that happened," said Nebraska's Don Bryant. "The increase in interest and exposure at that time was a real boost. People saw college football who had never seen it before. Schools made efforts to get on TV as the money started adding up."

The NCAA essentially maintained control of the television schedule until 1984, when Georgia and Oklahoma sued, claiming the NCAA's actions violated the Sherman

---

★ WOODY HAYES ★

LONG BEFORE WOODY HAYES PERFECTED HIS "THREE YARDS AND A CLOUD OF DUST" OFFENSIVE APPROACH AT OHIO STATE HE SHOWED AT LEAST A MOMENTARY APPRECIATION FOR THE PASSING GAME.

NORBERT WIRKOWSKI THREW FOR 1,000 YARDS DURING HAYES'S FINAL SEASON AT MIAMI OF OHIO. BUT HAYES EFFECTIVELY EXPUNGED THAT PIECE OF HISTORY THE DAY HE ARRIVED AT OHIO STATE, EVEN THOUGH HE DID RECRUIT EVENTUAL NFL ALL-PRO WIDE RECEIVER PAUL WARFIELD.

AND JUST TO BE CLEAR AS TO HIS FEELINGS ABOUT THE FORWARD PASS AND QUARTERBACKS WHO SPECIALIZED IN IT, HAYES'S ONLY ACT IN THE RECRUITMENT OF JOE NAMATH WAS TO OFFER HIM TO ANOTHER SCHOOL.

IN FAIRNESS TO HAYES, BY THE TIME NAMATH WAS DAZZLING COLLEGE SCOUTS, OHIO STATE ALREADY HAD PRODUCED A SERIES OF GREAT RUNNING BACKS AND WON THREE NATIONAL CHAMPIONSHIPS.

WOODY HAYES OHIO STATE COACH

FRED JACOBY, AN ASSISTANT DEFENSIVE BACKFIELD COACH AT WISCONSIN IN THOSE DAYS, REMEMBERS HAYES BRINGING HIS TEAM IN A DAY EARLY AND PRACTICING AT THE STADIUM. GIVEN THE BUCKEYES' APPROACH AND TALENT LEVEL, HAYES WASN'T EXACTLY CONCERNED ABOUT GIVING UP ANY SECRETS.

"ALL THE ASSISTANTS WOULD SAY, 'LET'S GO SEE WHAT THEY ARE GOING TO DO,'" RECALLS JACOBY. "I SAID, 'THEY ARE GOING TO BLOCK OFF TACKLE FOUR DIFFERENT WAYS.' I JUST HOPED THEY DIDN'T THROW THE BALL TO (PAUL) WARFIELD OUT THERE."

HAYES BECAME SUCH A STAUNCH BELIEVER IN THE RUNNING GAME, HE DIDN'T EVEN RECRUIT NAMATH, A TERRIFIC ATHLETE AND PASSING WHIZ OUT OF NEARBY PENNSYLVANIA. BUT JUST TO MAKE SURE NAMATH DIDN'T END UP THROWING PASSES AT HIS BUCKEYES, HAYES CALLED BEAR BRYANT AT ALABAMA.

"WOODY HAYES TOLD BRYANT TO RECRUIT NAMATH, BECAUSE HE WAS NOT GOING TO PLAY FOR HIM," SAID LEE ROY JORDAN, AN ALL-AMERICA LINEBACKER FOR BRYANT AT ALABAMA. "WOODY WOULD RATHER HIM PLAY FOR ALABAMA THAN TO PLAY FOR ANOTHER BIG TEN TEAM."

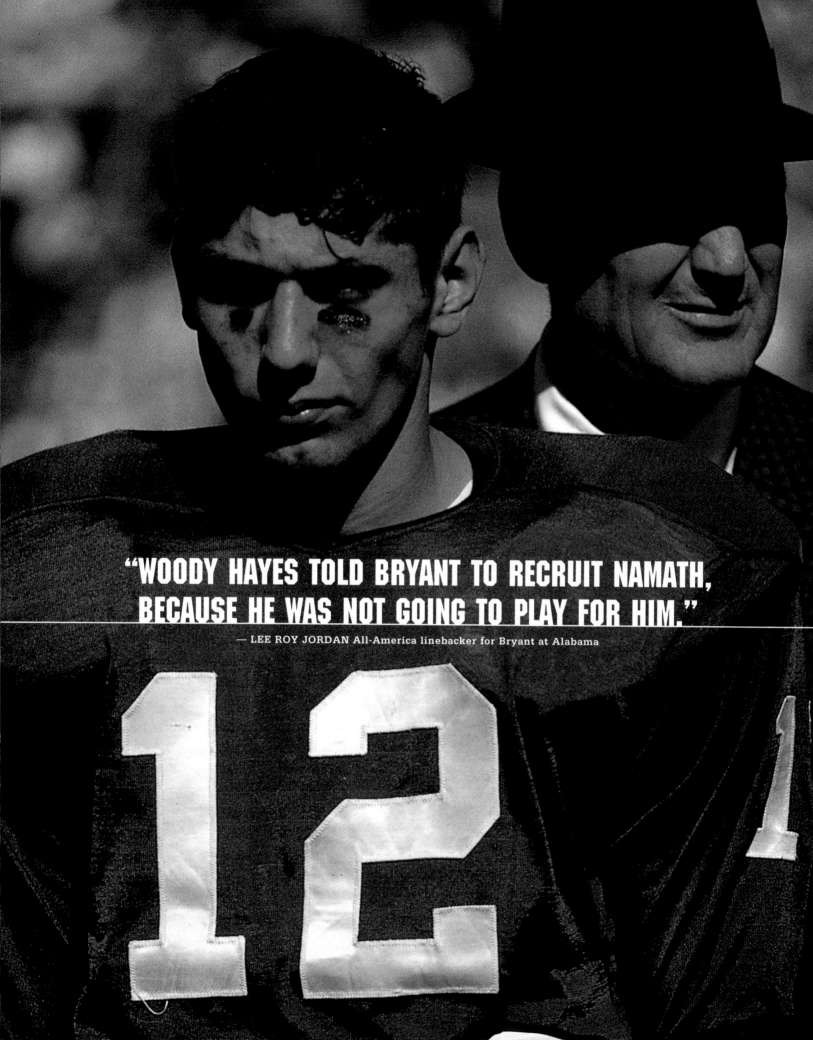

"WOODY HAYES TOLD BRYANT TO RECRUIT NAMATH, BECAUSE HE WAS NOT GOING TO PLAY FOR HIM."

— LEE ROY JORDAN All-America linebacker for Bryant at Alabama

COLLEGE FOOTBALL MIGHT HAVE BECOME MORE POPULAR TELEVISION PROGRAMMING QUICKER IF THE GAME HAD NOT RETURNED TO A SINGLE PLATOON FORMAT.

THANKS TO LIBERAL SUBSTITUTION RULES PASSED BEFORE WORLD WAR II, SCORING INCREASED FROM 26.6 POINTS A GAME IN 1940 TO 36.8 POINTS A GAME IN 1952. THE NUMBER OF PLAYS WENT FROM AN AVERAGE OF 114.4 TO AN AVERAGE OF 133.4. AND PASSING YARDS INCREASED FROM 156 YARDS TO 223.8 YARDS A GAME.

BUT SEVERAL OF THE AGING RULES MAKERS IN 1953, MOST NOTABLY FORMER TENNESSEE COACH GENERAL BOB NEYLAND, BELIEVED THE TWO-PLATOON SYSTEM WAS "CHICKEN SHIT FOOT-BALL." FORMER ALABAMA AND DUKE COACH WALLACE WADE AGREED

AS DID CHUCK BEDNARIK, WHO STILL BELIEVES THE GAME WAS MADE FOR TWO-WAY PLAYERS.

"COLLEGE FOOTBALL IN MY DAY, AS FAR AS I AM CONCERNED WAS COLLEGE FOOTBALL, " BEDNARIK SAYS. "IT WAS AN IRON-MAN SPORT. NOT LIKE TODAY. THESE KIDS ARE BIGGER, FASTER AND MAYBE BETTER, BUT THEY SPECIALIZE. I'D LIKE TO SEE THEM STAY OUT THERE THE ENTIRE GAME AND SEE HOW GOOD THEY ARE. WHAT YOU HAVE NOW IN COLLEGE AND PROS ARE KIDS WHO WEIGH 340, 350 POUNDS. THEY WOULD HAVE BEEN FALLING DOWN BACK IN THOSE DAYS. WATCH THEM AFTER FOUR PLAYS NOW. THEY WALK OFF TO THE SIDELINES AND PUT THE OXYGEN MASK ON."

FOR THE GREATER PART OF 12 YEARS, THE RULES COMMITTEE

"... KIDS WHO WEIGH 340, 350 POUNDS. THEY WOULD HAVE BEEN FALLING DOWN BACK IN THOSE DAYS."

— CHUCK BEDNARIK former University of Pennsylvania star

Anti-Trust Act. The Supreme Court concurred and Notre Dame eventually got its television deal.

"As the NCAA plan grew through the 1970s, there was one national game and four regional games each week," said Jacoby. "Basically it limited appearances and spread it around so more teams would be on. The thought was that if you limited the games it decreased the appreciable damage at the gate."

Chuck Neinas, former executive director of the College Football Association (CFA), said the NCAA plan often pro-hibited the best games from being shown during certain regional telecasts. Neinas once received a handwritten note from Alabama coach Bear Bryant, who complained he couldn't watch a key Michigan State–Notre Dame game on television. Instead, the state of Alabama received the Alabama A&M vs. Jackson State game in the regional time slot.

Still, college football thrived and tele-vision, limited as it was, played a role in driving fans into the stadiums. Starting with the 1954 season, attendance began an upward spiral that lasted 20 consecutive years.

With the game becoming more and more popular, every coach was looking for an edge. LSU's Paul Dietzel was no different. When he wasn't trying to manipulate the rules on the field he was looking for something a little extra off the field.

His teams were among the first to use weight training. LSU employed a Baton Rouge body builder to set up weight-

lifting machines for the Tigers. Given the lack of sophisti-cation at the time, most considered Dietzel's training methods misguided.

"We maybe had two or three guys on the team that ever lifted a weight," said former Nebraska coach Tom Osborne, who played football at Hastings College in Nebraska in the late 1950s. "They were looked upon as kind of odd. There was always the fear of getting muscle bound and that type of thing."

When Pepper Rodgers was an assistant coach at UCLA, Bruins head coach Tommy Prothro sent him into the press box to get plays off instant replay, a ploy that later was outlawed.

Of all the coaches in the 1950s and '60s, Prothro might have been the most forward looking. He took Oregon State to the Rose Bowl in 1957 and 1965 before taking over the UCLA program in 1966.

In 1962, Prothro's offensive innova-tions helped make quarterback Terry Baker the first Heisman Trophy winner from a West Coast school. Then, in 1966, Prothro's second Heisman-winning quarterback, Gary Beban, led UCLA to a stunning 14-12 upset of Michigan State in the Rose Bowl.

At UCLA, Prothro also came up with an idea to place a small headset inside Beban's helmet for transmitting sig-nals. But a concession stands walkie-talkie picked up the signals and The Football Rules Committee quickly passed a rule prohibiting electronic signaling devices.

THOUGH HORNUNG WAS A GREAT PLAYER, NOTRE DAME FINISHED 2-8 THAT SEASON AND HORNUNG REMAINS THE ONLY HEISMAN WINNER TO COME FROM A LOSING TEAM.

PAUL HORNUNG NOTRE DAME QUARTERBACK
1956 HEISMAN TROPHY WINNER

WRESTLED WITH SOMETIMES COMICAL SUBSTITUTION RULES BEFORE TWO-PLATOON FOOTBALL AND UNLIMITED SUBSTITUTION RETURNED IN 1965.

"THE RULES MADE THE OFFICIALS INTO SECRETARIES GETTING PLAYERS IN AND OUT OF THE GAME," SAID JOE ADAMS, THE NCAA FOOTBALL RULES COMMITTEE SECRETARY-EDITOR. "COACHES WOULD CREATE `DEAD' BENCHES FOR PLAYERS INELIGIBLE TO RE-ENTER THE GAME. CERTAIN PLAYERS WOULD WEAR RED OR GREEN ARMBANDS, DISTINGUISHING WHEN THEY COULD ENTER THE GAME."

AT OREGON STATE, BUD GIBBS, TIGHT-END COACH UNDER COACH TOMMY PROTHRO, HAD ONE JOB DURING GAMES, THAT WAS FLASH-ING SUBSTITUTION SCENARIOS WRITTEN OUT ON CARDS. FORMER DALLAS COWBOYS DIRECTOR OF PLAYER PERSONNEL, GIL BRANDT REMEMBERS GOING TO AN OREGON STATE GAME AND SEEING THE CARDHOLDER GETTING FLATTENED DURING A SIDELINE PLAY AND THE CARDS FLYING EVERYWHERE.

"THE THING OF IT WAS DURING THAT ERA, THAT WAS PART OF THE GAME," SAID TEXAS QUARTERBACK DUKE CARLISLE, WHO PLAYED BOTH WAYS AS A JUNIOR IN THE EARLY 1960S. "YOU WERE USED TO IT DURING HIGH SCHOOL BECAUSE THERE WEREN'T ENOUGH PLAYERS ON YOUR HIGH SCHOOL TEAM TO HAVE OFFENSIVE AND DEFENSIVE TEAMS. BUT THERE WAS CHAOS IN COLLEGE FOOTBALL. THERE WAS SWEARING AT EACH OTHER: 'HOW COULD YOU LET THAT GUY GO IN!' YOU MIGHT GET A FIVE OR 10-YARD PENALTY."

COACHES TRIED EVERYTHING TO GET AROUND THE SUBSTITU-TION RULES. THAT INCLUDED INSTRUCTING PLAYERS TO FAKE INJURIES. LSU COACH PAUL DIETZEL TOOK HIS TEAM TO THE NATIONAL CHAMPIONSHIP IN 1958 BY CREATING A UNIT CALLED THE "CHINESE BANDITS." HE HAD A WHITE TEAM, HIS STARTERS; A SECOND-TEAM TO BACK THEM UP, THEN THE BANDITS, WHICH WERE THE LEAST ATH-LETIC AND PLAYED ONLY DEFENSE.

PEPPER RODGERS COACHED COLLEGE FOOTBALL FOR MORE THAN 22 YEARS WITH HEAD COACHING STOPS AT KANSAS, UCLA AND GEORGIA TECH BEFORE WORK-ING WITH ABC SPORTS ON COLLEGE FOOTBALL TELECASTS.

AS THE COLLEGE GAME BECAME MORE COMPETITIVE IN THE 1950S AND 1960S, SO TOO DID THE TACTICS.

"A COACH WOULD SOMETIMES SEND A GRADUATE ASSISTANT OVER TO AN OPPOSING PRACTICE, AND HE'D LOOK LIKE A NORMAL STUDENT WHO BLENDED IN," SAYS RODGERS. "THAT GUY WOULD HAVE TO STAND THERE AND TRY TO MEMORIZE EVERYTHING HE SAW WITHOUT WRITING ANYTHING DOWN. OF COURSE, IF THE KID COULD MEMORIZE EVERYTHING, THEN MAYBE HE SHOULD HAVE BEEN THE HEAD COACH OF THE SCHOOL THAT SENT HIM."

RODGERS, HOWEVER, PREFERRED COUNTER INTELLI-GENCE, IN WHICH HE DABBLED AS AN ASSISTANT AT FLORIDA.

"WE WERE ABOUT TO SEND A GUY TO GEORGIA TECH WHEN SOMEONE SENT ME A POSTCARD SAYING TECH WAS WORKING HARD AT BLOCKING PUNTS," SAYS RODGERS. "THAT WAS NO BIG NEWS. SO I DECIDED TO SEND A POST-CARD TO GEORGIA TECH COACH BOBBY DODD SAYING I'D SEEN FLORIDA PRACTICE THROWING PASSES FROM A PUNT FORMATION. I SIGNED IT, `A TECH FAN.'

"WE GET INTO THE GAME THAT WEEK AND THE FIRST TIME WE DROP BACK TO PUNT EVERYONE ON THE TECH SIDE-LINE IS SCREAMING, `WATCH THE FAKE, WATCH THE FAKE.' THE REST OF THE YEAR, I SENT A POSTCARD TO EVERY COACH WE WERE ABOUT TO PLAY."

— **PEPPER RODGERS**

Prothro developed the "passing tree," which sent receivers on routes all over the field, instead of just deep down the sideline. He was among the first to splice game film into offensive and defensive reels, so coaches could go over specific parts of the game with specific players.

"I worked for Tommy as an assistant and replaced him at UCLA," said Pepper Rodgers. "First of all, in terms of football fundamentals I learned more about the techniques of the game from Tommy than anyone else. Tommy was-n't the greatest recruiter and in order to be the best coach, you had to be among the best recruiters. But in terms of pure intelligence he was as smart or smarter than most of the coaches. He and I would play chess by the hours. He said chess was more like football than any other game. He said in chess you don't win making moves, you win by making moves when the other guy makes a mis-take. In college football, when he beat you on long pass it was because the other guy made a mistake."

Off the field, the game's growth and popularity became fertile ground for marketing innovation. Indeed, with athletic scholarships came the need for schools to sell tickets and develop addi-tional revenue streams. Two of the all-time best were Michigan athletic director Don Canham and Liberty Bowl executive director Bud Dudley, who had been athletic director at Villanova.

"I've always considered Fritz Crisler the first real businessman athletic director," said Keith Jackson. "Don Canham came along in Crisler's wake and was even better. But Fritz built the

GARY BEBAN UCLA QUARTERBACK
1966 HEISMAN TROPHY WINNER

foundation. In 1970 I went out to do an interview with Fritz. At that time, all the academes were fighting with the athletic departments. The chemistry and English professors were whining over not getting enough publicity. Fritz had just had his first bout with cancer, but he agreed to meet. I really didn't know the man very well. I asked him about the academes accusing the athletic department of destroying young people because of the pressure to win. You could see his neck get red and the veins pop up. For a minute, he was the old coach again. He said, 'Well, what the hell do you propose we do, teach them to lose?' I hugged him. We went on to become close friends."

Canham had been Michigan's track coach before he took over the athletic department. But he relied on business principles learned while running a teaching supply business on the side to grow the Wolverine program. Among other things, Canham was among the first to popularize the Student Book Store concept by offering athletic gear, jerseys, T-shirts, caps and cups with the school's logo. He also

purchases of $10 or more. Eventually, the store came back for 50,000 more tickets. Dudley pulled off the "grocery store" games for five years with various opponents and drew more than 460,000 fans in the process.

"One year at the Liberty Bowl, I was given permission as an on-the-field reporter for ABC to interview the then Vice President, Spiro Agnew, who was in the stands," said Bill Flemming. "At halftime, I went up to where he was seated and as I approached him I reached into my coat pocket for my handkerchief. It was a very chilly day. All of a sudden, I was grabbed by two of the strongest Secret Service guys I have ever seen. They pinned my arms behind me until they had me in a vice-like grip. I guess they thought I was an assassin.

"The Vice President quickly came to my rescue, and my arms were black and blue for a week. I was so embarrassed I forgot the Vice President's name."

In terms of acceptance and growth, nothing matched the 1960s. Attendance increased by nearly 50 percent

"THE MOST OUTSTANDING GAME I DID FOR ABC WAS THE 1969 MICHIGAN–OHIO STATE GAME. OHIO STATE WAS FAVORED BY THREE TOUCHDOWNS AND THEY CAME TO MICHIGAN, WHICH HAD LOST TWO GAMES. ON THE AFTERNOON BEFORE THE GAME WE WOULD SHOOT STILLS OF PLAYERS. CHET FORTE LINED UP ALL THE GUYS. UP WE CAME TO A BIG TACKLE, A GUY WHO HAD BEEN HANDLING A ROSE. THE KID HELD IT UP TO HIS CHIN FOR THE PICTURE. WOODY WENT BALLISTIC. THE GUY WAS 6-FEET-6, 290 POUNDS. WOODY GRABBED THAT ROSE AND HE WAS CHIN TO CHIN WITH HIM, ALTHOUGH THE GUY'S CHIN AT WOODY'S HEAD. I NEVER SAW ANYBODY SO UPSET ABOUT SOMEONE COUNTING HIS CHICKENS BEFORE THEY HATCHED. MICHIGAN BEAT OHIO STATE, 24-12. ACCORDING TO WOODY, THAT WAS THE MOST HUMILIATING DEFEAT HE EVER HAD IN COACHING."

— BILL FLEMMING
former ABC Sports announcer

tied concerts to athletic events and marketed football tickets through newspaper ads and local department stores.

Dudley created the Liberty Bowl in 1959 by negotiating a five-year contract with NBC before the first game was even played. It was Dudley who gave Paul "Bear" Bryant his first and last bowl bids at Alabama.

"He was a visionary," says Gene Corrigan, former Atlantic Coast Conference commissioner.

But Dudley's most ingenious move might have come at Villanova when he scheduled a game against Georgia in Philadelphia. Despite having only a 9,000-seat stadium on campus, Dudley guaranteed Georgia coach Wally Butts $25,000. Dudley figured he would move the game to cavernous Philadelphia Municipal Stadium and fill the place. But six weeks before the game, only 2,300 tickets had been sold.

Dudley had read about grocery store giveaways and convinced a chain in the area to buy 40,000 tickets at 35 cents each. The grocery stores gave away the tickets with

from 1960 to 1970. The two-platoon game increased scoring and television, thanks in part to ABC Sports, broadened the game's appeal throughout the country. The NFL's increasing popularity only proved to drive even more fans to the colleges.

"It was two different games," said Bob Griese, ABC Sports announcer. "Now, you have unlimited substitution where you can take guys out in mass whenever you want to. You can take a back out and put three receivers in, or take receivers out and put backs in. It used to be that you could only put one guy in at a time. When the rules changed, you could do whatever you wanted to do. Those rules changes and the NFL changed everything in college football. The NFL went to varied formations and a lot of passing. Colleges have always followed the pros so they started doing some of the things that were happening in the NFL and it really helped the colleges."

Nearly every corner of the country had a dominant team with USC, Texas, Nebraska, Michigan, Alabama and Ohio State among them. Canham's marketing genius was filling Michigan Stadium and when Bo Schembechler became the Wolverines' coach in 1969, Ohio State's Woody Hayes had a true rival.

As the power shifted to large state universities, so did the ability to generate money. With no rules regulating the number of players on a team, large state schools could attract equally large blocks of talent. That was especially true of schools such as Alabama which made a commitment to football by upgrading facilities and creating multiple revenue streams through alumni, television and large gate receipts.

"Schools would stockpile players," says Gil Brandt. "Before the NCAA started legislating the number of players you could have, you'd have a pair and a spare. At the big schools, you'd have a coach for the right guard and one for the left guard."

With plenty of players, modern facilities and a school's commitment, about the only thing left was to find the right coach. And Alabama did just that in 1958 when it hired Paul "Bear" Bryant away from Texas A&M to start the greatest dynasty in the history of college football in the South.

"I was in high school when he was going strong," said Dick Vermeil, former ABC Sports accouncer who guided the St. Louis Rams to the 2000 Super Bowl title.

"I remember reading his book, going to his clinics, watching his teams on television. I think his book was called *Championship Football*. When it came out

BLUE RIBBON PANEL ★

"**I** WAS IN ANN ARBOR TO ANNOUNCE A IOWA–MICHI-GAN GAME. THE DAY BEFORE THE GAME, I WAS SPEAK-ING WITH IOWA COACH HAYDEN FRY. I ASKED HIM ABOUT HIS MOST VIVID MEMORY AT THE STADIUM.

"HE SAID THAT WHILE HE WAS COACHING AT SMU HIS TEAM WAS A HEAVY UNDERDOG AGAINST MICHIGAN. THEY LOST A CLOSE, HARD FOUGHT GAME TO THE WOLVERINES. AFTER THE GAME, A PROMINENT FORD MOTOR COMPANY EXECUTIVE ASKED TO SPEAK TO THE SMU TEAM. THE MAN SAID HE WAS SO IMPRESSED WITH THE WAY SMU BATTLED MICHIGAN HE DECIDED TO NAME A NEW CAR AFTER THEM.

"LEE IACCOCA CALLED IT THE 'MUSTANG,' AND THE REST IS HISTORY.

— **ROGER TWIBELL**
ABC Sports announcer

BO SCHEMBECHLER
FORMER MICHIGAN COACH

WOODY HAYES
FORMER OHIO STATE COACH

PAUL "BEAR" BRYANT
ALABAMA HEAD COACH

"I VERBALLY COMMITTED TO BRYANT TO PLAY QUARTERBACK AT ALABAMA. ONE OF MY DAD'S BIGGEST THRILLS WAS WHEN BEAR BRYANT CALLED TO WISH US HAPPY NEW YEAR FROM THE SUGAR BOWL IN 1967. I WAS OUT AND MY DAD TOOK THE CALL. BUT I GOT SO MUCH PRESSURE FROM MY BROTHER, FAMILY AND FRIENDS TO GO TO MARYLAND, I HAD TO CALL BRYANT AND TELL HIM I WAS GOING TO MARYLAND. BUT WHEN HE CALLED US FROM THE SUGAR BOWL, THE PRESIDENT CALLING COULD NOT HAVE MADE A BIGGER IMPACT ON MY DAD."

— **TIM BRANDT played linebacker at Maryland**

it was like the Bible. The thing about Bear, he had that aura about him. Maybe it was more an image than a reality. He was a master at knowing how to get the most out of an athlete. Those who played for him ended up being the best athletes they could have been with the God-given talents they possessed. To do that, you had to have a certain kind of discipline. And he instilled that."

At Texas, the Longhorns brought in Darrell Royal. At USC, it was John McKay. And, at Nebraska, Bob Devaney drove the program.

Bryant took the Crimson Tide to 24 straight bowl games after failing to do so in his first season. Alabama went 83-10-6 from 1959 to 1967 and won three national championships. From 1963 to 1967, Alabama didn't lose a home game. Bryant's teams were smart, quick and often directed by unusually talented quarterbacks such as Joe Namath, Kenny Stabler, Jeff Rutledge, Steve Sloan, Scott Hunter and Richard Todd.

"He taught loyalty, class, character, team work," said Lee Roy Jordan, former Alabama linebacker. "His philosophy was that he was there to teach his players the game of life. He seldom lost his temper. But he was pretty much in control. He had this presence about him. You didn't want to disappoint him."

But Bryant also was as wily and sly as any coach in any sport.

"I always said any time you wanted to know about circumventing a rule — legally — just give me five minutes and I'll find out, because I'll call Coach Bryant," said Charlie McClendon, former LSU coach, who played for Bryant at Kentucky. "Because of him the Football Rules Committee had to get rid of the tackle-eligible rule. They had to change the uniform numbering system because Coach Bryant would stick a 68 on a wide receiver and confuse the heck out of your defense. He was the first to run a quarterback on the field to deliver the play to the huddle, and then back off. They changed the rule to make (the quarterback) stay in the game."

"Mel Allen and I worked a Texas A&M–Texas game at College Station in 1957," said Bill Flemming. "Bear Bryant was A&M's coach and he asked Mel to come to his house the night before the game. I stayed at the motel. Mel knocked on my door at 1 or 2 a.m. He told me Bear was resigning after the game the next day. Mel was an Alabama graduate and he told me Bear had requested him not to say anything on air. I was a rookie compared to Mel, who said he hadn't even told the producer. I told Mel we should sleep on it and meet for breakfast. And we did. I told him I thought he ought to bring the producer into this. We decided we would sign off as soon as the game was over. We would give a real brief summary, go off air and come back with a special report. We were fulfilling the coach's request. Bear had gone into the dressing and room and told his team he was going to Alabama and we reported the news."

More than anything, Bryant was a student of the game. He was known to read the rules book before every season and remained strategically flexible to the end. He passed when he had good quarterbacks, pulled back and ran the ball when he did not. When USC and running back Sam Cunningham hammered Alabama 42-21 to open the 1970 season, Bryant realized he had to recruit the black athlete. The next season he had running back Wilbur Jackson and

"**I** NEVER SAW MYSELF AS A POTENTIAL PROFESSIONAL FOOTBALL PLAYER UNTIL THE SUMMER BEFORE MY SENIOR YEAR. UNTIL TITLE IX MANDATED SCHOLARSHIP REDUCTIONS, TEAMS LIKE NEBRASKA, OKLAHOMA, FLORIDA, TEXAS AND USC WOULD HAVE 120 GUYS ON THE TEAM. YOU HAD 40 OR 50 GUYS WHO HAD BEEN HIGH SCHOOL ALL-AMERICANS. YOU WALKED INTO THAT REALITY AND KNEW THERE WERE ONLY GOING TO BE SO MANY OPPORTUNITIES. IT WASN'T UNTIL I WATCHED THE 1973 COLLEGE ALL-STAR GAME AND SAW WHAT SOME OF THE RECEIVERS DID OR DIDN'T DO THAT I THOUGHT I HAD A CHANCE. MY COACH AT USC, JOHN McKAY, COACHED THAT TEAM AGAINST THE MIAMI DOLPHINS. I THOUGHT, 'I'M WATCHING THESE ALL-AMERICANS AND SEEING THE MISTAKES THEY'RE MAKING. MAYBE I COULD BE A FIRST ROUND PICK.'"

LYNN SWANN, ABC SPORTS ANNOUNCER, PLAYED ON A NATIONAL CHAMPIONSHIP TEAM AT USC AND THEN WON FOUR SUPER BOWLS WITH THE PITTSBURGH STEELERS.

— **LYNN SWANN ABC Sports announcer won four Super Bowls with the Pittsburgh Steelers**

Alabama won the national championship. When Oklahoma played Alabama to a 24-24 tie in the 1970 Bluebonnet Bowl, Bryant knew it was time for the Wishbone as well.

"Oklahoma and Alabama were the only teams in the 1970s that won more than 100 games each," said Barry Switzer, former Oklahoma coach. "So Bear Bryant didn't care if Texas invented it. It was after we (Oklahoma) put 500 yards on them in the Bluebonnet Bowl that they went to the Wishbone."

Darrell Royal made himself a Texas state treasure by executing the Wishbone in the 1960s. He arrived in 1957 at the age of 32 after a 5-5 season at Washington and two 6-4 campaigns at Mississippi State. Of all the coaches being talked about at the time, Royal most certainly wasn't one of them. But Texas athletic director D. X. Bible saw something

"WHEN MONEY BECOMES A FACTOR, IT CHANGES THE CONSOLIDATION OF TEAMS AT THE HIGHEST LEVEL. THE PRESSURE IS GREAT TO RAISE THE FINANCES NECESSARY TO SUPPORT THE PROGRAM AS REFLECTED IN STADIUMS, WORKOUT FACILITIES AND RECRUITING BUDGETS. WITH SO MANY ATHLETES WANTING TO ENTER PRO FOOTBALL, AND WITH SO FEW PRO OPPORTUNITIES, THE SERVICE ACADEMIES HAD A DIFFICULT TIME BECAUSE OF THEIR REQUIRED POST-COLLEGE MILITARY COMMITMENT."
— ROGER STAUBACH Navy Quarterback

THE SERVICE ACADEMIES ENJOYED ONE OF THEIR LAST MOMENTS IN THE BIG-TIME FOOTBALL SPOTLIGHT IN 1963 WHEN NAVY QUARTERBACK ROGER STAUBACH BECAME THE LAST MILITARY PLAYER TO WIN THE HEISMAN TROPHY.

"ONE OF MY FAVORITE COLLEGE GAMES WAS THE FIRST ARMY–AIR FORCE GAME, WHICH WAS PLAYED AT YANKEE STADIUM IN 1959," SAID MERLE HARMON. "THERE HAD BEEN SUCH A BIG BUILDUP. NEW YORK HAD AT LEAST ONE BIG GAME AT YANKEE STADIUM EACH YEAR. AIR FORCE HAD RICH MAYO AT QUARTERBACK AND THE GAME WAS A SELLOUT. THERE WAS SUCH COMPETITION AMONG THE ACADEMIES AND AIR FORCE WAS SUPPOSED TO BE SO SUPERIOR TO NAVY AND ARMY.

"AIR FORCE WAS THE GLAMOUR ACADEMY THEN. BUT ARMY BROUGHT IN ALL THE CADETS THEY COULD FIND FROM WEST POINT TO YANKEE STADIUM, THEY EVEN HAD GUYS IN WHEEL CHAIRS ON SIDELINES. AIR FORCE BROUGHT IN 300 OR 400 FROM THE ACADEMY ON CHARTERED FLIGHTS. BEFORE THE GAME, THE AIR FORCE CADETS MARCH BRISKLY DOWN FIELD. OUR BROADCAST BOOTH WAS AT MID FIELD, AT THE 50, DOWN THE THIRD-BASELINE.

"THE TOP BRASS FROM BOTH SERVICES WERE RIGHT THERE. THEN CAME THE ARMY CADETS AND THEY COVERED THE FIELD SIDELINE TO SIDELINE. THEY MARCHED ONTO THE FIELD AND THEY SALUTED. THEN, ONE CADET BREAKS RANKS, AND GOES CLEAR OUT OF FORMATION. HE TAKES OFF HIS COAT AND UNIFORM AND UNDERNEATH HE WAS AN AIR FORCE CADET. HE GOES AND JUMPS INTO THE AIR FORCE SECTION AND THE PLACE GOES CRAZY. AIR FORCE WON THE GAME."

STAUBACH PLAYED AT PENSACOLA NAVAL STATION AFTER GRADUATING FROM NAVY IN 1964. BECAUSE OF HIS SERVICE COMMITMENTS, STAUBACH DIDN'T JOIN THE DALLAS COWBOYS UNTIL 1969 WHEN HE WAS 27 YEARS OLD.

ROGER STAUBACH

"**W**HEN I FIRST WENT TO WORK ON THE SIDELINES IN 1975, I WAS A 25-YEAR-OLD KID STRAIGHT OUT OF GRADUATE SCHOOL AT NORTH CAROLINA. I WAS JUST GETTING MY FEET WET AND DOING SOMETHING THAT HAD NEVER BEEN DONE BEFORE. BEAR BRYANT AND DARRELL ROYAL TOOK ME UNDER THEIR WING AND TREATED ME LIKE A FRIEND. THEY TOOK AN INTEREST IN WHAT WE WERE DOING AND HELPED US ALONG. BEFORE LONG, I WAS SITTING IN THEIR OFFICES IN THE MIDDLE OF THE WEEK TALKING TO THEM AND EATING LUNCH WITH THEM. THEY REALLY TOOK ME IN AND TOOK AN INTEREST IN WHAT WE WERE DOING.

"ARA PARSEGHIAN WAS RESISTENT TO (A SIDELINE REPORTER) WHEN IT FIRST CAME OUT IN 1974. THEN, IN 1975, HE CAME ON BOARD TO DO TELEVISION AT ABC AND HE QUICKLY CONVERTED TO THE IDEA.

"NOT EVERYBODY WAS SO WILLING TO ADJUST. SPORTSWRITERS, WITH JUSTIFICATION, WERE FURIOUS ABOUT WHAT

BEAR BRYANT

ABC HAD DONE WITH BEING ALLOWED TO PUT A REPORTER ON THE SIDELINE WITH A SIDELINE MIKE. AT THE TIME, WHAT WENT ON DURING THE GAME WAS NOT READILY REPORTED ON TELEVISION. THAT INSIDE SKINNY WAS THE HEART OF WHAT SPORTSWRITERS WERE DELIVERING TO THEIR READERS ON SUNDAY MORNING. THEY WOULD TALK TO THE COACHES AND PLAYERS AND GET THE INFORMATION AND DELIVER IT THE NEXT DAY. NOW, THEY WERE BEING SCOOPED. THE WRITERS' ASSOCIATION INFORMALLY ASKED THE COACHES' ASSOCIATION IF THEY WOULD GET US TAKEN OFF THE SIDELINES. AT THE TIME, THE PRESIDENT OF THE COACHES' ASSOCIATION WAS BEAR BRYANT AND THE INCOMING PRESIDENT WAS ROYAL; SO THAT PUT AN END TO THAT. OBVIOUSLY, I APPRECIATED THAT. I OWE MY CAREER TO THEM."

— **JIM LAMPLEY**
former ABC Sports announcer

in Royal, who had played for Bud Wilkinson at Oklahoma.

"He was very bright and very organized," said Carlisle, the former Texas quarterback. "He had the ability to choose the best assistants. I always thought before a game that we were very well prepared. I didn't expect somebody to be better prepared than we were. He paid a lot of attention to details."

Royal coveted the Texas job because he knew of the state's vast recruiting riches. As the largest school in the state, Texas also had extraordinary resources. And those had barely been tapped when Royal took over.

"I didn't have any name when I got here," said Royal. "Nobody knew me. They took a pretty good chance on me. What would I have been if I had not come to the University Texas? I might have been fired if I was at some other place, doing the same thing, trying just as hard."

But it wasn't until 1968 that one of Royal's assistants, Emory Bellard, devised what became the Wishbone offense.

Out West, John McKay preferred the I-formation that allowed a great back to break down opposing defenses. The offense produced a series of Heisman Trophy winners starting with Mike Garrett. O. J. Simpson, Charles

DARRELL ROYAL

WOODY HAYES

White and Marcus Allen followed with Ricky Bell and Anthony Davis equally qualified.

McKay installed the "I" in 1962 after two losing seasons and USC won the national title. By the time McKay left for the NFL, USC had won four national titles and compiled a 127-40-8 record in his 16 seasons.

At Nebraska, Bob Devaney put the Cornhuskers on the map quickly with a come-from-behind 25-13 victory at Michigan in 1962.

A gregarious Irishman, Devaney injected fun into a program that had been defined by its brutal practices. He quit scrimmaging during game week and shortened the legendary practice sessions. And he listened to a bright, young assistant named Tom Osborne and switched to the I-formation in 1969 after back-to-back 6-4 seasons. Nebraska won the national championship in 1970 and 1971.

Nebraska eventually became the model for the big-time college football program. Coaches used red-shirting, which allowed a player to practice but not play for a full season without losing any eligibility, developed an entire

MIKE GARRETT

O. J. SIMPSON

CHARLES WHITE

MARCUS ALLEN

OUT WEST, JOHN MCKAY PREFERRED THE I-FORMATION THAT ALLOWED A GREAT BACK TO BREAK DOWN OPPOSING DEFENSES. THE OFFENSE PRODUCED A SERIES OF HEISMAN TROPHY WINNERS STARTING WITH MIKE GARRETT. O. J. SIMPSON, CHARLES WHITE AND MARCUS ALLEN FOLLOWED WITH RICKY BELL AND ANTHONY DAVIS EQUALLY QUALIFIED

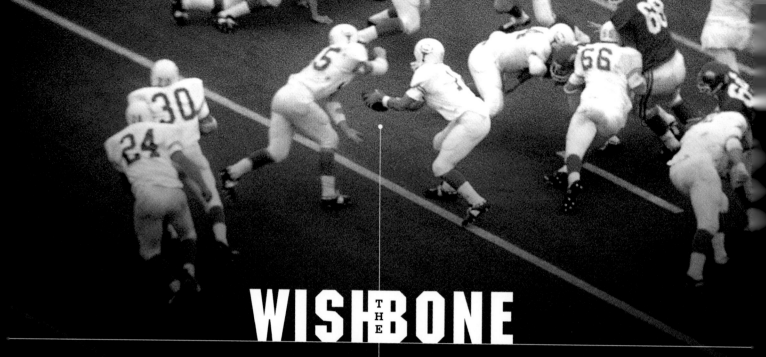

WISH THE BONE

Imagine Microsoft giving up the source code for Windows after a couple dominating years in the market.

That approximates what Darrell Royal did with the most dominant offense in the history of college football. Texas assistant, Emory Bellard, who had run a triple-option, three-back offense as a high school coach, developed the Wishbone in 1968.

"I spent a lot of time up in my office during the summer doodling with the idea," said Bellard. "It was not uncommon to be working on ideas with a pencil and pad. I wrote it up, and then gathered a group of players and demonstrated it on the field to Coach Royal. It wasn't too hard to sell because I had an option background and Coach Royal had seen enough 6-4 seasons."

Keith Jackson called the Wishbone, "the penultimate creator of indecision." By forcing the defense to react one way or another on every play, the Wishbone could be overwhelming. After Texas played Houston to a 20-20 tie and lost to rival Texas A&M to open the 1968 season, the Longhorns ran the Wishbone to 30 straight victories.

Meanwhile, Royal shared the offense with Alabama's Bear Bryant, Pepper Rodgers at UCLA and even Barry Switzer at Oklahoma.

"Coach Royal was pretty liberal in spreading it around," said Bellard. "His good friend, Chuck Fairbanks, was fixin to lose his job at Oklahoma. Coach Royal came into my office one day and said, 'Barry Switzer (OU's offensive coordinator at the time) is going to be calling. Give him whatever information they need.' I said, 'Are you sure?' He said, 'Yes. We need to help them.'

"I told him I'd do it but that I didn't think we should be so benevolent. Barry called a couple times every week and two years later we had trouble chasing down those jackrabbits. And they did it with all Texas kids - Jack Mildren, Billy Sims and Joe Washington. I don't mind telling the story because it says a lot about Darrell. But I probably wouldn't have been so generous."

After the 1970 season, Royal never beat Oklahoma again.

"It was tougher to run and pass when I played than it is today. That's why it's tough to compare people in different eras. The rules were so different that it's a different game. Not only can you extend your arms, but you can open your hands. It's not a lot of blocking. It's a lot of shoving."

— BOB GRIESE
1966 All-America Quarterback at Purdue

program for walk-ons and an elaborate strength and conditioning program.

"Nebraska's consistency is similar to that of Joe Paterno at Penn State," said Todd Blackledge, former ABC Sports announcer and quarterback under Paterno. "In terms of execution, Nebraska was always better than everybody. They got good when they finally got the athletic ability and speed to go along with that consistency"

In 1966, ABC Sports became the first network to broadcast a full slate of regular season games. Meanwhile, players were getting bigger, stronger and faster. Offenses were becoming more diversified. The Wishbone gave way to the veer, the run-and-shoot and the four-back, one receiver set.

"My brother was playing at Maryland in one of the early ABC games," said Tim Brandt. "It was Maryland against Oklahoma in Norman. My dad rented four TV sets and put them in different rooms and he invited everybody he knew over to the house. My brother, Mike, was the starting right cornerback at Maryland. On the first or second play, Oklahoma threw a deep pass and they called pass interference on my brother. It was a big gain and they went into score. Then the floodgates opened. My dad was sick."

By the time college football moved into the 21st century, the game had become as sophisticated as a chess match.

Running backs routinely cover 40 yards in less than 4.5 seconds and offensive linemen such as Jonathan Ogden and Tony Boselli remained cat-quick despite standing 6-feet-8-inches and weighing more than 300 pounds.

But on all fronts, it's the speed that dazzles even those geniuses who drove the evolution of college football decades ago.

"The game is much tougher today," says Frank Broyles, athletic director at Arkansas. "The collisions are much harder. At the Tennessee–Arkansas game in 1999, I went down to the field. I hadn't been down to the field for a few years. The speed of the game was unbelievable."

So too is the atmosphere, tradition and sense of purpose that has colored the background of college footall games from Yale to USC for more than 130 years.

"I love the intensity, the pomp and circumstance of college football," said Jack Arute. "I love the fact that on any given Saturday the lowliest of teams can upset the biggest on the block. I don't think you can say that week in and week out in pro football.

"Take Missouri's near upset of Nebraska in 1998, or Florida State steam-rolling to a national title and getting upset by Miami. Every time you go into a stadium, you can sense the excitement with the fans, see it with players. It's something tangible you can taste. Athletes talk about 'juice' or the high. I think that is the 'juice' in our business."

"THE GAME IS MUCH TOUGHER TODAY. THE COLLISIONS ARE MUCH HARDER."
— **FRANK BROYLES** player for Georgia Tech in the 1940s and athletic director at Arkansas

PASS-BLOCKING RULES CHANGED OVER FOUR SEASONS STARTING IN THE MID-1970S. THE FIRST CHANGE ALLOWED OFFENSIVE LINEMEN "HALF EXTENSIONS" OF THEIR ARMS TO BLOCK. LATER, THEY WERE ALLOWED FULL EXTENSION AND THE ILLEGAL HANDS PENALTY WAS REDUCED TO FIVE YARDS. THE RULES NOT ONLY PROVIDED BETTER PROTECTION FOR QUARTERBACKS, BUT THEY LED COACHES FAVORING THE PASSING GAME ALSO TO FAVOR HUGE OFFENSIVE LINEMEN.

"THE BIGGEST CHANGE IN THE GAME FROM WHEN I WAS COACHING IS THAT YOU COULDN'T USE YOUR HANDS," LSU'S McCLENDON SAID. "SO YOU HAD TO GET RID OF THE BALL QUICK IN THE PASSING GAME. NOWADAYS, THEY CAN PUSH AND SHOVE AND GIVE THE QUARTERBACK MORE TIME. THAT'S GOOD BECAUSE PEOPLE LIKE TO SEE THE WIDE-OPEN GAME."

"MONTE CLARK, OUR OLD OFFENSIVE LINE COACH WITH THE DOLPHINS, CALLS TODAY'S BLOCKING THE LAMAZE WAY OF BLOCKING BECAUSE THERE'S A LOT OF PUSHING AND SHOVING. IN THE '60S AND '70S, OFFENSIVE LINEMEN HAD TO KEEP THEIR HANDS CLOSED INTO A FIST. YOU DON'T HAVE TO DO THAT NOW AND SO IT'S MUCH EASIER TO PASS BLOCK. AND THAT'S WHY TEAMS ARE THROWING ALMOST EXCLUSIVELY AND NOT MAKING AN EFFORT TO RUN THE BALL."

★ **BLOCKING RULES** ★

QB JOHN ELWAY
RB O. J. SIMPSON
   HERSCHEL WALKER
   ARCHIE GRIFFIN
OL ORLANDO PACE
   RON YARY
   DAVE RIMINGTON
   JOHN HANNAH
   TONY BOSELLI
WR ANTHONY CARTER
   JOHNNY RODGERS
TE KEITH JACKSON
K SEBASTIAN JANIKOWSKI

ABC SPORTS COLLEGE

FIRST TEAM

| QB | ELWAY | RB | SIMPSON | RB | WALKER | RB | GRIFFIN | OL | PACE | OL | YARY | OL | RIMINGTON |

| DL | SMITH | DL | SELMON | DL | WHITE | DL | SMITH | DL | GREEN | LB | TAYLOR | LB | SINGLETARY |

ALL-TIME ALL

DL BUBBA SMITH
   LEE ROY SELMON
   RANDY WHITE
   BRUCE SMITH
   HUGH GREEN
LB LAWRENCE TAYLOR
   MIKE SINGLETARY
   JACK HAM
DB DEION SANDERS
   CHARLES WOODSON
   RONNIE LOTT
   JACK TATUM
P REGGIE ROBY
C BEAR BRYANT

FOOTBALL AMERICA TEAM

OL HANNAH	OL BOSELLI	WR CARTER	WR RODGERS	TE JACKSON		K JANIKOWSKI

LB HAM	DB SANDERS	DB WOODSON	DB LOTT	DB TATUM	P ROBY	C BRYANT

"ABC SPORTS PRESENTS
ALL THE COLOR AND EXCITEMENT OF NCAA COLLEGE FOOTBALL.

WHAT A WAY TO SPEND AN AUTUMN AFTERNOON"

— CHRIS SCHENKEL

Chris Schenkel was a veteran of more than 18 years

in television when he became the first voice of ABC Sports college football coverage in 1964.

When ABC Sports became the first network to telecast a full schedule of games in 1966, Schenkel and Bud Wilkinson,

the legendary Oklahoma player and coach, manned the booth. And it was Schenkel's signature line —

"ABC Sports presents all the color and excitement of NCAA college football.

What a way to spend an autumn afternoon" —

that opened The Game of the Week telecasts and forever connected Schenkel to the college game. As warm and gracious

off the air as he was on, Schenkel recalled some of those days more than 30 years ago.

Roone Arledge was a Columbia guy, so he appreciated college football. He also was a New York (football) Giants fan, which is how I got to know him because I was doing their games for CBS when Roone brought me to ABC. He had great sense about him and he knew college football was ripe because pro football was coming along.

It took a lot of money at that time, but ABC Sports threw the book at the game. We had every resource available to us and we took advantage of those tools. I had the privilege of working with Bud Wilkinson on the first Game of the Week broadcast in 1966. Bud gave college football great dignity as a coach and he was wonderful to work with in the booth. The Game of the Week was a luxury because, with few exceptions, we had the best game every week no matter where it was. And we were never more warmly welcomed anywhere than we were at those schools. Bud and I had the pleasure of having dinner with one of the two coaches the night before the game. All of them, except one, would give us the game plan. The only exception was Woody Hayes. We were doing an Ohio State–Purdue game in West Lafayette, Indiana and staying in the same hotel as the team. Woody sees Bud in the lobby and says, "Here's the game plan, Bud." Later on, we get a knock on the door. It's Woody. He says, "Bud, Chris, you're both a little older now and you guys might forget that game plan when you go out to dinner. I think I better take it back." Really, it was because I was a Purdue guy. Woody never said anything because he was so diplomatic. But I'm sure that's why he came back to get the game plan.

I remember spending three days with John Wayne and Bear Bryant ahead of a USC – Alabama game in Birmingham. I never had three days like that in my life. I got to know John earlier and he and Bear were good friends. They were the same type. It was incredible. When you were around them at the same time all you did is listen. I wish I had had a tape recorder. Then throw Bud in there who knew how to get them to open up, and it was just wonderful.

But I can't say enough what doing college football for ABC Sports meant to all of us and the lives of the viewers we touched each week. Soon after I started at ABC, I came up with a saying that I would use to begin each telecast. To this day, wherever I go someone will shout that to me from out of a crowd. I would say: "ABC Sports presents all the color and excitement of NCAA college football. What a way to spend an autumn afternoon."

We did games everywhere regardless of the size of the schools. We were looking for the best game and it didn't matter if it was Yale–Harvard or USC–Notre Dame. We did a Grambling–Southern University game in Yankee Stadium before a standing room only crowd. It was great fun. I had done a Giants game in Yankee Stadium from the right field photographer's pit. ABC decided we needed to be closer to the game.

They created a temporary booth on the opposite side of the field, which is where you wanted to be. They also put a tarp over our heads. It rained that day from start to finish. Around the start of the second half that big canvas tarp burst and wiped out everything. I did the second half of that game blind.

One of the biggest games we ever did was the Arkansas–Texas game Dec. 6, 1969. Texas was No. 1 and Arkansas was No. 2 and the two coaches – Darrell Royal and Frank Broyles – were best friends. I interviewed President Richard Nixon at halftime. He would have liked to stay in the booth the entire game. We had the same business managers when he was vice president so we knew one another. It was the best interview I had ever done. And he knew the game. Bud Wilkinson was Nixon's Physical Fitness Director at the time and they were friends as well. Texas won 15-14.

Everyone was a part of the process in those days and we had some wonderful people. Roone and Walter Byers, who was head of the NCAA at the time, understood the need for cooperation. Chuck Howard was our chief producer. Bill Flemming handled the sidelines and added so much class to the telecasts. My spotter, Bill Friel, and I did more than 600 games together. And Bud was just an amazing man.

I am so proud that I was able to help establish a series that is still going. College football…what a wonderful way to spend an autumn afternoon.

— **CHRIS SCHENKEL**

BLUE RIBBON PANEL

Jack **ARUTE**, Terry **BOWDEN**, Dean **BLEVINS**, Tim **BRANDT**, Gary **DANIELSON**, Dan **FOUTS**, Terry **GANNON**, Bob **GRIESE**, Keith **JACKSON**, Brent **MUSBURGER**, Brad **NESSLER**, John **SAUNDERS**, Lynn **SWANN**, Roger **TWIBELL**;

FORMER ABC SPORTS ANNOUNCERS:

Gary **BENDER**, Todd **BLACKLEDGE**, Frank **BROYLES**, Beano **COOK**, Steve **DAVIS**, Bill **FLEMMING**, Lee **GROSSCUP**, Merle **HARMON**, Jim **LAMPLEY**, Pepper **RODGERS**, Darrell **ROYAL**, Chris **SCHENKEL**, Bo **SCHEMBECHLER**, Dick **VERMEIL**, Steve **ZABRISKIE**.

QUARTERBACK

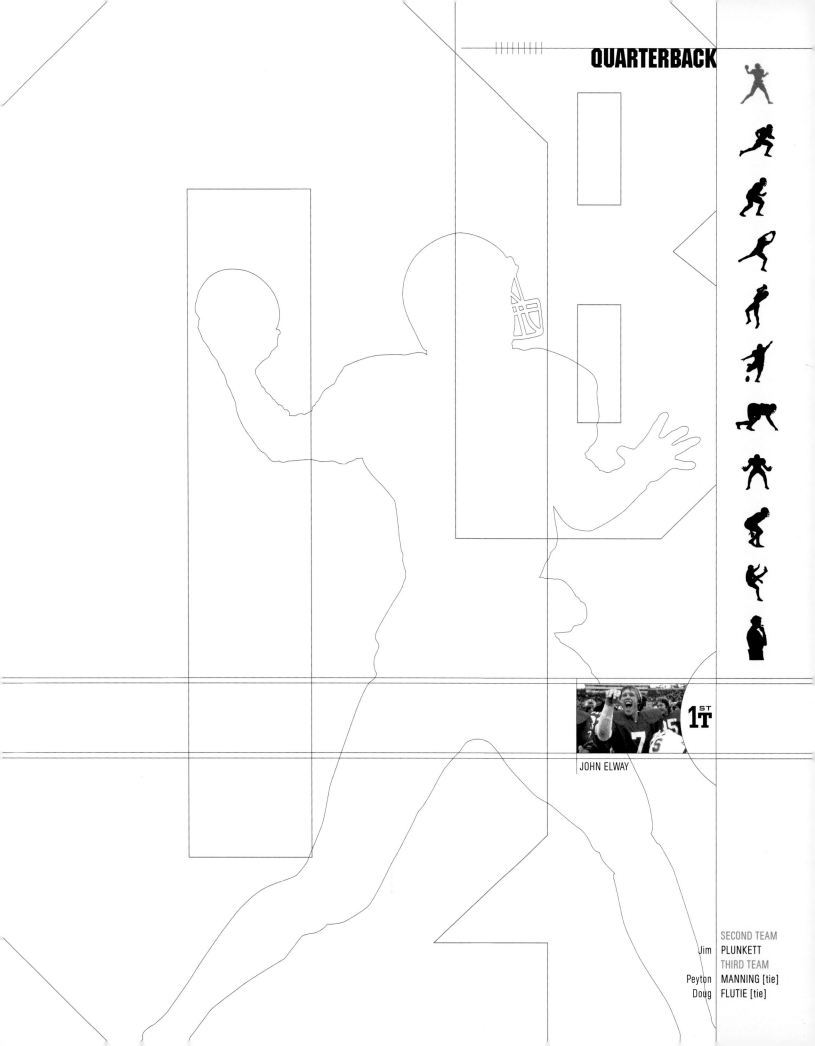

JOHN ELWAY

1ST T

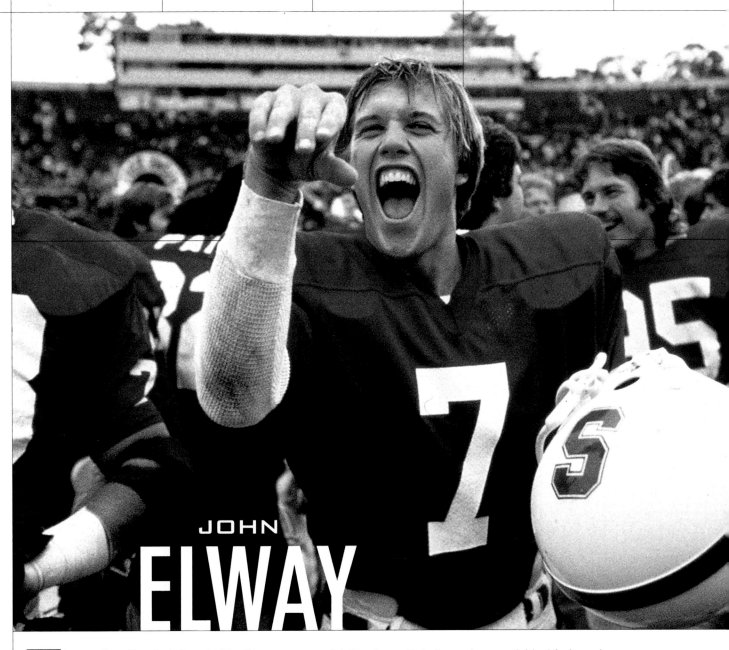

"...HE'S PROBABLY THE BEST COLLEGE QUARTERBACK I HAVE EVER SEEN."
— LEE GROSSCUP former ABC Sports announcer

JOHN ELWAY

The son of a college football coach, John Elway grew up around the smell of autumn and the rhythm of the college game. Though a gifted baseball player, it was on the football field that Elway's natural ability combined with the education he received at home.

"Elway had the best pure release that I had ever seen," said Lee Grosscup, former ABC Sports announcer. "I liked him as a competitor. I liked his courage. Not only could he throw from the pocket, but he could throw moving to his left or right. He had the 'stuff' early on."

"The difference is raw physical talent," said Andre Tyler, a Stanford wide receiver at the time. "There are situations in a game when most quarterbacks would not be physically able even to think about doing what Elway does routinely. You can be surrounded by defenders and John will get the ball to you. He can throw that hard and that accurately. He could throw it on a line for 40, 50 yards, and he could throw it 85 yards if he had to."

Said Paul Wiggin, former Stanford All-America and the school's head coach during the Elway years, "I've been standing behind quarterbacks all my life and I've never seen anybody who can make it happen like this kid does."

In 1981, as a sophomore playing right field for Stanford's baseball team, Elway hit .361 with nine homers and 50 RBI in 49 games. In the NCAA Central Regionals, he hit .444 and was voted onto the all-tournament team.

SCHOOL	NICKNAME	MILES PER HOUR ON FASTBALL	CAREER (COLLEGE) BATTING AVERAGE	SINGLE GAME TOUCHDOWN PASSES
STANFORD	THE ARM	92	.321	6

#7 | 6'3" | 215

JOHN
ELWAY **1**ST
quarterback

"Elway is the one who stands
out for me. I was working in
Baltimore when he was drafted
by the Colts. The Colts thought so
highly of him, they drafted him even
though he said he wanted no part
of playing in Baltimore. That had
nothing to do with the city.
The team was in sorry shape. And
(Frank) Kush had been a college
coach not known for throwing it
much. In the college game, it is
hard to argue there has ever been a
better quarterback than Elway."

— **JOHN SAUNDERS**
ABC Sports announcer

77 TOUCHDOWN PASSES

A STANFORD SCHOOL RECORD

"The hero is a poor Mexican-American kid. He delivers newspapers to help support his parents, both of whom are blind. At age 14, he entered a schoolboy contest, and, while officials look on in disbelief, he flips a football 63 yards. He soon becomes a star high school quarterback, rushing from practice each day to work long hours as a gas station attendant and grocery store clerk. A scout from a big college watches the hero passing and shouts: 'Lookit the ball! Lookit where the ball is! Right on the chest every time!' The hero wins a scholarship to a big college and, overcoming injuries and a serious operation, wins a starting assignment. A crisis arises when pro scouts storm the hero's frat house and try to persuade him to turn pro. But the hero refuses. He tells his coach that he will play out the final year to help the team and set a good example for youth. 'I rate team achievements,' he says, 'above individual achievements.' The hero breaks school, conference and national passing records, wins the Heisman Trophy as the most outstanding college football player in the U.S. Then, in a slambang finale, he leads his team to a thrilling upset victory in the Rose Bowl." *Time* magazine, Dec. 3, 1970

JIM PLUNKETT

| 2ND T | JIM PLUNKETT *quarterback* | #16 | 210 | 6'3" |

They played at the same school and attacked opposing defenses with the same wide open offense. Jim Plunkett and John Elway set records, Elway breaking many of those created by Plunkett. But in the end, Plunkett was the foundation upon which Elway perfected his craft.

Plunkett grew up in San Jose, just 18 miles south of Stanford. He might as well have been on another planet. His mother was blind and his father, who had limited vision, died during Plunkett's junior year in college. A thyroid operation during his freshman year helped make Plunkett's first Stanford season so unimpressive that coach John Ralston nearly switched the 6-foot-3-inch, 210-pounder to defensive end. Plunkett, as he had done through virtually every moment of his life, persevered and marched forward. Two years later, after being red-shirted as a sophomore, Plunkett took over and never let go.

In his first varsity start, he drilled San Jose State, which was coached by Elway's father, Jack, for 277 yards and five touchdowns, four of those passing. When his Stanford career ended, Plunkett had broken the existing NCAA record for passing yards by 468. Given the obstacles, it seems only fitting Plunkett's idol as a child was Zorro, the Spanish Robin Hood.

"Jim Plunkett was such a big, strong-armed guy that even on blitzes he was able to throw guys off him," said Tim Brandt. "I picked Doug Flutie No. 2, but he didn't have the complete package Plunkett had. Jim could hang in the pocket or run the option. He could do most anything."

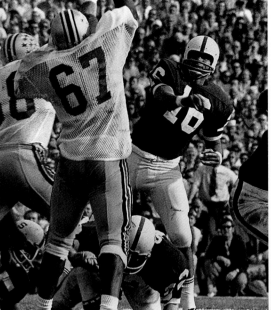

1968
FIRST COLLEGE START

5
10 OF 13 PASSING 277 YARDS
TOTAL TOUCHDOWNS
4 PASSING, 1 RUSHING

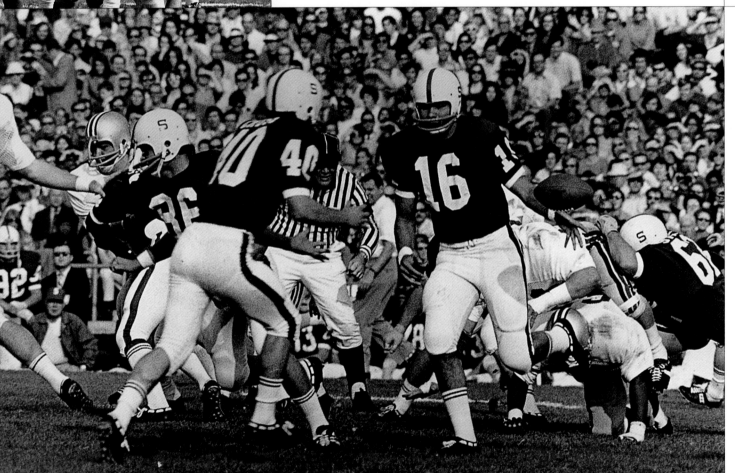

"If anyone ever got by me and hurt Jim,
I think I'd turn in my uniform."

— **BILL MEYERS Stanford offensive tackle**

40   30   20   10   G

PEYTON
MANNING

#16 | 6'5" | 230

3RD T PEYTON **MANNING**
quarterback

Just as his father had more than 25 years earlier in Mississippi, Peyton Manning became the most famous man in an entire state before his 23rd birthday. When Peyton decided to bypass the NFL and return for his senior season at Tennessee, a Knoxville television station interviewed schoolchildren as to what they had learned from such a moral stand. Billboards were covered with "Thank you, Peyton" signs and an entire state let out a collective sigh. But not before Manning consulted everyone from Michael Jordan and Tim Duncan to Hank Stram and Fran Tarkenton.

| #18 | 6'3" | 212 |

ARCHIE MANNING
quarterback

ARCHIE MANNING

Full name: Elisha Archie Manning III
Hometown: Drew, Mississippi
Population: 2,143

In the South, college football is the religion everyone practices on Saturday. And in Mississippi, Archie Manning was church and state in the late 1960s and early 1970s. The elevation of Manning to the status of living legend became official when he led Ole Miss to an upset victory over Arkansas in the 1970 Sugar Bowl. Archie's Army buttons blanketed the state.

When Tennessee fans came up with an "Archie Who?" button, Lamont Wilson, a postal clerk in Magnolia, Miss., took the tune to Johnny Cash's "Folsom Prison Blues" and created "The Ballad of Archie Who?" for the Hoddy Toddy record label. A group of guitar pickers known as the Rebel Rousers recorded the song and sold more than 35,000 copies. The fact Ole Miss hammered Tennessee 38-0 only added to the hysteria.

"I think Archie Manning was another one of those guys who built college football into a national phenomenon," said Brad Nessler, ABC Sports announcer. "I lived in Minnesota, the heart of Big Ten country, and I knew what Archie Manning was doing every Saturday in Mississippi."

As a junior, Manning won the Walter Camp Memorial Award as the outstanding college back. A gifted athlete, Manning could run a 10.2-second 100-yard dash and was drafted by the Atlanta Braves.

Manning and his son, Peyton, who turned Ole Miss rival Tennessee around and elicited the same kind of hero worship a generation later, remain the greatest father-son combination — regardless of position — in college football history.

ON TURNING PROFESSIONAL

TROY AIKMAN:
I'VE SEEN YOU A LOT ON TELEVISION. I THINK YOU'RE READY.

DREW BLEDSOE:
PEYTON, PRO FOOTBALL IS THE BEST JOB IN THE WORLD, BECAUSE YOU'RE PLAYING FOOTBALL AND THAT'S ALL YOU HAVE TO CONCENTRATE ON.

PHIL SIMMS:
I WATCHED YOUR BOWL GAME, AND I KNOW YOU'RE READY.

ROGER STAUBACH:
PEYTON, IT WAS AN HONOR TO WIN THE HEISMAN, BUT IT DIDN'T MAKE ME A BETTER NFL PLAYER. PLEASE DO NOT GO BACK JUST TO WIN THAT.

RICK MIRER:
I WOULDN'T TRADE MY LAST YEAR AT NOTRE DAME FOR ANYTHING.

| #22 | 5'9" | 174 |

3RD T DOUG FLUTIE
quarterback

DOUG
FLUTIE

College Career STATS

10,519 Total PASSING Yards

739 Total RUSHING Yards

74 Total TDs

"I have had the privilege of covering many great events in virtually every sport, college and professional but perhaps the most memorable was the Boston College 47-45 victory over Miami when Doug Flutie connected on a 48-yard 'Hail Mary' pass to Gerard Phelan as time ran out. That was a special play made by a special player in a very special game."

— BRENT MUSBURGER
ABC Sports announcer

The pass covered at least 64 yards and sliced through the gusting wind and dark gray mist of a late afternoon Miami sky. The ball exploded out of the hand of Doug Flutie, who on that day not only had out-dueled Bernie Kosar of the defending national champion Hurricanes, but had become the first 10,000-yard passer in NCAA history. That he should heave the ball into the heavy air and that it might find his roommate, wide receiver Gerard Phelan, in the end zone amid the long arms of four Miami defenders seemed wholly reasonable to Flutie.

"I've been lucky all my life, so why not?" he asked. Said Phelan: "You get on the same frequency with Doug and somehow things happen. You can't always explain it."

Legendary Dallas Cowboys executive Gil Brandt tried to explain the consistently spectacular events Flutie orchestrated during four seasons at Boston College this way: "With Doug Flutie, life is a magic show. He never loses, he only runs out of time."

In Flutie's case, a little luck and a whole lot of magic converged for a remarkable college career. Flutie had been turned down for a Boston College scholarship and ultimately received the last one available in 1981 when the Eagles made a coaching change. Four games into his college career and deep into the depth chart, Flutie got the call. Boston College was losing 31-0 in the fourth quarter and coach Jack Bicknell looked down the bench and motioned Flutie into the game. He passed for 135 yards in a game Penn State's Joe Paterno would learn to remember. In the next three seasons, Flutie scorched the Nittany Lions for 520, 380 and 447 yards respectively.

G   10   20   30   40

Maybe you can't come home again, but Troy Aikman proved you can at least visit. His family moved from suburban Southern California to a farm five miles outside Henrietta, Oklahoma, a town of 6,000, when Aikman was 12. Six years later, Oklahoma coach Barry Switzer told Aikman the Sooners would pass more with him in the backfield.

"I really knew nothing about Troy Aikman. But I figured Barry had had enough No. 1 picks (in the NFL draft) to know what one looked like, so I said we'd be real interested." — **TERRY DONAHUE UCLA'S head coach**

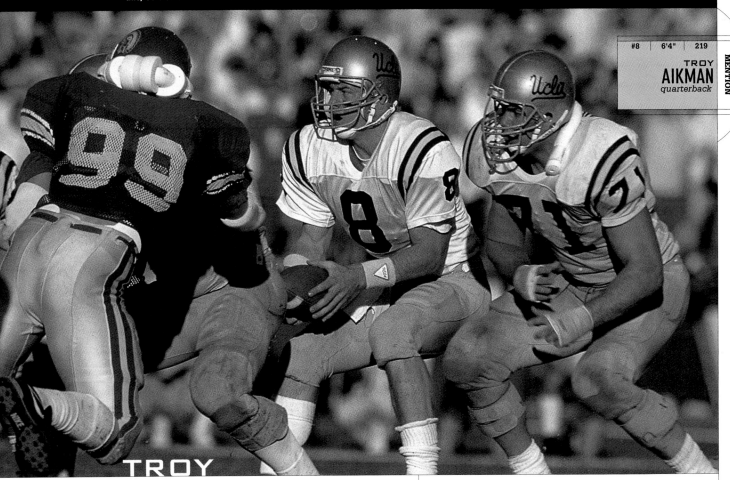

| #8 | 6'4" | 219 |

TROY
AIKMAN
quarterback

HONORABLE MENTION

TROY
AIKMAN

Aikman took over the Sooner offense as a freshman after an injury to the starter. His debut, however, only cemented Switzer's confidence in the Sooner running game. Aikman connected on just 2 of 14 passes for eight yards and threw three interceptions. When Aikman went down with an injury early in his sophomore season, Switzer turned the team over to Jamelle Holieway, who led Oklahoma to a national title. But Switzer, who would reunite with Aikman at the Dallas Cowboys, knew what he had when he called UCLA on Aikman's behalf.

TY DETMER

"I had heard of his numbers in high school (8,005 passing yards), but we hadn't really recruited him, didn't have film on him. So I'm thinking John Elway, and in walks Pee Wee Herman."

— LAVELL EDWARDS, BYU COACH

Ty Detmer had the greatest season of any quarterback in college football history in 1990. He broke 31 NCAA records, including most passing yards in a single season (5,188), tied five others and won the Heisman Trophy as a junior. Detmer concluded his career with 24 straight 300-yard passing games and remains the all-time leader in career passing yardage with 15,031. To put that number in perspective, John Elway threw for 9,349 yards at Stanford and Peyton Manning had 11,201 at Tennessee.

STEVE YOUNG

By the time Steve Young arrived at BYU in 1980, the quarterback succession process had been decided. Jim McMahon was completing one of the most brilliant college careers in any sport and Eric Krzmarzick was on deck with Gym Kimball as understudy. Young had been a bruising option quarterback in high school and, despite being recruited by LaVell Edwards, Young was destined for another position, most likely running back or wide receiver on offense with an outside shot at defensive back. Incidentally, Young's father, LeGrande, had set a single season rushing record as a fullback for BYU in 1959, so a switch seemed destined.

"We weren't sure when we recruited him that he had the arm to be a BYU-type quarterback," says Dick Felt, BYU's defensive coordinator at the time.

Edwards was of the same opinion given Young's size, 6-1 and 198 pounds, and speed, 4.5 in the 40. Edwards wanted Young on the field, but he never really considered him behind center.

"I think we have our quarterbacks for the future," Edwards told Young, then a freshman.

G   10   20   30   40

JIM
McMAHON
quarterback

HONORABLE MENTION

McMahon's NCAA Records

9,536 YARDS PASSING

84 TOUCHDOWNS

156.9 PASSING EFFICIENCY

1,060 ATTEMPTS

653 COMPLETIONS

34 INTERCEPTIONS

JIM McMAHON

By the time Jim McMahon left Brigham Young, he had 70 NCAA total offense or passing records. McMahon became a quarterback at the age of 10 when the coach asked all the youngsters to throw the ball. When McMahon stepped up and launched the ball 50 yards — twice as far as anyone else — he became a quarterback.

By the time he was ready for college, the one school he wanted never called. "If Notre Dame had called, I would have gone," says McMahon. "But anyplace else I wanted to play baseball, too. It was my favorite sport at the time."

BYU went 11-1 with McMahon at quarterback in 1980. He set 32 NCAA passing or total offense records and brought BYU back from a 21 point deficit in the final 2:33 for a 46-45 victory in the Holiday Bowl.

BYU QUARTERBACKS HEISMAN VOTING

YEAR	1979	1981	1983	1984/1985	1990/1991
PLAYER	MARC WILSON	JIM McMAHON	STEVE YOUNG	ROBBIE BOSCO	TY DETMER
FINISH	3rd	3rd	2nd	3rd	1st/3rd

"We'd like to move you to safety. We need defensive backs. I think you can play quarterback, but you're too good of an athlete to sit around."

After Young's freshman season, an assistant coaching change provided him the slimmest of openings during spring practice. Listed as a top defensive back in the depth charts, Young threw passes anyway. And he threw them so well that Edwards couldn't help but notice.

"I went out and watched him," says Edwards, "and it was evident he could throw. The decision was made."

History would follow.

In a process that would repeat itself in San Francisco with Joe Montana, Young replaced an injured legend in Jim McMahon for two games as a sophomore. Young completed 45 of 60 passes for 579 yards and was ordained the heir apparent. Said Edwards following Young's All America junior season, "I think a lot of his success is ahead of him." Indeed.

Six Generations of Separation
Steve Young shared more than a last name with Brigham Young, the leader of the Mormon Church. Steve is the great-great-great-grandson of Brigham, who in 1847 led 148 of his Latter-Day Saints to Utah's great Salt Lake valley. Steve's road to stardom, first at Brigham Young University and later in the NFL, was no less unlikely.

Six Degrees of Separation — The Family
Brigham Young made Emily Dow Partridge his third wife; together they had a daughter, Emily Augusta Young, who married Hyrum Clawson; their daughter, Carly Louise Clawson, married Seymour B. Young, Jr., who was Brigham's nephew. Their son, Scott Richmond Young, married Louise Leonard; together they had LeGrande Young, who married Sherry Steed and they had a son, Steve.

Five Degrees of Separation — The Football Field
Gary Sheide became the first of a string of great Brigham Young quarterbacks developed under the leadership of head coach LaVell Edwards. Gifford Nielsen came next, followed by Marc Wilson, who was followed by Jim McMahon and then Young. Robbie Bosco followed Young, who was in turn followed by Ty Detmer and Steve Sarkisian.

If Charlie Ward isn't the most heralded athlete in the history of college football then he's certainly among the most heralded never to play the game professionally.

Ward led Florida State to the 1993 National Championship and set 19 school and seven Atlantic Coast Conference records in just two seasons as the Seminoles' starting quarterback. He completed 62.3 percent of his passes, has the school's lowest interception rate (2.90) and threw for 27 touchdowns as a senior. But it was Ward's personality, approach and intelligence that tied all the athletic success in a bow. In addition to the Heisman, Ward became only the second football player in history to win the prestigious Sullivan Award as the nation's top amateur athlete.

Ward's skill on the basketball court eventually led him off the football field and into the National Basketball Association.

HONORABLE MENTION

#17 | 6'2" | 190

CHARLIE
WARD
quarterback

The Year of Charlie Ward
PARTIAL LIST OF INDIVIDUAL AWARDS IN 1993

HEISMAN TROPHY WINNER

AAU SULLIVAN AWARD WINNER

DAVEY O'BRIEN AWARD WINNER

JOHN UNITAS GOLDEN ARM AWARD WINNER

WALTER CAMP PLAYER OF THE YEAR

CHEVROLET OFFENSIVE PLAYER OF THE YEAR

SCRIPPS HOWARD PLAYER OF THE YEAR

ACC PLAYER OF THE YEAR

TOYOTA LEADER OF THE YEAR

THE SPORTING NEWS PLAYER OF THE YEAR

UPI PLAYER OF THE YEAR

ACC OFFENSIVE PLAYER OF THE YEAR

FOOTBALL NEWS OFFENSIVE PLAYER OF THE YEAR

ASSOCIATED PRESS ALL-AMERICAN

WALTER CAMP ALL-AMERICAN

THE SPORTING NEWS ALL-AMERICAN

UPI ALL-AMERICAN

FOOTBALL WRITERS' ALL-AMERICAN

SCRIPPS HOWARD ALL-AMERICAN

FOOTBALL NEWS ALL-AMERICAN

KODAK ALL-AMERICAN

ALL-ATLANTIC COAST CONFERENCE

FOOTBALL NEWS ALL-ATLANTIC COAST CONFERENCE

ALL-ATLANTIC COAST ACADEMIC TEAM

CHARLIE
WARD

G   10   20   30   40

RUNNING BACK

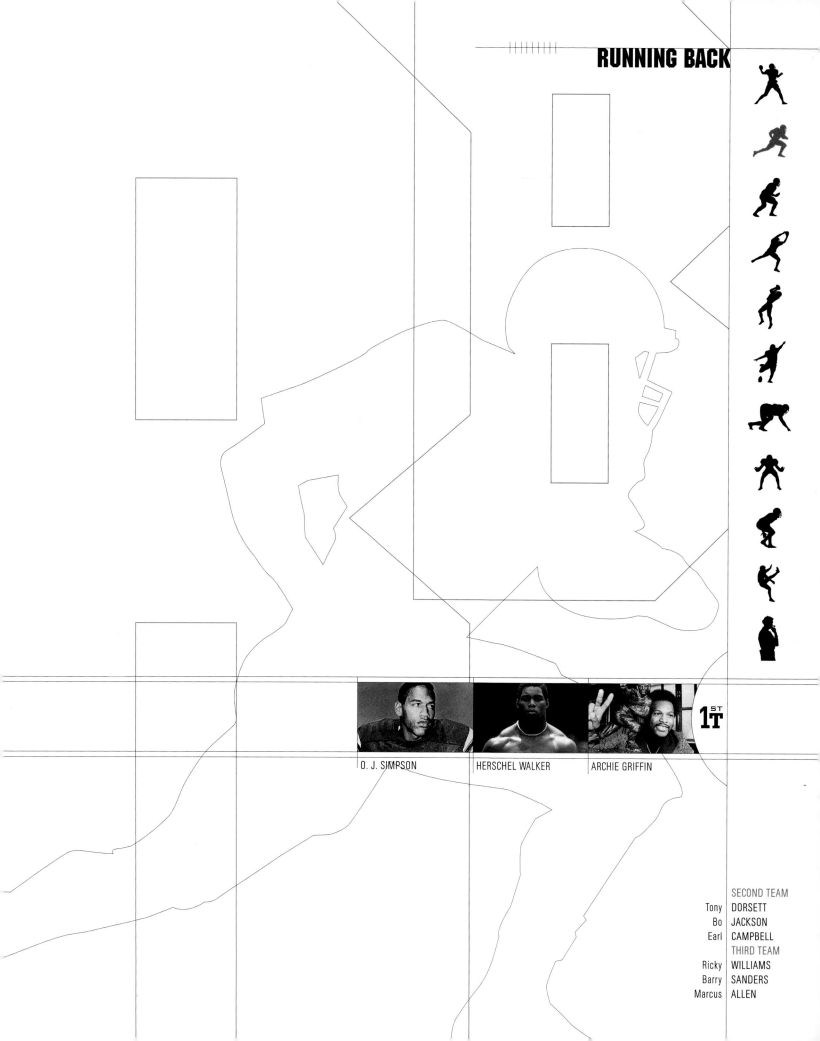

O. J. SIMPSON   HERSCHEL WALKER   ARCHIE GRIFFIN

1ST
T

SECOND TEAM
Tony DORSETT
Bo JACKSON
Earl CAMPBELL
THIRD TEAM
Ricky WILLIAMS
Barry SANDERS
Marcus ALLEN

Even at the University of Southern California, where tailbacks already had become a dominant theme in the school's football legacy, O. J. Simpson was a unique package. Months before he stepped onto the football field as a Trojan, Simpson had teamed with three other USC sprinters to break the world record in the 440-yard relay. The combination of size, power and speed was matched only by Simpson's vision, balance and footwork.

That he ever made it out of San Francisco and into the larger culture's collective history, much less USC, can be traced to a single decision on an otherwise lazy afternoon in the shadows of a clouding future. At San Francisco's Galileo High, Simpson said he played every position including

"O. J. Simpson is the greatest running back in the history of college football. He's just the greatest, that's all."

— BEANO COOK, Former ABC Sports announcer

GENERALLY CONSIDERED ONE OF THE TWO OR THREE BEST EVER AT HIS POSITION, SIMPSON WORE ONLY THE MOST BASIC PADDING. HE RARELY WORE ELBOW PADS, NEVER WORE FOREARM PADS AND ESCHEWED TRADITIONAL HIP AND TAILBONE PADS OPTING INSTEAD TO TAPE SMALL KNEE PADS TO HIS HIPS WHILE LEAVING HIS BACKSIDE UNPROTECTED.

"I FEEL MORE LOOSE THAT WAY," SIMPSON SAID. "I TRY TO HIT THE TACKLER BEFORE HE HITS ME. I WANT TO BE THE PUNISHER, NOT HIM. RUNNING IS A FEELING. I DON'T WEAR A LOT OF PADS BECAUSE I WANT TO 'FEEL' THE GAME, THE CONTACT. IT HELPS TO BE ABLE TO FEEL A TACKLER HITTING YOU AND GRABBING YOU. YOU KNOW WHERE HE IS AND WHAT TO DO."

O. J. SIMPSON

#32	6'1"	212

SIMPSON 1ST
running back

defensive tackle because most of the other kids were "kinda small." The team lost far more than it won and Simpson went largely unnoticed by the major schools he wanted to attend. Slowly and without much notice, Simpson moved toward a military career. He was on the verge of joining the Army when a friend bet him he couldn't make the football team at San Francisco's two-year City College. Simpson enrolled for the fall semester on the last day of registration. Two years and 54 touchdowns later, Simpson headed off to USC. Standing 6-foot-1-inch and weighing a little more than 200 pounds, Simpson could cover 100 yards in less than 9.4 seconds. While others saw him as a flanker with open field skills, USC coach John McKay saw a tailback.

#34   6'1"   225   HERSCHEL **WALKER** *running back*   1ST 1T

HERSCHEL **WALKER**

"WHEN I COVERED THE GEORGIA–GEORGIA TECH GAME IN 1982, I MET BEFORE THE GAME WITH GEORGIA COACH VINCE DOOLEY AND ASKED HIM TO DESCRIBE HIS OFFENSE. 'WE HAVE A SIMPLE OFFENSE,' SAID DOOLEY.

'WE GO HERSCHEL RIGHT, HERSCHEL LEFT, AND HERSCHEL UP THE MIDDLE.'

EVERY TIME WALKER CARRIED THE BALL, BULLDOG FANS CHANTED: 'LET THE BIG DOG EAT!' THE BIG DOG FEASTED THAT DAY EN ROUTE TO AN EASY VICTORY AND THE HEISMAN TROPHY."

— LEE GROSSCUP

L ike mothers all over America, Christine Walker feared for her son on the football field. Actually, that's not quite right. Mrs. Walker's fears had more to do with what might happen to the other players.

"I was afraid he would hurt somebody," she said. With good reason.

Her son had grown into a man at the tender age of 18. As a high school senior, Herschel Walker was as big and as strong as 95 percent of the running backs in the National Football League. And he might have been faster than all of them. Gil Brandt, the former Dallas Cowboys director of player personnel, didn't need to see much more to know what Walker would become.

"Walker and Earl Campbell were the only two players who could have gone directly into the NFL from high school," said Brandt.

It certainly looked that way at Georgia. Walker broke the freshman rushing

record set by Tony Dorsett, finished third in the Heisman Trophy voting, (highest ever for a freshman) and became the only freshman ever voted to the Football Writers' All-America Team. On the football field at least, few freshmen have ever dominated to the extent Walker did in his first season. He capped the stunning debut with 150 yards and two touchdowns in a 17-10 victory over Notre Dame in the Sugar Bowl, despite playing with a severely separated shoulder. Take away Walker, the rest of the Bulldogs contributed 23 yards to a victory that sealed the 1980 national championship.

"The things Herschel Walker did and the way he did them as an 18-year old kid were mind-boggling," said Brad Nessler. "His first year at Georgia was my first year living in Atlanta. I had never seen one guy take a conference by storm like he did. I loved what O. J. did and I grew up in the Big Ten and saw Archie Griffin. But Herschel Walker was superman in everything he did in college."

HOMETOWN: WRIGHTSVILLE, GA.
POPULATION: 2,350
HEIGHT: 6'1"
WEIGHT: 225
WAIST: 31"

ARCHIE GRIFFIN

Archie Griffin was the centerpiece of a college football offensive rotation toward powerful, dominant runnning backs. Tony Dorsett, Griffin, USC's Ricky Bell, Texas sophomore Earl Campbell and California's Chuck Muncie were churning up yardage all over the country during the 1975 season, which culminated in Griffin's second Heisman Trophy. Red Grange, Tom Harmon, Glenn Davis, Hopalong Cassady and Jim Brown never gained 1,000 yards in a season. More than 30 players did it in 1975. In fairness to the older stars, a myriad of rules changes altered the playing field. Freshman eligibility, an increase in the number of games played and the two-platoon system benefited the running game starting in the 1960s. Still, Griffin's performance stands on its own regardless of the era. He is the only player to win back-to-back Heisman Trophies. Starting in his sophomore season, Griffin peeled off 31 consecutive 100-yard games.

Standing just 5-foot-8-inches and weighing only 182 pounds, Griffin never missed a game at Ohio State despite carrying the ball nearly 1,000 times in his career.

BACK-to-BACK

HEISMAN TROPHIES

"ARCHIE GRIFFIN IS THE GREATEST RUNNING BACK I'VE EVER SEEN IN COLLEGE.

G   10   20   30   40

IN FACT, I'VE NEVER SEEN A GREATER FOOTBALL PLAYER." — WOODY HAYES

40 30 20 10 G

ony Dorsett was not a young man of shallow ambition. After shredding Navy's defense for 180 yards midway through the 1976 season to break the NCAA rushing record, Dorsett listened as Bill Hillgrove of Pittsburgh's WTAE radio gushed, "In my estimation, you are the greatest back ever to play the game." Responded Dorsett, "Well, my stats prove it."

There were still four games remaining in Dorsett's final season at Pittsburgh when he broke Archie Griffin's career rushing record. But Dorsett wasn't finished. He wanted to "put the new record out of reach," which it would be for the next 22 years. Dorsett thought 6,000

yards sounded reasonable so he did the math. He would have to average 195 yards a game, including the regular season finale against rival Penn State, which wasn't about to be the doormat for Dorsett's run to 6,000.

But four weeks later, not even Joe Paterno could come up with enough bodies to stop Dorsett's charge. He sliced through the Nittany Lions for 224 yards in a 24-7 Pitt victory. Dorsett finished with 18 NCAA records, including the rushing mark of 6,082 yards, more than 900 yards more than Griffin, tied three more and set 37 school records.

"Pitt was playing at Notre Dame in 1976, the year Pitt won the national championship," said Keith Jackson. "I walked into the stadium and started to laugh. The grass must have been three inches deep. I walked over to the athletic office and caught Dan Devine, who was the coach at Notre Dame. I said, 'When are you going to cut the grass?' He said, 'What do you mean? The grass is trimmed. The field is perfect and ready to play. 'I thought, 'Sure, if you've got mules and you're playing thoroughbreds.'

"Bill Flemming was on the sidelines that day and we opened the telecast with Bill dropping a golf ball onto the field. The ball disappeared. Early in the game, Tony Dorsett went 61 yards to set up a touchdown. End of story."

#33 | **5'11"** | **192**

2ND T TONY
DORSETT
running back

TONY **DORSETT**

1976

37 SCHOOL RECORDS

6,082 YARDS RUSHING

G   10   20   30   40

BO
JACKSON

If Herschel Walker represented a natural evolution that traced its roots to O. J. Simpson, a running back of intimidating size and world class speed, then Bo Jackson represented a whole new species. Surrounded by a national championship team as a freshman at Georgia, Walker's impact was immediate and long term. But the depth and breadth of Jackson's heroics remain the standard by which all other multisport superstars will be measured. Like Walker, Jackson ran on his school's track team after the football season. But unlike anyone of his generation, Jackson also displayed potential few professional baseball scouts had ever seen at the collegiate level.

Jackson turned down a $150,000 signing bonus from the Yankees out of high school after matching the national scholastic record with 20 home runs in 25 games as a senior despite rarely practicing due to track commitments. Though Jackson did not have the supporting case Walker enjoyed, he none the less matured into a punishing multi-dimensional tailback. He gained 829 yards as a freshman, 1,213 as a sophomore and won the Heisman Trophy as a senior after averaging nearly seven yards (6.62) a carry for his career. All the while, Jackson split off-seasons between track and baseball.

The depth of Jackson's extraordinary talent and work ethic became clear to virtually every baseball scout in the country in the spring of his junior year. Jackson hit .401 with 17 homers in 42 games including mammoth shots that have become a part of Auburn baseball lore.

But it was on the football field that Jackson came to define his position. Jackson gained more than 4,300 yards including 1,786 his senior season, and scored 43 touchdowns. All that despite missing all or parts of 10 games.

> "In seven years of pro baseball, I saw four or five guys, total, who had the type of power Bo possessed. Three or four guys who could hit like he could; and three or four who could throw like he could. But those were 12 different people...he was the closest thing to Mickey Mantle since Mickey Mantle. As far as the total package of skills, I've never seen anyone remotely close to Bo."
>
> **— HAL BAIRD Auburn's baseball coach and a pitcher in the Kansas City Royals system in the 1970s**

#34	220	6'2"

JACKSON BO **2**ND
running back **T**

RICKY WILLIAMS	TONY DORSETT	CHARLES WHITE	HERSCHEL WALKER	ARCHIE GRIFFIN
Texas	Pittsburgh	USC	Georgia	Ohio State
1995-98	1973-76	1976-79	1980-82	1972-75
6,279	6,082	5,598	5,259	5,177

There were three games remaining in Ricky Williams' senior season at Texas and he had already scored more points and touchdowns than any player in Division I history. He would finish the 1998 season having moved from 37th to first on the NCAA career rushing list and blowing by Tony Dorsett's 22-year-old mark in the process. Dorsett thought he had put the rushing record out of reach by skipping past the 6,000 yard mark. And he had until Williams, cut from a mold that produced Herschel Walker and Bo Jackson before him, decided to come back to Texas for his senior season.

Despite finishing 5th in the 1997 Heisman voting and being projected as a certain Top 10 draft pick, Williams wanted one more run. Though he had been brilliant in former coach John Mackovic's pro-style offense, Williams was never the first option. "I was so excited to be the man," said Williams. "And I believed we could be a good team."

He also saw a chance to add to the Texas backfield legacy by erasing Dorsett's mark. Williams won the Doak Walker Award, named after another Texas legend, as the nation's top back as a junior. He was so taken by Walker, who was on hand to deliver the award, that Williams put a No. 37 decal, Walker's number, on his helmet prior to the 1998 season. When Walker died just weeks into the season, Williams switched from his usual No. 34 to a No. 37 jersey for the Oklahoma game. When he burst into the end zone for a fourth quarter score, Williams pointed to the number, looked into the sky and shouted, "That's for you, Doak."

RICKY **WILLIAMS**

40-YD DASH : 4.4 SECONDS | BENCH PRESS : 406 POUNDS

3RD T

| #34 | 5'10" | 236 |

RICKY **WILLIAMS**
running back

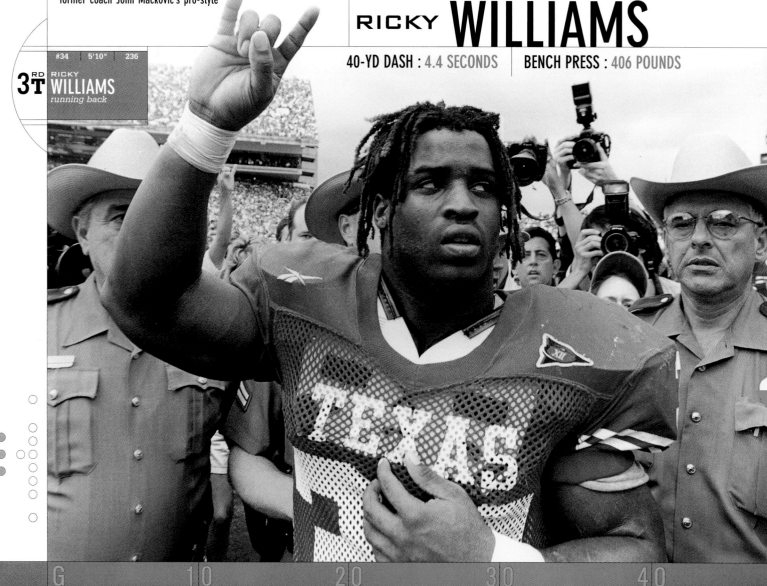

G | 10 | 20 | 30 | 40

#20 | 6"1" | 225

EARL CAMPBELL 2ND T
running back

EARL
CAMPBELL

> "Earl was good enough as a freshman to go into pro football. He wouldn't have been a star right away, but no one would have had the guts to cut him, because you could see the raw talent there."
>
> **— DARRELL ROYAL,**
> **former Texas coach**

Earl Campbell had spent one season at the University of Texas, a school with as much football history as the game itself, when the 1975 season started.

This is how Jones Ramsey, Texas' director of sports information at the time, opened his Sept. 10, 1975 release to the state's newspapers:

"Some folks say they're self-made men and others are products of their environment, but God made Earl Campbell, friend, and if you don't believe it, you're gonna have to argue with Earl. He carries a bible in one hand and a football in the other, and you have a much better chance of keeping him out of the end zone than you do changing his religious convictions."

They write country songs about guys like Earl Campbell, but in Texas guys like Earl Campbell become icons.

That's especially true when the guy loves country music enough to want to name his second son "Country," and so admires Texas that he eventually names the boy "Tyler," in honor of his hometown. But when you become the first Longhorn to win the Heisman Trophy, not even a country song comes close to capturing the piece of Texas you have become.

Until Tony Dorsett came along, Campbell was the most dominating freshman back in history, averaging more than 5.7 yards a carry. He only got better.

At 6-feet-1-inch and weighing 225 pounds, Campbell was as fast as any player that size has ever been.

"When I got to the ninth grade," says Campbell, who is a member of the National Football League Hall of Fame, "that's when I began to realize that God gave me a talent that he didn't give Johnny down the street."

TROJAN TRADITION

Marcus Allen says he was just like a lot of kids growing up in Southern California in the 1980s. "I grew up loving USC football and UCLA basketball," says Allen. "But I was going to play football, not basketball, so there was no choice."

But Allen was much different than all those other kids. As a high school senior, Allen threw for 1,900 yards, ran for 1,198 yards — averaging 12.4 yards a carry — scored 12 touchdowns on offense, intercepted 11 passes — four of which he converted into touchdowns — and led the team in tackles.

Though USC recruited Allen as a defensive back, coach John Robinson needed just four practices to decide Allen was a tailback. Allen played behind All-American Charles White as a freshman and then moved into the starting lineup as a sophomore. At 185 pounds, Robinson made Allen a fullback whose primary responsibility was to clear the lanes for White.

As it turned out, two Heisman Trophy winners came out of that move. White won the 1979 Heisman and Allen, who learned more than he cared to learn as a fullback, won in 1981.

"I realized later that it was a great thing for me and that it helped me to become a better and more complete back," says Allen. "But at the time, I didn't like it at all."

Once Allen took over, he left all the others who had come before him in his wake. Not even O. J. Simpson dominated the position like Allen did as a senior. He set 15 NCAA records and tied another — including most rushing attempts (403), most yards (2,342) most touchdowns (22), highest per game average (212.9), most 200-yard games in a season (8) and most consecutive 200-yard games (5). He also led the nation in all-purpose yardage (rushing, receiving, returns) and caught 34 passes to lead the Trojans in that category.

To put those numbers in perspective, Earl Campbell had a total of three 200-yard games at Texas. Ricky Williams, who broke the career rushing mark in 1999, never had more than six 200-yard games in a season. When Allen became the first 2,000-yard back in NCAA history, he broke Tony Dorsett's existing record by almost 400 yards.

* Led nation   ** NCAA record

YEAR	PLAYER	ATT	YARDS	AVG	TD	RANK	HEISMAN VOTING
1963	MIKE GARRETT	128	833	6.5	3	7	
1964	MIKE GARRETT	217	948	4.4	9	6	
1965	MIKE GARRETT	267*	1,440*	5.4	13	1	Won
1967	O. J. SIMPSON	266*	1,415*	5.3	11	1	2nd
1968	O. J. SIMPSON	355	1,709*	4.8	22	1	Won
1972	ANTHONY DAVIS	184	1,034	5.6	16	26	
1973	ANTHONY DAVIS	260	1,039	4.0	13	31	
1974	ANTHONY DAVIS	288	1,354	4.7	13	7	2nd
1975	RICKY BELL	357*	1,875*	5.3	13	1	3rd
1976	RICKY BELL	276	1,417	5.1	14	4	2nd
1977	CHARLES WHITE	264	1,291	4.9	7	14	
1978	CHARLES WHITE	342*	1,760	5.1	12	4	4th
1979	CHARLES WHITE	293	1,803*	6.2	18	1	Won
1980	MARCUS ALLEN	354*	1,563	4.4	14	2	
1981	MARCUS ALLEN	403**	2,342**	5.8	22*	1	Won

G   10   20   30   40

#33 | 6'2" | 210

MARCUS
ALLEN 3RD T
running back

MARCUS
ALLEN

"Because of the tradition at
tailback, a lot of weight is on
the shoulders of whoever is at
that position. But the pressure
gave me more incentive to do
well. I didn't want to be the one
who failed. So I always felt that
I had to work harder than
anyone else at practice."

— MARCUS ALLEN

40   30   20   10   G

BARRY SANDERS

3RD 3T BARRY SANDERS
running back

#21 | 5'8" | 203

2628 YARDS
37 TDS
12 GAMES

Barry Sanders left Oklahoma State after one of the best seasons in college football history. As a junior on a mediocre Cowboys team, Sanders set NCAA records with 2,628 rushing yards and a remarkable 37 touchdowns in 12 games.

But there was more than NFL money behind Sanders' decision to leave college. The Heisman Trophy winner was destined to become even more of a target thanks to the Cowboys' supporting cast — the graduation of the entire offensive line.

OFFENSIVE LINE

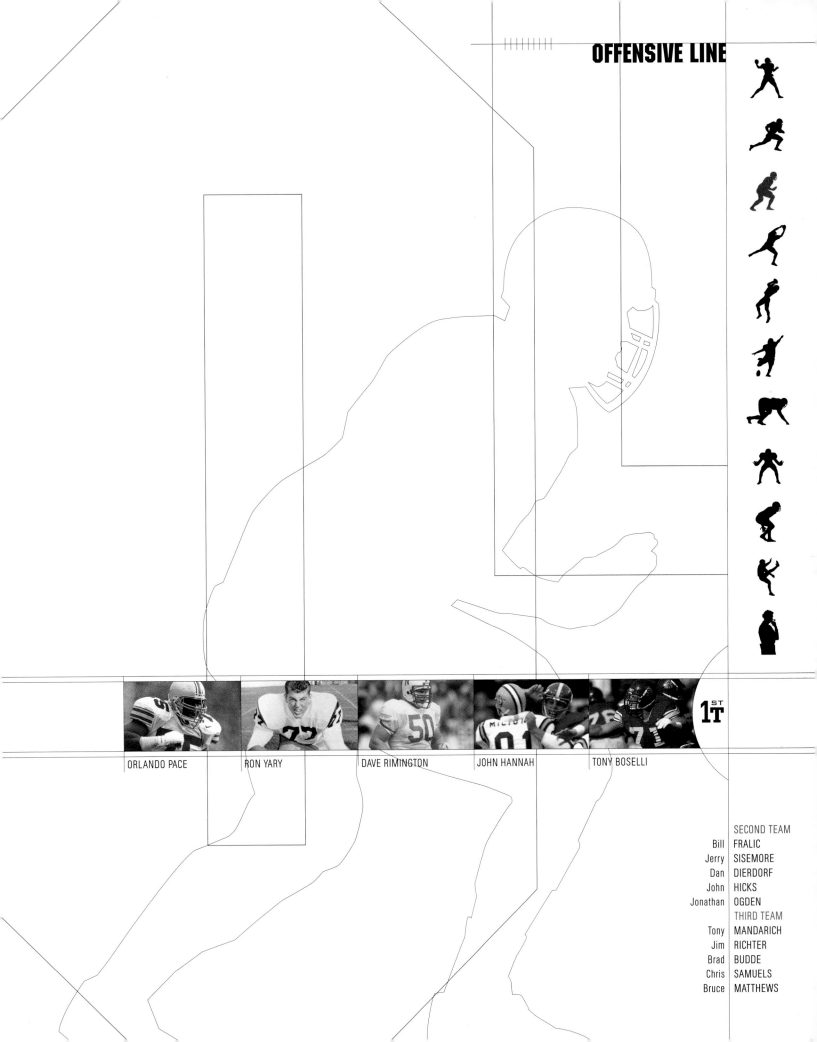

ORLANDO PACE   RON YARY   DAVE RIMINGTON   JOHN HANNAH   TONY BOSELLI

1ST T

SECOND TEAM
Bill FRALIC
Jerry SISEMORE
Dan DIERDORF
John HICKS
Jonathan OGDEN

THIRD TEAM
Tony MANDARICH
Jim RICHTER
Brad BUDDE
Chris SAMUELS
Bruce MATTHEWS

1995

LOMBARDI AWARD

LOMBARDI AWARD
OUTLAND TROPHY

1996

#75 | 6'7" | 320

1ST
1T

ORLANDO
PACE
offensive lineman

ORLANDO

PACE

G   0   30   40

"To me, Orlando Pace is the best lineman of all time. I have never seen an offensive lineman with that type of speed off the snap. This guy could have been a running back on third-down situations. You would see him making pancake blocks down field and the running back would not break stride running behind him. At the time, he was a a freak of nature."

— JOHN SAUNDERS

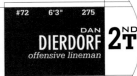

#72   6'3"   275

DAN
DIERDORF   2ND T

offensive lineman

DAN
DIERDORF

In the state of Ohio, Dan Dierdorf's football sins were of the most serious nature. Not only did he decide to leave the state for college, but he left for the University of Michigan. If that wasn't enough, Dierdorf became a two-time All-Big Ten tackle and consensus All-American as a senior for Bo Schembechler.

"Any football player who leaves Ohio is considered a traitor," said Dierdorf. "They even have the coaches of the smaller colleges trying to convince you to go to Ohio State."

The opposite was true for Reggie McKenzie, who in 1971 teamed with Dierdorf on one the greatest offensive lines in Michigan history. McKenzie ended up at Michigan almost by default after only a handful of schools expressed interest.

Playing guard opposite Dierdorf's tackle, the Wolverines averaged more than 400 yards a game on offense.

"Guys like Dan Dierdorf and Ron Yary had quick feet and great mobility," said Tim Brandt. "They could have played in any era. They didn't lift weights, but they were naturally strong."

Ohio State used Pace on both sides of the ball, shifting him to the defensive line in short yardage and goal-line situations. At one point, there was even some consideration — at Pace's suggestion — of putting the 320-pounder in the backfield on short yardage plays.

"The hitting," says Pace, "that's what I enjoy. When I was little, I played football because I was big, so I had to play. But I've grown to love the game, the physical part of it."

"The guy is unbelievable. I mean, he's got the whole package: great feet, great hands, long arms. I try to tell people that you just don't see guys who are this big and this good." said Jim Lachey, a former All-America at Ohio State and three-time Pro Bowler in 11 NFL seasons.

#77	6'3"	265

1ST T

RON YARY
offensive lineman

It All Started With Yary

YEAR	PLAYER	POSITION	DRAFT*
1968	Ron Yary	Tackle	1
1968	Mike Taylor	Tackle	10
1970	Sid Smith	Tackle	26
1971	Marv Montgomery	Tackle	12
1973	Pete Adams	Tackle	22
1974	Steve Riley	Tackle	25
1977	Marvin Powell	Tackle	4
1980	Anthony Munoz	Tackle	3
1980	Brad Budde	Guard	11
1981	Keith Van Horne	Tackle	11
1983	Bruce Matthews	Guard	9
1983	Don Mosebar	Tackle	26
1985	Ken Ruettgers	Tackle	7
1986	James Fitzpatrick	Tackle	13
1988	Dave Cadigan	Tackle	8
1991	Pat Harlow	Tackle	11
1995	Tony Boselli	Tackle	2

*Overall First-Round NFL Draft Position

RON YARY

If O. J. Simpson is the dominant link in USC's chain of remarkable tailbacks, then the man who cleared the way for him in 1967 represents the lock. But like Simpson, Ron Yary took a circuitous route to stardom at USC.

After spending his freshman season at a junior college, Yary joined the Trojans and became a starter on the defensive line. He was good enough to be named All-West Coast defensive tackle. But when Yary showed up in 1966, coach John McKay decided Yary would go across the line.

"McKay called me before the season and told me they were going to play me both ways that year," says Yary, who became a perennial All-Pro for the Minnesota Vikings. "They were going to work me into it slowly. I really wanted to do it, but it never came about. Defense was more fun, but your longevity is better playing the offensive line."

The same was true for the USC backs who ran in front of Yary. Indeed, it was Yary's work on behalf of Simpson that established Yary as one of the very best the college game ever has produced. Yary was considered so instrumental to Simpson's first-year success that the Minnesota Vikings traded quarterback Fran Tarkenton for the first pick in the 1968 draft, which they used on Yary.

Though Simpson had an equally brilliant season without Yary, he also averaged nearly a half-yard less per rushing play in 1968.

G   10   20   30   40

> "John Hannah is the finest offensive lineman I've been around in 30 years as a coach and that covers a lot of games and a lot of players. He has all the physical tools of greatness, plus he has a burning desire to excel. I've seen him do things on the football field I couldn't believe, especially for a man who stands 6-foot-3-inches and weighs over 260 pounds."
>
> — PAUL "BEAR" BRYANT

JOHN
HANNAH

Considered one of the greatest offensive linemen to play the game at any level, John Hannah has been named to every all-time team of merit. Hannah was a consensus All-America in 1972 and so dominated his position that New England made him the fourth pick overall in the 1973 NFL Draft. Before the draft, however, Hannah was unsure of himself and visited Alabama coach Bear Bryant for advice.

"I went to Coach Bryant and told him it looked like I would get drafted real high," says Hannah. "I asked him if I needed to get an attorney, or what I should do. Coach looked at me and said, 'Shoot, John, you ain't good enough to need an attorney.'"

In retrospect, Hannah thought Bryant merely was trying to keep him hungry. After all, by the time Hannah left Alabama, Bryant considered Hannah the best offensive lineman he had ever coached.

The Hannah pedigree might be the most pure in all of college football. John's father, Herb, was an Alabama offensive lineman from 1948 through 1950 and played one season for the New York Giants. John's two brothers, Charles and David, were All-Southeastern Conference offensive linemen at Alabama as well.

But at Alabama Hannah was far more than a football player. Indeed, he might be one of the most successful three-sport athletes in the history of college athletics. Entering his senior year, Hannah was the defending Southeastern Conference shot put and discus champion and he held the conference indoor shot put record. As a freshman wrestler in the heavyweight division, Hannah was unbeaten.

"He's one of the greatest iron men to play the game," said Terry Bowden. "He was just an iron man out there, game in and game out. I think I'm a little biased because I come from Alabama. But to me he was a dead gum go-to-work blue-collar guy. He was dominant from the beginning to the end of his career."

#73 6'3" 265
JOHN
HANNAH 1ST
offensive lineman

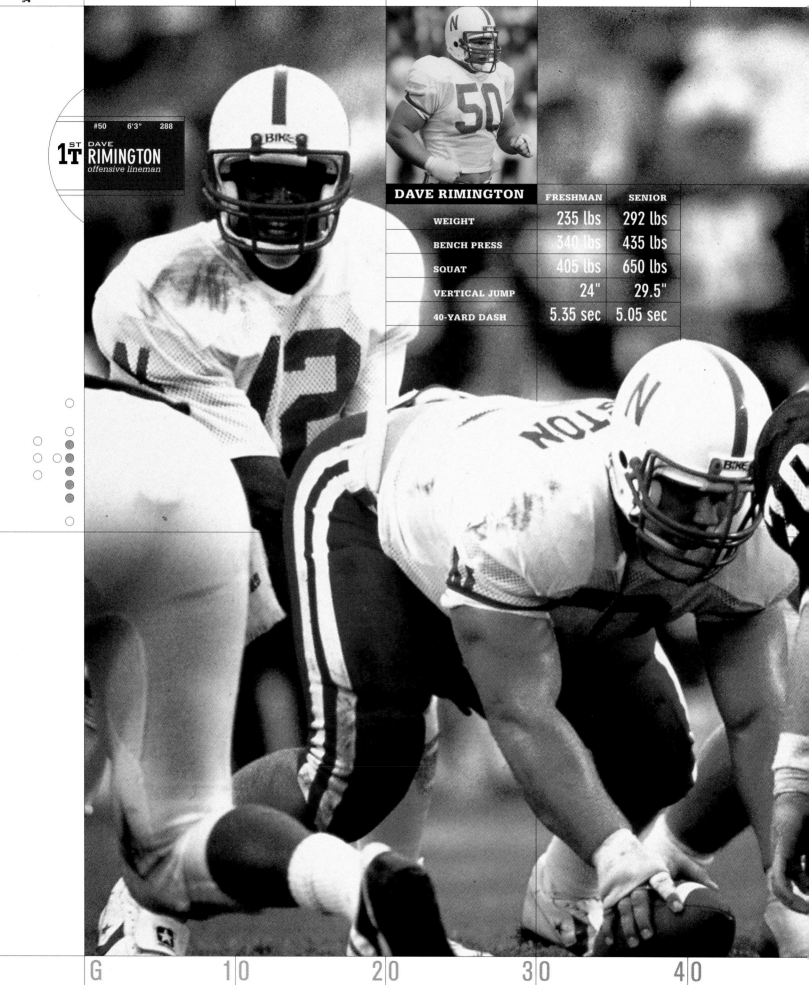

1ST T

#50   6'3"   288

DAVE
RIMINGTON
offensive lineman

DAVE RIMINGTON	FRESHMAN	SENIOR
WEIGHT	235 lbs	292 lbs
BENCH PRESS	340 lbs	435 lbs
SQUAT	405 lbs	650 lbs
VERTICAL JUMP	24"	29.5"
40-YARD DASH	5.35 sec	5.05 sec

G   10   20   30   40

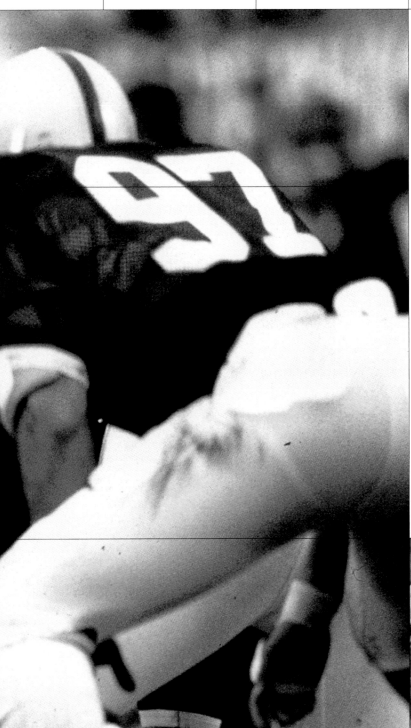

The best way to appreciate what Dave Rimington had become by his senior season at Nebraska was to look at where he had come from.

Between Rimington's freshman and senior seasons, he lowered his time in the 40 by 3/10ths of a second despite adding 57 pounds of muscle. And if there is any question about the extra weight having turned into pure strength, the numbers provided confirmation: 435-pound bench press and 650-pound squat.

Rimington, at the time only the third junior to win the Outland Trophy (as the nation's best lineman), was so dominant as a junior that he was mentioned as a potential Heisman Trophy candidate as a senior.

"He blows holes in the line you could send the backs through three abreast," said former Nebraska offensive line coach Clete Fischer.

Rimington was a two-time Academic All-American with a 3.25 grade point average in economics.

DAVE
RIMINGTON

"He blows holes in the line you could send the backs through three abreast."
— CLETE FISCHER former Nebraska offensive line coach

Tony Boselli might be the only player in the history of college football to turn a severe knee injury into an improved position in the NFL draft.

In 1993, the 6-foot-8-inch, 305-pound Boselli found himself face down in the Arizona Stadium grass on his way to an early exit from USC. Boselli had been named to a handful of All-America teams as a sophomore and by the second month of his junior season, he was leaning toward the NFL at the expense of his senior year. All that changed when Boselli looked down and saw his left knee cap decidedly out of place. He missed the rest of the season and USC seemed to do much the same.

But the injury proved only to serve the interests of all concerned. Boselli came back bigger and stronger and USC followed his lead.

"I have great admiration for him," said John Robinson, who was twice coach at USC and spent nine years coaching in the NFL. "In order for us to get back to the championship level, we needed to set a standard, and Tony set that."

Actually, Boselli fell in step with a standard that had been set long before by USC linemen. A consensus All-American, he was the No. 2 pick overall in the 1995 draft.

"At USC, we are as appreciated as any other position on the field. Maybe not by the people on the outside, but by the staff and the other players, and that's more important than anything."

— TONY BOSELLI

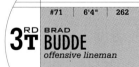

#71	6'4"	262

3RD **BRAD**
T **BUDDE**
offensive lineman

BRAD
BUDDE

Of all the schools and all the positions on a football field, playing tailback for the University of Southern California has a glamour and history unlike any other. Between Mike Garrett in 1965 and Marcus Allen in 1981, USC backs won four Heisman Trophies and might have won at least two more (Ricky Bell and Anthony Davis) with better timing.

But for the Trojans and their marquee backs, it's always been what's up front that matters most. And Charles White, No. 3 in the USC Heisman lineage, knows that better than any of the great runners before him. In his 1979 race to the Heisman, White ran behind a Trojan offensive line that included Anthony Munoz, Keith Van Horne and Brad Budde.

#71   6'8"   305

TONY
BOSELLI 1ST
offensive lineman

TONY
BOSELLI

Of the trio, none played better than Budde that season. The first four-year USC starter since World War II, Budde became the first Trojan to win the Lombardi Award, given to the nation's top lineman. He also finished second in the Outland Trophy voting and anchored what might be the greatest offensive line in college football history.

USC scored 389 points, which was its highest total in 28 years entering the 2000 season, and averaged almost 5 1/2 yards every time it ran the ball. The Trojans finished 11-0-1 and second in the nation behind Alabama. Meanwhile, Munoz was the third player taken in the 1980 NFL Draft, Budde was selected eight spots later at No. 11 and White was the No. 27 selection. A year later, Van Horne was chosen by Chicago with the 11th pick overall.

40   30   20   10   G

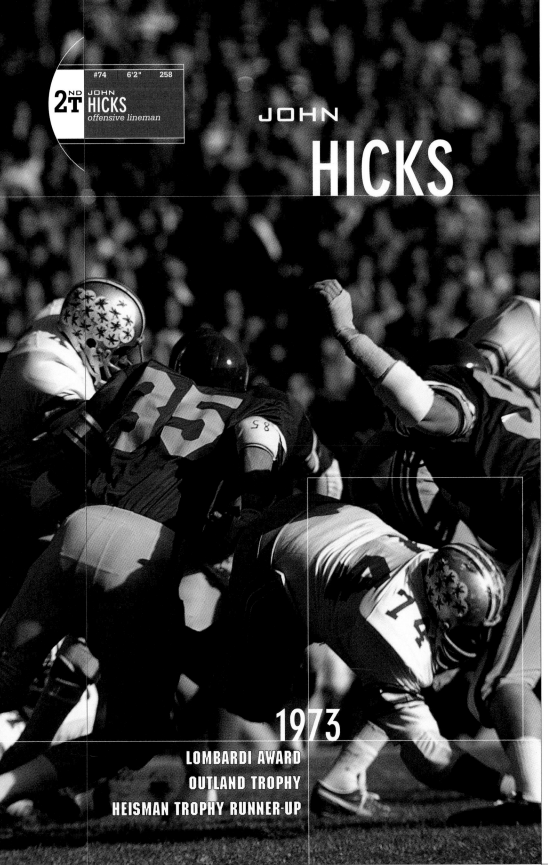

#74 6'2" 258

2ND T

JOHN

HICKS

offensive lineman

JOHN

HICKS

1973

LOMBARDI AWARD
OUTLAND TROPHY
HEISMAN TROPHY RUNNER-UP

It wasn't enough that Ohio State's John Hicks became the first player ever to start in three Rose Bowls, but he nearly completed the greatest triple crown season in college football history in 1973.

And he did it all after major knee surgery eliminated nearly 50 percent of his college career.

Hicks didn't become a starter until his sophomore season because freshmen still weren't eligible in 1969. But midway through the 1970 season, Hicks went down. Knee injuries have always been serious, but they were particularly so given the surgical procedures in the early 1970s. Hicks missed the final six games in 1970 and all of the 1971 regular season.

By the time he returned to the starting lineup in 1972, Hicks had matured into one of the most dominant offensive tackles of his era. He was an All-American in 1972 and 1973, the latter on one of the school's greatest teams. The Buckeyes won consecutive Big Ten titles and in 1973 beat USC 42-21 in the Rose Bowl to finish 10-0-1.

But to put Hicks' performance and that of the Buckeyes in perspective you have to consider the numbers and, in Hicks's case, those of his teammates. Ohio State outscored the opposition 413-64, or by an average of approximately 38-6. The Buckeyes defense, led by linebacker Randy Gradishar, had four shutouts and six games in which they didn't allow a touchdown. The offense churned out an average of more than 355 yards a game, most of it coming on the ground behind Hicks.

When it was over, all eyes were on Hicks. He won the Outland Trophy and the Lombardi Award, a rare double in itself. Then he finished second to Penn State's John Cappelletti and ahead of teammates Archie Griffin (fifth) and Gradishar (sixth) in the Heisman Trophy voting.

Better than most, Joe Moore knew a great offensive lineman when he saw one. After all, Moore was an assistant at the University of Pittsburgh and the one common denominator when Mark May, Russ Grimm and Jim Covert passed through.

But when Moore talks about the greatest of the group, the discussion starts and ends with Bill Fralic, who is credited with being the man behind the term "pancake block." The Pitt sports information office coined the term as a way to describe Fralic's dominance to potential Heisman Trophy voters in 1983. Fralic finished eighth in the Heisman voting in 1983 and sixth in 1984, two of the highest finishes for an offensive lineman.

"I haven't had anyone play for me for four years the way Bill Fralic did," says Moore. "There was never anyone even close to being the complete player he was for his four seasons in college. From his first day as a freshman, everything he did was to make himself a great football player. He just came in and dominated like no one I have ever seen on the offensive line."

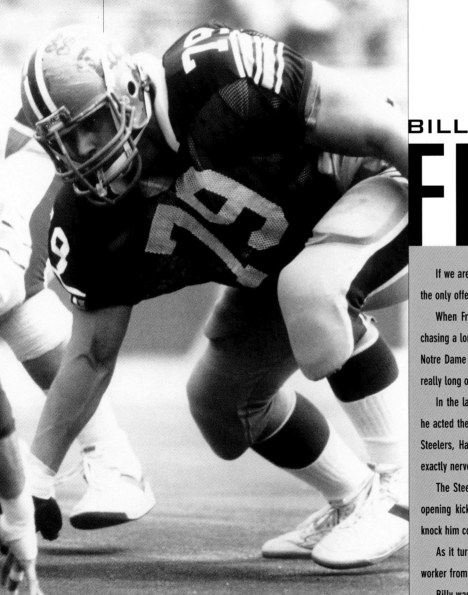

#79	6'5"	280

BILL
FRALIC **2ND**
offensive line

BILL
FRALIC

If we are separated only by degrees, then Bill Fralic's connection to the only offensive lineman to with the Heisman Trophy makes sense.

When Fralic finished sixth in the Heisman voting in 1984, he was chasing a longshot. The only offensive lineman to win the Heisman was Notre Dame tight end Leon Hart in 1949. But if you want to talk about really long odds, consider Fralic's 25-year connection to Hart.

In the late 1940s, Hart was considered a giant at 265 pounds. And he acted the part. Before his professional debut against the Pittsburgh Steelers, Hart, who played for Detroit, was quoted saying he wasn't exactly nervous about the National Football League.

The Steelers no doubt were informed of Hart's bravado and on the opening kickoff, 200-pound Charlie Mehelich hit Hart hard enough to knock him cold.

As it turned out, Mehelich's sister, Dorothy, married a rugged steel worker from Pittsburgh named William Fralic.

Billy was their third son.

"He's one of the greatest players at his position in the history of college football."
— FOGE FAZIO former Pittsburgh coach

#75 6'4" 260

2ND T JERRY SISEMORE
offensive lineman

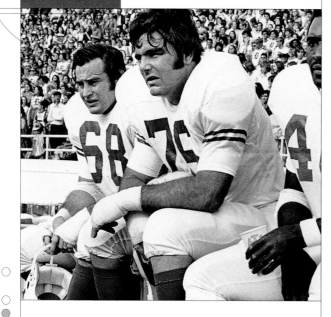

To appreciate Jonathan Ogden's performance at UCLA during his senior season you have to understand what Tony Boselli did a year before at USC. Boselli anchored a USC offensive line that cleared the way for a running game that averaged more than 394 yards in 1995. Boselli was so impressive that the Jacksonville Jaguars made him the No. 2 pick in the first round of the 1995 NFL Draft. What does all this have to do with Ogden? There were many, including former San Francisco offensive line coach Bob McKittrick, who found Ogden even more impressive than Boselli.

"He's the best I've seen," said McKittrick. "This guy runs faster, jumps higher and bench presses more than (Tony) Boselli. Everything you can measure athletically, he's a little bit better."

That includes throwing the 16-pound shot put. Ogden finished fifth at the NCAA Indoor Track and Field Championships in 1994 and 1995 and finished fifth outdoors in 1995 when he qualifed for the 1996 Olympic Trials. All this without ever concentrating on the event year-round. At the time, UCLA throws coach Art Venegas told anyone who would listen that Ogden was good enough to win a gold medal at the 2000 Olympic Games if track and field became Ogden's focus. It didn't, but Ogden has done just fine on the football field where he, like Boselli, has become an All-Pro in the NFL.

JERRY
SISEMORE

There are two things you need to know about Jerry Sisemore if you want to understand his stance on the state of Texas and defensive players.

First, Sisemore was described by the University of Texas as "an orange-blooded high school star" when he arrived in Austin out of Plainview. That's because Sisemore committed to Texas before the school even had a chance to recruit him. Second, Sisemore, a 6-foot-4-inch, 260-pound two-time All-America tackle who started as a sophomore on the Longhorns' 1970 national championship team, is said to have once knocked down five SMU defenders on the same play.

That fact was outlined on the school's 1980 Longhorn Hall of Honor Selection Ballot. The brief bio also noted, "his deeds were many."

Indeed.

FAST FACTS

79 Jonathan Ogden is one of just eight players to have his football number (79) retired at UCLA

1 He allowed one quarterback sack over his final two seasons at UCLA

61'1 1½" Ogden's longest shot put (61'1 1/2") came in the 1995 NCAA Outdoor Track and Field Championships

#79 | 6'8" | 318

JONATHAN
OGDEN **2ND**
offensive line

JONATHAN
OGDEN

"He's a beautiful athlete to watch."
—**TERRY DONAHUE** former UCLA coach

40   30   20   10   G

It's likely no offensive lineman in the history of college sports cut a more impressive figure than the 6-foot-6-inch, 324-pound Tony Mandarich. By the time the 1989 NFL draft rolled around, Mandarich's legend had outgrown comparison. He had bench pressed 220 pounds an astounding 39 times in pre-draft workouts. But Michigan State coach George Perles, a defensive coach for the Pittsburgh Steelers when they won four Super Bowls in the 1970s, put the Mandarich hype into overdrive when he said, "As a junior he could have started on any of our Super Bowl teams. He may be the best offensive tackle ever."

The Packers selected Mandarich with the No. 2 pick in the 1989 NFL Draft. Barry Sanders and Deion Sanders followed.

6'6"

| #79 | 6'6" | 324 |

3RD T TONY
MANDARICH
offensive lineman

Boxing promoters Shelly Finkel and Dan Duva saw Tony Mandarich on the cover of *Sports Illustrated* and had an idea.

How about stepping into the ring with heavyweight champion Mike Tyson? "It would be the biggest pay-per-view event ever," gushed Finkel. During contract negotiations with the Green Bay Packers, Mandarich said he would consider taking a season off to prepare for Tyson.

Both were 22 at the time. Although Mandarich would have had more than six inches and nearly 100 pounds on Tyson, the champ was something considerably less than concerned. "I've never heard of him," said Tyson, "but he'll experience something he has never experienced before."

TONY
MANDARICH

WIDE RECEIVER

1ST T

ANTHONY CARTER   JOHNNY RODGERS

SECOND TEAM
Tim   BROWN
Lynn   SWANN
THIRD TEAM
Randy   MOSS
Peter   WARRICK

ANTHONY
CARTER

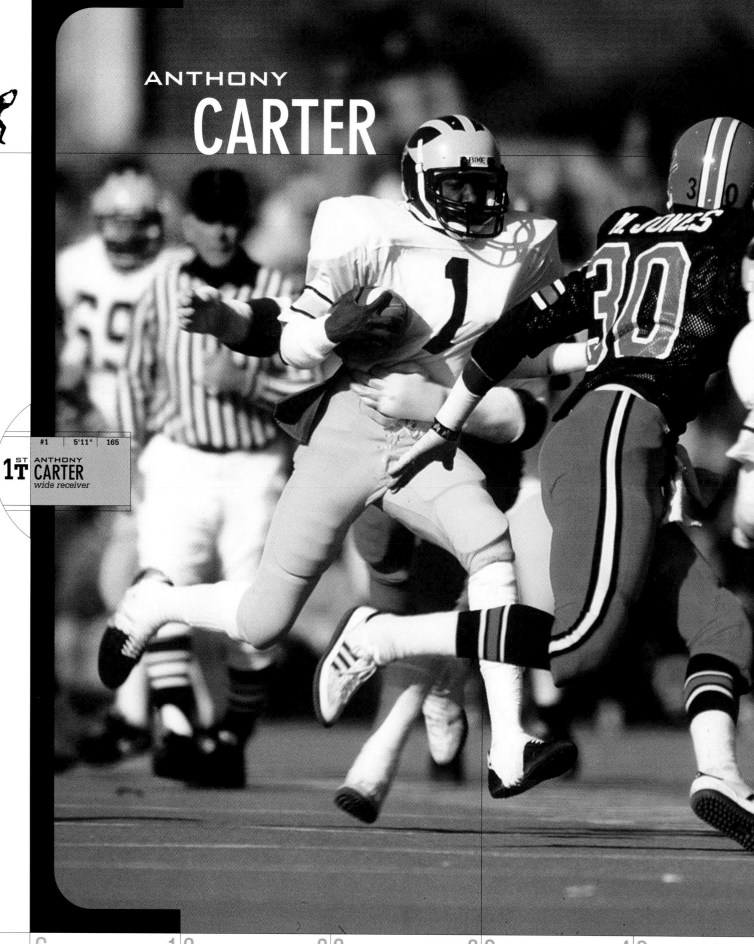

1ST **#1** | **5'11"** | **165**
ANTHONY
CARTER
wide receiver

Just under 6 feet tall and weighing all of 165 pounds, Anthony Carter became the first three-time All-American in the Big Ten Conference in 36 years. With incredible quickness and break away speed, Carter scored a Big Ten record 37 touchdowns and set an NCAA record by averaging 17.4 yards per play in all-purpose yardage.

But the numbers don't come close to explaining the impact Carter had on Michigan and the fear he put into every Wolverine opponent. He averaged less than four catches a game and finished 100 receptions behind the NCAA record holder at the time (Howard Twilley caught 261 at Tulsa). But no player had a higher quality quotient than Carter. He turned nearly one in every four catches into a touchdown. And while he didn't come close to the record for total career receptions, his 33 touchdown receptions ranked second.

NEARLY ONE OUT OF FOUR CATCHES WERE FOR
TOUCHDOWNS

What if Carter had played for a pro-style passing team such as Stanford, Florida State or Brigham Young?

"I suspect he would have broken every pass-receiving record in the book."

— **HAYDEN FRY former Iowa coach**

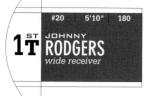

#20   5'10"   180

1ST T JOHNNY
RODGERS
wide receiver

Though named a starting wide receiver on the ABC Sports All-Time All-America First Team, Johnny Rodgers could have made the team at any of three positions.

Despite Nebraska's bruising running game, Rodgers' performance as a receiver, running back and special teams player was so dramatic that he won the 1972 Heisman Trophy over All-America running back Greg Pruitt without setting a single NCAA record. Indeed, Rodgers might have been the most electric punt and kick returner ever to play the college game.

"Everywhere they put him," one pro scout said, "at slot, wing, flanker, anywhere, you can see the defense lean a little."

wr

143 CAREER RECEPTIONS,
26 TOUCHDOWNS

rb

130 CAREER RUSHING ATTEMPTS,
11 TOUCHDOWNS

JOHNNY

RODGERS

Rodgers averaged 15.5 yards on 98 career punt returns with seven touchdowns, returned one kickoff for a touchdown, converted 11 of his 130 career rushing attempts into touchdowns and had 26 touchdown receptions in 143 career receptions. Between punt returns, runs from scrimmage and receiving, Rodgers touched the ball 152 times as a senior and turned more than 11 percent into touchdowns.

Rodgers capped off his career against Notre Dame in the Orange Bowl. Nebraska hammered the Fighting Irish 40-6 with Rodgers scoring four touchdowns and passing for another.

How did Rodgers learn to run so fast in so many different directions?

"By dodging trash cans and telephone poles" in his Omaha neighborhood, says Rodgers.

98 CAREER PUNT RETURNS,
7 TOUCHDOWNS

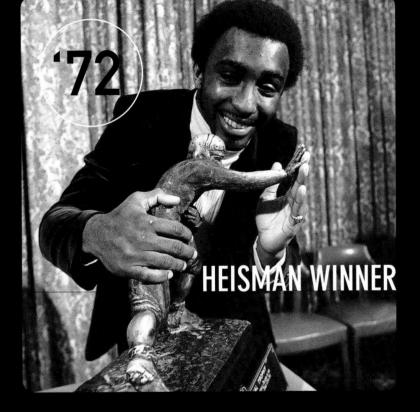

'72

HEISMAN WINNER

11% TD RATIO

"Johnny Rodgers was as good as I've ever seen returning kicks. He had a wonderful hesitation move. Before he would start, you would say, 'Oh, my God, he's going to get clobbered.' But it was his acceleration from a standing position that was so incredible. He had get-off-the-mark quickness. He was almost breathtaking."

— CHRIS SCHENKEL

40 30 20 10 G

THE HEISMAN TWINS

Tim Brown vs. Johnny Rodgers
(last two college seasons)

	BROWN '86-87	RODGERS '71-72
Rushing	4.3	5.6
Receiving	20.9	16.8
Punt Returns	13.2	16.2
Kickoff Returns	24.0	27.1
Yards on TDs	45.4	29.1
On all Plays	14.5	13.7

It had been 15 years since college football had seen a player create so much electricity from so many angles. Nebraska's Johnny Rodgers won the 1972 Heisman Trophy by returning punts, kickoffs, pass receptions and handoffs into mad dashes toward the end zone.

But Rodgers had very little on Notre Dame's Tim Brown. Though bigger than Rodgers, Brown was just as fast and he had the same arsenal of moves. Over his final two seasons at Notre Dame, Brown averaged 14.5 yards every time he touched the ball and an amazing 45.4 yards on 16 touchdowns. As a junior, Brown scored on kickoffs (2), receptions (5) and rushes (2). Then, two games into his senior year, Brown needed less than five minutes to return two Michigan State punts — 71 yards and 66 yards — for touchdowns, the first by the Irish in 14 years.

TIM BROWN

#81	6'0"	195

2ND T
TIM BROWN
wide receiver

"I've only known one other football player who brought the crowd to its feet every time he touched the ball — Gale Sayers when he was with the Bears." — PAUL HORNUNG former Notre Dame and Green Bay Packers star

G   10   20   30   40

As one of the most spectacular players in Michigan history, Desmond Howard wanted everyone to know what he knew: "I want them to hold their breaths every time I touch the ball." And so they did. Michigan teammates called Howard's remarkable dashes to the end zone "HOCUS POCUS," and referred to Howard's uncanny ability to deliver big at the biggest moments "The Magic Show." Howard won the 1991 Heisman Trophy after scoring 138 points to shatter Michigan's scoring record, which Tom Harmon had set 51 years earlier. Although only 5-feet-9-inches and 176 pounds, Howard scored on kickoff returns, punt returns, passes and runs. Off the field, Howard was just as unique. He meditated 10 to 15 minutes a day, lived alone in an off-campus apartment, rarely socialized with teammates and spent much of his time away from football satisfying his intellectual curiosity. "To work at something until it looks easy defines my relationship to the word magic," said Howard. "It's the one aspect where I deserve the nickname."

DESMOND
HOWARD

"I want them to hold their breaths every time I touch the ball."

— DESMOND HOWARD

| #21 | 176 | 5'9" |

DESMOND
HOWARD
wide receiver

HONORABLE MENTION

40 30 20 10 G

LYNN
SWANN

| #82 | 5'11" | 180 |

2ND T LYNN
SWANN
wide receiver

Maybe all you really need to know about how good Lynn Swann was at USC is the fact he was named the team's Most Valuable Player as a senior in 1973. This at a school known for running backs and the offensive linemen that helped make them.

"I have no style," Swann said at the time. "I just do what's needed at the time to get the job done."

And that included just about everything for coach John McKay's Trojans. In USC's first two games of the 1973 season, Swann scored four times — though penalties negated two of the touchdowns — on 50 and 73-yard punt returns, a 15-yard pass reception and a 76-yard run off a screen pass.

Like Nebraska's Johnny Rodgers, Swann could pick apart a defense from virtually any spot on the field. He averaged 12.2 on punt returns, 16.4 yards per catch and 7.7 yards carrying the ball.

"Lynn was as valuable to us as Johnny Rodgers was to Nebraska," says McKay. "We asked him to do more things in our offense than anyone else and he excelled at all of them."

"Lynn was one of those great athletes you recognize because they are so fluid. I'd always judge a receiver by the way he was able to make the quarterback look like he never threw a bad pass. Lynn was like a shortstop or a center fielder in baseball. He had that instinctive ability to get to the ball wherever it was thrown. He had a rhythm that he would just cruise to the spot where he knew the ball was going and make the quarterback look like he threw a perfect pass every time, which we all know is impossible."

— GARY DANIELSON

G 10 20 30 40

#3 | 6'4" | 210

KEYSHAWN
JOHNSON
wide receiver

He was called "the immodest receiver" by a local newspaper and that suited USC's Keyshawn Johnson just fine. "I know I'm the best in the country," he said prior to the 1995 season, "but I knew I was the best last year." Just in case nobody was listening, Johnson went out and proved it. He caught 102 passes for 1,434 yards against constant double teams and then blistered Northwestern for a Rose Bowl record 216 yards on 12 catches in his USC finale. The immodest receiver also was right.

40   30   20   10   G

RANDY MOSS

| #88 | 6'5" | 198 |

3RD **RANDY**
T **MOSS**
wide receiver

THE FREAK

What else do you call a 6-foot-5-inch wide receiver who can run 40 yards in 4.25 seconds and leap 39 inches straight up into the air? Despite personal problems that cost him scholarships to Notre Dame and Florida State, Randy Moss finally settled into his college career at Marshall University in Huntington, West Virginia. Away from the spotlights and big-school hype, Moss quietly became a legend. As a freshman, Moss shattered various NCAA records with 1,709 receiving yards. His 28 touchdown catches tied the NCAA record established by Jerry Rice when he was a senior. If that wasn't enough, Moss entered the Southern Conference indoor track championships after just three days of practice. He won the 55 meters and the 200 meters, the latter 2/100ths of a second off the conference record. Said Florida State coach Bobby Bowden, "He was as good as Deion Sanders. Deion's my measuring stick for athletic ability and this kid was just a bigger Deion."

> "The way I see it, God has a magic wand and he taps just a few on the head."
> **— RANDY MOSS**

N.TERRY
28

39"
VERTICAL

40   30   20   10   G

On a national scale, the memories of Peter Warrick's Florida State career are born from late-night highlights. Warrick bouncing off tackles like a pinball, diving for a catch, weaving around defenders on an impossible punt return or sprinting around end on a reverse.

But Warrick did even more than that for Florida State's 1999 national championship team. He produced touchdowns as a running back, punt returner, receiver and quarterback. At quarterback, Warrick threw for one score and ran for two others.

And he still finished as the Atlantic Coast Conference's all-time receiving yardage leader with 3,517.

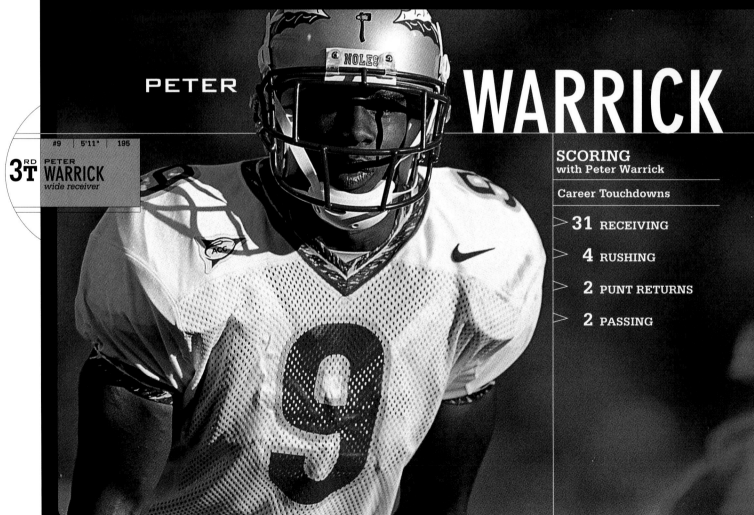

PETER **WARRICK**

3RD T

#9 | 5'11" | 195

PETER
WARRICK
wide receiver

SCORING
with Peter Warrick

Career Touchdowns

> **31** RECEIVING

> **4** RUSHING

> **2** PUNT RETURNS

> **2** PASSING

TIGHT END

1ST

KEITH JACKSON

SECOND TEAM
Kellen WINSLOW
THIRD TEAM
Dave CASPER

1ST 1T
KEITH
JACKSON
tight end

#88   6'3"   250

"It would have been hard for anyone to make more big plays than Keith Jackson. He didn't have many thrown his way, but when his number was called he always came up with a big play. When a guy catches only three passes a game and is voted first team All-America, that should tell you something. He had the skills of cornerback in a large frame. That's why he looked like he was kind of going in slow motion. But he would run away from defensive backs. No one was going to catch Keith Jackson from behind."

— DEAN BLEVINS ABC Sports announcer

For most of Keith Jackson's three seasons at Oklahoma, particularly the last two, opponents were pleased to accept a bone-shaking block from the 6-foot-3-inch, 250-pound tight end as the lesser of three evils. The worst of them being a Jackson reception followed closely by a run from scrimmage.

| #83 | 6'5" | 251 |

KELLEN
WINSLOW 2ND
tight end

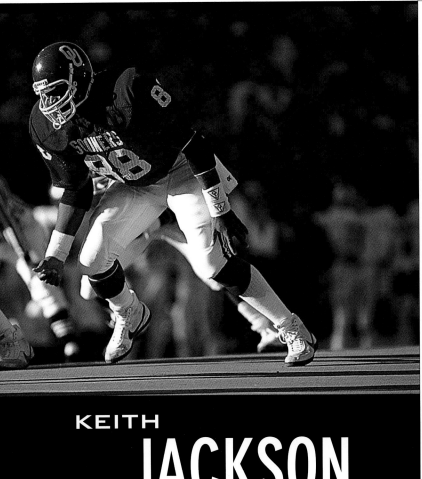

KEITH
JACKSON

KELLEN
WINSLOW

Not even Kellen Winslow knew for sure how he wound up at the University of Missouri. In East St. Louis, Illinois, a troubled town with a future not nearly as bright as its past, Winslow was so shy that he might have moved through four years of high school and on into a career at UPS where he worked on the weekends if a coach hadn't talked him into football pads as a senior.

Winslow's athletic ambitions to that point included one season of baseball and a starting spot on the school's chess team. The physical education teacher also happened to be the football coach of one of the state's most dominant teams. He put Winslow at tight end and East St. Louis made it all the way to the state finals.

Despite playing for a school that ranked last in the NCAA in passing for much of the 1986 season, Jackson averaged 28.8 yards a reception and converted five of his 14 catches into touchdowns. He also carried the ball 66 yards for another touchdown against Minnesota. As a senior, Jackson was no less intimidating as he turned four of his 13 catches into touchdowns and averaged 27.5 yards a catch.

All told, Jackson converted 14 of his 62 career receptions, an amazing 23 percent, into scores.

DAVE
CASPER

| #68 | 6'4" | 240 |

3RD T
DAVE
CASPER
tight end

When Ara Parseghian moved his left offensive tackle to tight end for the 1973 season, he already knew there was nothing tight about the guy making the switch.

Dave Casper, "Ghost" at Notre Dame, might have been one of the looser spirits ever to roam the football field in South Bend. As gifted intellectually as he was athletically, Casper once nodded off in class and then stunned an irritated professor by repeating the 14 points of the lecture he had just slept through — in order. He cut his hair once a year and started the football season almost bald. In interviews, he routinely included the fact that at least two toes on each foot were longer than his big toes. If he sensed any doubt, Casper would gladly take off his shoes and socks for an inspection. He preferred talking about anything other than football off the field and would often answer "No" when people noted his size and asked if he played the game. He tried to quit football as a high school junior but said the coach came "bugging my parents all the time and my older brother was captain of the team. So I gave in."

As a senior at Notre Dame, Casper was asked about his "first love." He responded, "in sports, baseball." While others worked themselves into a pre-game frenzy, Casper said "I don't try to get psyched up for a game because I don't think it helps. I would rather be assignment conscious so that I don't make any mistakes."

By the way, Parseghian, who later worked on college football with ABC Sports, considered Casper one of the best athletes he coached at Notre Dame.

"He was the most complete player at the position," said Lee Grosscup. "If I had to pick one tight end, Casper would be the one because he also was a great blocker."

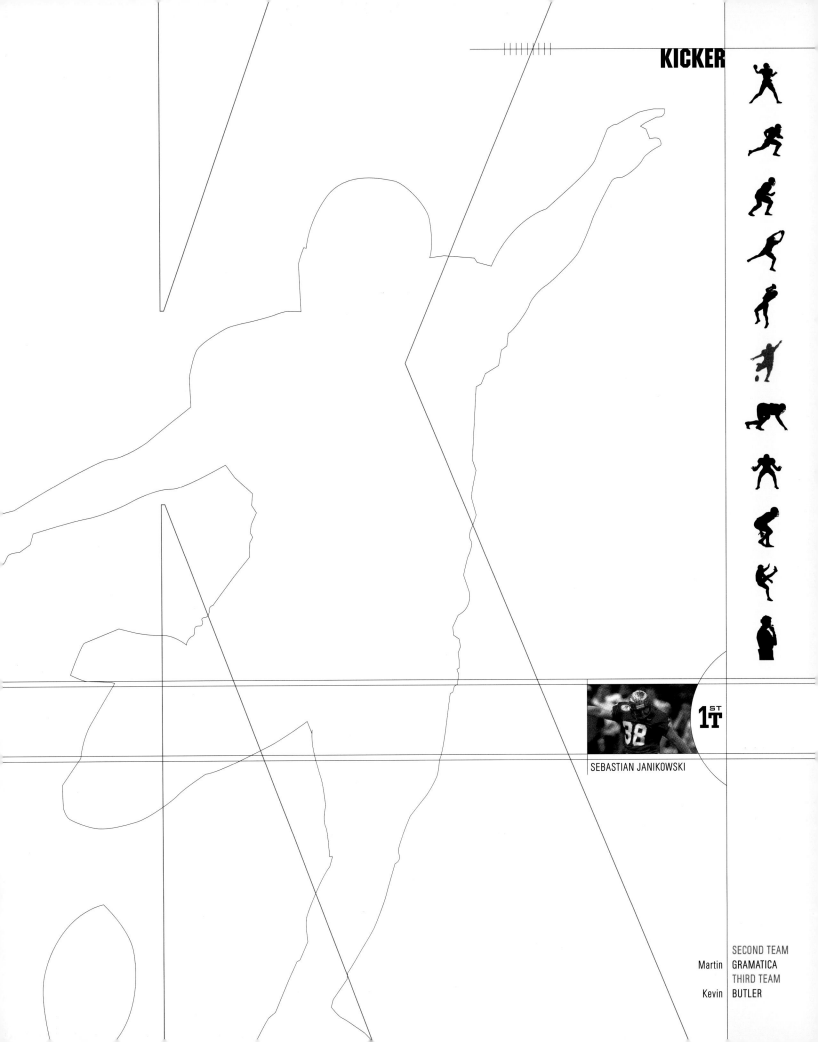

KICKER

1ST

SEBASTIAN JANIKOWSKI

SECOND TEAM
Martin GRAMATICA
THIRD TEAM
Kevin BUTLER

Bill Gramatica had added himself to a family legacy when he took over the kicking duties at Florida State in 1996. His brother, Martin, had been an All-American at Kansas State and one of college football's most accomplished specialists. But life for Bill Gramatica and FSU coach Bobby Bowden already was in the process of changing.

At Seabreeze High School in Daytona, a young Polish senior named Sebastian Janikowski decided to try out for the football team. He had moved to Florida from Poland only three years earlier to spend more time with his father. The fact he would go on to set the Florida High School record with 69 goals on the soccer field surprised no one.

Janikowski had been a member of the Polish National Under-17 Team. Upon graduation from Seebreaze, he would turn down various offers to play soccer professionally in South America.

But in the high stakes world of college football where recruiting has become highly sophisticated and national in scope, no one knew a thing about Janikowski. Even in Florida, a state that annually produces three of the nation's top 20 teams, recruiters were focused elsewhere.

At least they were until Janikowski started kicking footballs. As a high school senior, he sent 80 percent of his kickoffs through the end zone and just two of his kicks were returned. He also converted all 31 extra point attempts. But it was his 15 field goal attempts that made Janikowski a national name and eventually changed the career of Bill Gramatica.

Five times Janikowski lined up for a field-goal attempt of 51 yards or longer. Four times he converted including kicks of 60, 56, 53 and 51. His lone miss: a 71-yard bomb that narrowly missed.

A year later, Janikowski replaced Gramatica at FSU early in his freshman season. Janikowski nailed a FSU record 56-yarder, turned half of his 84 kickoffs into touchbacks and converted 16 of 21 field goal attempts.

And that was just the beginning. As a senior, 68.7 percent of his kickoffs were touchbacks. Of the 24 that were returned, only two made it past the 24-yard line. For Janikowski's career, he converted nearly 80 percent of his field goal attempts, including better than 72 percent from 40 yards or longer.

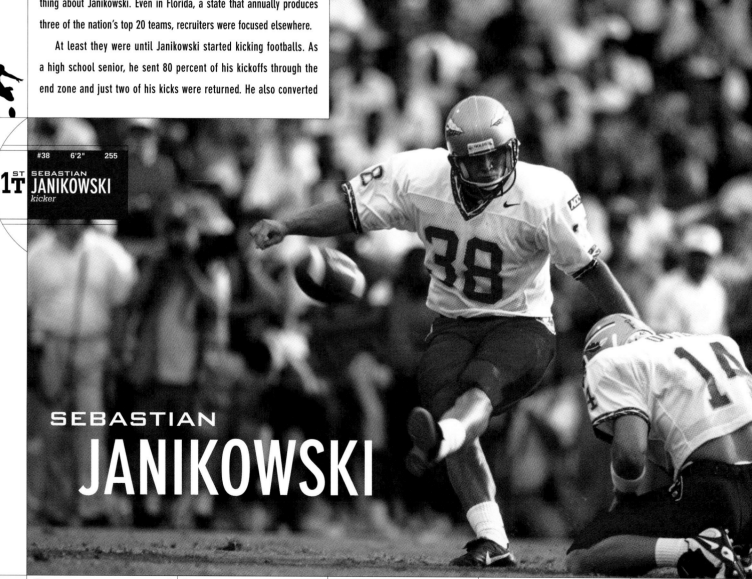

#38 6'2" 255

1ST

SEBASTIAN
JANIKOWSKI
kicker

SEBASTIAN
JANIKOWSKI

G   10   20   30   40

The pain Martin Gramatica inflicted on Kansas State opponents was born from an injury that might have ended most careers.

During Gramatica's first two college seasons, he connected on just 3-of-9 field goal attempts beyond 30 yards. Then, in 1996, a year after hitting 7 of 10 field goals and converting 43 of 46 extra points, Gramatica went down with a torn ACL in his kicking leg. The knee injury eliminated Gramatica's junior season before it started.

But Gramatica found gain amid pain. The rehabilitation actually strengthened his knee, if not his resolve, and in 1997 Gramatica became the dominant kicker in college football. He hit 37 of 39 extra points and a stunning 19 of 20 field goal attempts, including three of 50 yards or more. His 65-yard field goal against Northern Illinois remains an NCAA record.

Then again, given Gramatica's background and home-schooling, the success was not surprising. He grew up playing soccer in Argentina before his parents moved to the United States. Once in America, William Gramatica put up goal posts on the family's 15-acre farm. The uprights were two feet closer than regulation and a 10-foot-high bush approximated a leaping defensive lineman.

Martin became the oldest and most successful of three kicking Gramatica brothers and as a senior at Kansas State, earned the nickname "Automatica."

#10 | 5'8" | 170

MARTIN
GRAMATICA **2**ND**T**
kicker

MARTIN
GRAMATICA

✳ **65** YARD FIELD GOAL ✳ **37/39** EXTRA POINTS ✳ **19/20** FIELD GOAL ATTEMPTS

40 30 20 10 G

KEVIN

BUTLER

3T RD	KEVIN BUTLER
	kicker

#5 | 6'1" | 195

78.6%
CAREER FIELD GOALS

71.4%
FROM 50+ YARDS (1984)

52.4%
PERCENTAGE OF FIELD
GOALS MADE FROM 50+

Former Clemson coach Danny Ford sounded like somebody who had just run a personal best and lost to a guy setting the world record.

What can you do?

Ford, like others in the 1980s, simply watched as Georgia's consensus All-American kicker, Kevin Butler, drilled another field goal. In the 1984 game at Clemson, Butler converted an SEC record-tying 60-yarder to beat the Tigers 26-23.

"He busted the ball," said Ford. "I'll bet the ball is flat. He kicked the fool out of it. You're always aware of him. He's done it several times before against a lot of people."

Butler connected on 78.6 percent of his attempts at Georgia despite launching more than 20 percent of his kicks from beyond 50 yards. In his final game for the Bulldogs, Butler had field goals of 57, 50 and 34 yards and added an extra point (his 72nd straight). Butler made 5 of 7 from beyond 50 yards as a senior, including the 60-yarder against Clemson and left Georgia with 13 school records, seven SEC records and four NCAA marks, including highest percentage of field goals made from 50 yards and beyond (52.4 percent).

"When you talk about kicking, you talk about Bill Hartman when you come from Georgia," says Butler. "Coach Hartman would use the expression, 'the art of the jewel,' and that's something we'd talk about every day. Getting real consistent, being consistent in what you do. No matter if it was football or if it's business or just life. You have to be consistent to create stability and confidence in yourself, and to this day, I still think about things he told me before I kicked."

G | 10 | 20 | 30 | 40

DEFENSIVE LINE

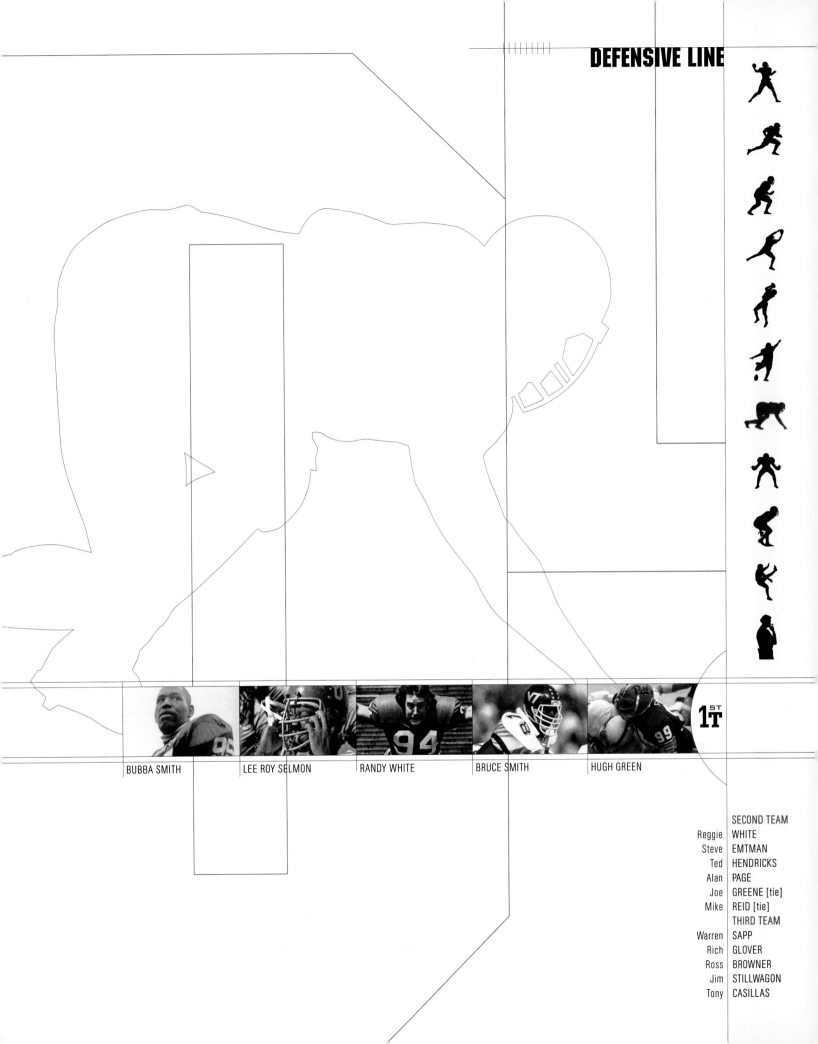

BUBBA SMITH   LEE ROY SELMON   RANDY WHITE   BRUCE SMITH   HUGH GREEN

1ST

	SECOND TEAM
Reggie	WHITE
Steve	EMTMAN
Ted	HENDRICKS
Alan	PAGE
Joe	GREENE [tie]
Mike	REID [tie]
	THIRD TEAM
Warren	SAPP
Rich	GLOVER
Ross	BROWNER
Jim	STILLWAGON
Tony	CASILLAS

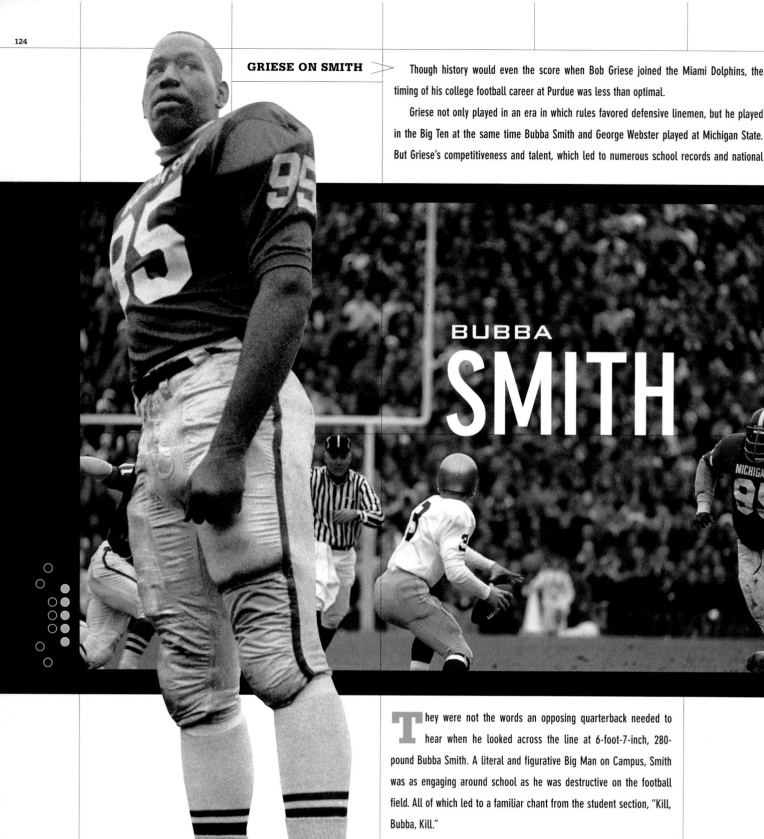

GRIESE ON SMITH >

Though history would even the score when Bob Griese joined the Miami Dolphins, the timing of his college football career at Purdue was less than optimal.

Griese not only played in an era in which rules favored defensive linemen, but he played in the Big Ten at the same time Bubba Smith and George Webster played at Michigan State. But Griese's competitiveness and talent, which led to numerous school records and national

BUBBA
SMITH

They were not the words an opposing quarterback needed to hear when he looked across the line at 6-foot-7-inch, 280-pound Bubba Smith. A literal and figurative Big Man on Campus, Smith was as engaging around school as he was destructive on the football field. All of which led to a familiar chant from the student section, "Kill, Bubba, Kill."

Smith controlled the defensive line of one of the greatest defensive teams in college football history at Michigan State in 1965 and 1966. Indeed, four players — including George Webster — from those teams were among the first eight players picked in the 1967 NFL Draft.

But it was Smith's presence that made Michigan State so dominant. He was fast enough to chase down a running back who had broken into accolades, left an impression on virtually every Purdue opponent, but particularly Smith.

"At the end of the game, we were giving up short passes," said Smith, following Michigan State's 1966 game against Purdue. "It wasn't as big a thing to stop them then as it was in the first half. But that Bob Griese! He releases the ball so fast it is tough to get to him. I'll tell you, I hope we don't face another one like him again. He's the greatest."

All of which underscores just how good Michigan State was and how good Griese must have been. The Spartans won the game, 41-20.

"I watched Bubba Smith on television and I remember just his dominance in the middle of the line. Everyone remembers the game he had in 1966 against Notre Dame. He was unbelievable. But even more impressive was that week-to-week he disrupted Big 10 teams. That Michigan State team was the best collection of defensive talent I have ever seen." — JIM LAMPLEY

| #95 | 6'7" | 280 |

BUBBA
SMITH 1ST
defensive lineman

the clear. And he was big enough and strong enough to completely alter the game as teams routinely ran away from Smith, or assigned two and sometimes three players to distract him.

"He could play in today's time," said Bob Griese. "There is no question about that. He was huge when he played. The thing about Bubba was that not only was he big, but he was so fast. He was a forerunner to the big linemen that you see today. We didn't have anyone at Purdue who could block him. I played against him for three years in college, then I played against him in the pros.

"In both places, he was a guy that on offense you had to know where he was at all times because he could disrupt the play. It didn't matter if you were running or passing. You had to have two guys on him. You couldn't block him by yourself, in college or in the pros. He was a dominant player."

And Michigan State was a dominant team with Smith moving around the line — he played defensive end, tackle and middle guard — and Webster patrolling the fringe. In 1965, the Spartans held Michigan to minus-51 yards rushing, Ohio State to minus-22 and Notre Dame to minus-12. In 1966, Michigan State was even better, going undefeated and winning its second Big Ten title. The Spartans of Smith and Webster played Notre Dame to a 10-10 tie in 1966, a game widely considered the greatest in college football history.

#94   6'4"   257

1ST T RANDY
WHITE
defensive lineman

RANDY
WHITE

Barry Switzer called Lee Roy Selmon the "greatest player" he ever coached. The accolade would have had the same bite if Switzer had merely called Lee Roy the best Selmon he ever coached.

Though he followed older brother Lucious to Oklahoma, Lee Roy was the leader of the greatest trio of brothers to ever play college football for the same school at the same time. Lee Roy and Dewey, older by 11 months, were starters on Oklahoma's national championship teams in 1974 and 1975. Each was a consensus All-American and they ranked first and second on the team in tackles both seasons before departing for the NFL's Tampa Bay Buccaneers in 1976, Lee Roy in the first round, Dewey in the second.

Lucious, their older brother, had been a consensus All-American in 1973, and until Lee Roy came along, Switzer considered Lucious "the best down lineman" he had ever coached. All three brothers started on Oklahoma's defensive line in 1973 and together they combined for 234 tackles, 26 of them for losses.

"We compared different schools," said Lee Roy, "but Dewey and me concluded that OU had everything the other teams had plus Lucious was already there. That gave OU the one plus that helped us decide."

Of the three, Lee Roy turned out to be just a little better than his two brothers. He won the Outland Trophy and Lombardi Award as a senior and was a consensus All-America pick in each of his final two seasons.

"When I was at Oklahoma my first year as a true freshman, we were playing against the first team defense which had Lee Roy and his

LEE ROY
SELMON

brother, Dewey," said Dean Blevins, a former Oklahoma quarterback. "I was running the second team offense and we drove down inside the 20. I thought there was nothing to this college football. We got down to the 2 yard line and ran an option play to the left.

"There was a wide open hole. I thought, 'we're in goodshape.' Then this big hand came out of nowhere, grabbed my jersey and threw me down. My head snapped back to the turf. It was Lee Roy. Today, they call it a concussion. I had a migraine for a month.

"Lee Roy was a gentle giant. Never has there been a guy who was more opposite on the field than off. He is of impeccable character, polite and somewhat shy. But on the football field he was a raging bull. He had cat-like quickness and he could beat off the double teams consistently. He was a combination of size, strength and speed. If you were putting together a team in the year 3000, I would bet Lee Roy would be on that team."

andy White and the Maryland football team resembled one another when he arrived as a freshman in 1971. White had promise, which was about all you could say for a varsity team that was finishing another 2-9 season.

When Jerry Claiborne took over as head coach before the 1972 season he decided to spend a little time with White. It didn't take long for either of them to figure out they were on the same page.

"My first look at Randy White was of a player with good speed and movement, but of someone who wanted to get better," says Claiborne. "I asked Randy if he wanted to be an All-American, and he said yes. I told him he could be one of the five best linemen in the U.S. if he wanted to, but he had to realize how much work that would take. The ability was naturally there, but he was a worker. He never missed any time in the weight room, and he made himself bigger and faster. By the time he was a senior, he was as fast as some offensive backs I had coached."

He also was the No. 1 lineman in the country. In 1974 White won the Outland Trophy, the Lombardi Award and was named ACC Player of the Year.

"He was the best player that I ever coached," says Claiborne. "In his prime he was as good as anybody who ever played defensive line, college or pro."

"Randy was a very quiet guy off the field, but he played with a viciousness and intensity unlike anything I have ever seen. He came in as a fullback and played there as a freshman. Jerry Claiborne was trying to build a top notch defense and he took most of the top athletes and put them on the defensive line. Even as a defensive lineman, Randy could outrun most of the running backs."

— TIM BRANDT

LEE ROY SELMON   BARRY SWITZER   DEWEY SELMON

#93	6'3"	256

LEE ROY
SELMON 1ST
defensive lineman

First there was Leroy Selmon. Then came LeRoy followed by Lee Roy.

With three Selmons playing football at the same school, some confusion was inevitable. But not getting the name right of the biggest and best of them all?

As it turned out, no one spelled Lee Roy Selmon's name right around Oklahoma until he had finished playing. Why? No particular reason if you ask Lee Roy. He arrived at Oklahoma as Leroy. Selmon says his first grade teacher had changed the spelling on his first day of class.

"This is not the way to spell LeRoy," Selmon recalled the teacher saying. "You should spell Lee Roy LeRoy."

Somehow it turned into Leroy. Then, just prior to his final season at Oklahoma, the sports information office issued a correction to the spelling of Selmon's name. Accordingly, Leroy became LeRoy.

It wasn't until the spring of 1976 that Lee Roy corrected everyone. On the many awards and certificates he won during his four seasons at Oklahoma, the spelling bounced between Leroy and LeRoy.

"Actually," said Selmon when asked about the issue, "my name is Lee Roy — two words — Lee Roy. It's spelled right on my driver's license."

And it's spelled right in the National Football Foundation Hall of Fame as well.

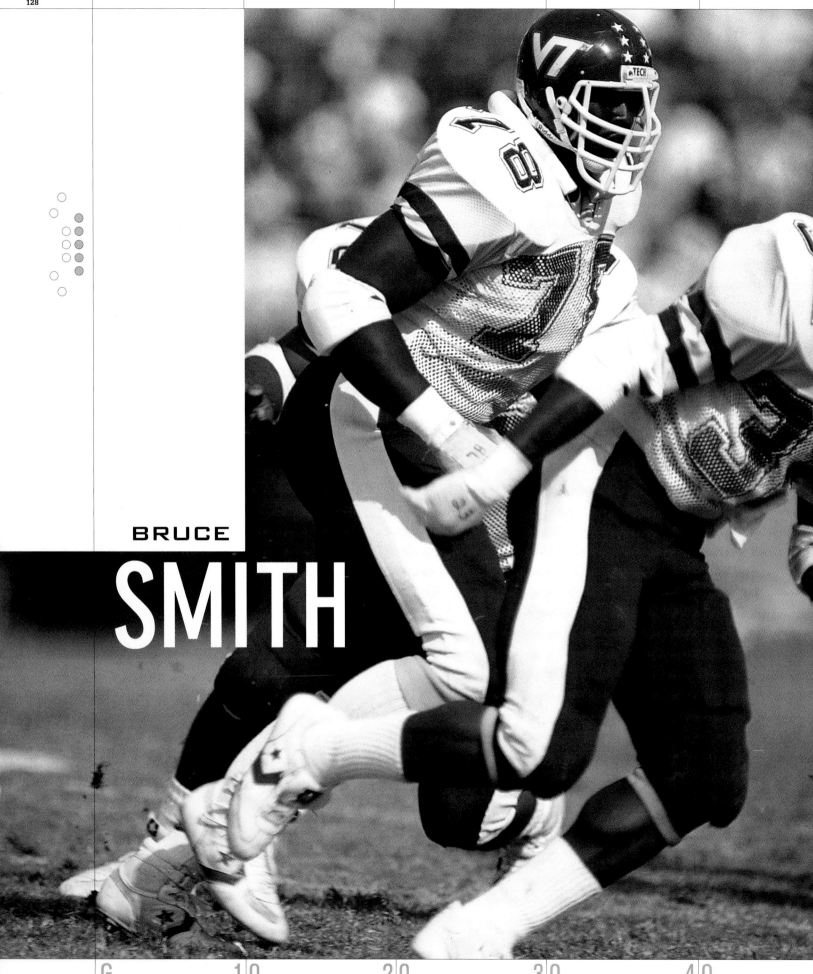

BRUCE
SMITH

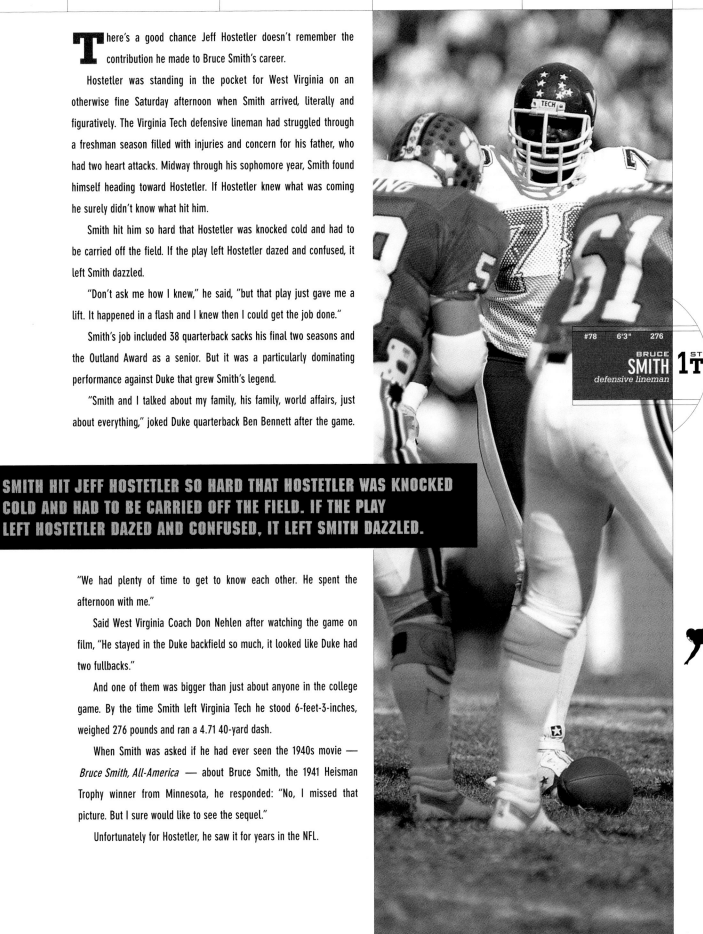

There's a good chance Jeff Hostetler doesn't remember the contribution he made to Bruce Smith's career.

Hostetler was standing in the pocket for West Virginia on an otherwise fine Saturday afternoon when Smith arrived, literally and figuratively. The Virginia Tech defensive lineman had struggled through a freshman season filled with injuries and concern for his father, who had two heart attacks. Midway through his sophomore year, Smith found himself heading toward Hostetler. If Hostetler knew what was coming he surely didn't know what hit him.

Smith hit him so hard that Hostetler was knocked cold and had to be carried off the field. If the play left Hostetler dazed and confused, it left Smith dazzled.

"Don't ask me how I knew," he said, "but that play just gave me a lift. It happened in a flash and I knew then I could get the job done."

Smith's job included 38 quarterback sacks his final two seasons and the Outland Award as a senior. But it was a particularly dominating performance against Duke that grew Smith's legend.

"Smith and I talked about my family, his family, world affairs, just about everything," joked Duke quarterback Ben Bennett after the game.

#78   6'3"   276

BRUCE
SMITH 1ST
defensive lineman

SMITH HIT JEFF HOSTETLER SO HARD THAT HOSTETLER WAS KNOCKED COLD AND HAD TO BE CARRIED OFF THE FIELD. IF THE PLAY LEFT HOSTETLER DAZED AND CONFUSED, IT LEFT SMITH DAZZLED.

"We had plenty of time to get to know each other. He spent the afternoon with me."

Said West Virginia Coach Don Nehlen after watching the game on film, "He stayed in the Duke backfield so much, it looked like Duke had two fullbacks."

And one of them was bigger than just about anyone in the college game. By the time Smith left Virginia Tech he stood 6-feet-3-inches, weighed 276 pounds and ran a 4.71 40-yard dash.

When Smith was asked if he had ever seen the 1940s movie — *Bruce Smith, All-America* — about Bruce Smith, the 1941 Heisman Trophy winner from Minnesota, he responded: "No, I missed that picture. But I sure would like to see the sequel."

Unfortunately for Hostetler, he saw it for years in the NFL.

STEVE
EMTMAN

The only way to understand what Steve Emtman might have been is to understand what he was at the University of Washington.

Emtman grew up on a 2,000-acre ranch amid 200 head of cattle and fields of wheat, barley, lentils and alfalfa. Though he was big and farm-tough, the locals told him to stay clear of the big school in Seattle.

Better to find a smaller place where he actually might get a chance to play.

Emtman listened and marched off to Washington. Four years later, the 6-foot-4-inch, 290-pound defensive tackle had become the most decorated player in school history. The 1991 team, which revolved around Emtman's defensive exploits, went 12-0 and shared the national championship. If there was an award to be won, Emtman won it and he did so decisively.

Dennis Green, Stanford's head coach at the time, described Emtman as "probably the best defensive lineman in college football the last 10 years."

With Emtman controlling the defensive line, Washington allowed just 67.1 yards rushing and 9.2 points a game. Indeed, the Huskies were in the top five in virtually every defensive category including rushing defense, pass-efficiency defense, total defense, scoring defense and turnovers.

Ultimately, the one element of Emtman's approach that defined his place in college football proved contrary to self-preservation in the NFL. Known to go full speed on every play in every game at Washington, Emtman's approach encouraged injury at the professional level and eventually ended his career prematurely.

"The NFL doesn't compare to college; it's not even the same thing, they're two different animals," said Emtman in 1999. "Maybe it was the extra pressure put on me when I first got into the league or the injuries.

"But nothing can compare to my college days."

Still, Emtman provided a glimpse of what he might have become. He intercepted a Dan Marino pass and returned it 90 yards for a touchdown, the longest ever by a defensive lineman.

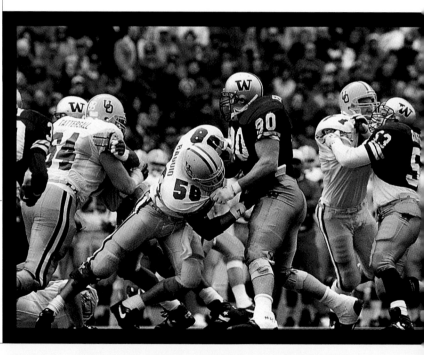

91 The Washington Monument

Steve Emtman's 1991 Honors

AWARDS

Outland Trophy winner   **Lombardi** Trophy winner   **Heisman** Trophy finalist (4th place)

Walter Camp First Team All-America **Football Writers of AMERICA** First Team All-America

Playboy First Team All-America   **UPI Defensive Player** of the Year

Kodak First Team All-America   **Pac-10** Defensive Player of the Year

G   10   20   30   40

#90 | 6'4" | 290

STEVE ENTMAN 2ND T
defensive lineman

"PROBABLY THE BEST
DEFENSIVE LINEMAN
IN COLLEGE FOOTBALL
THE LAST 10 YEARS."
— DENNIS GREEN

Associated Press First Team All-America   **United Press International** First Team All-America

The Football News First Team All-America   **The Sporting News** First Team All-America

Football News Defensive Player of the Year   **Chevrolet Defensive Player** of the Year

Rose Bowl Co-Outstanding Player

AWARDS

40   30   20   10   G

TED
HENDRICKS

At the University of Miami the only thing predictable about Ted Hendricks was his performance.

He stood 6-feet-8-inches and played defensive end as well as anyone in college football history.

He had good enough hands to play tight end on offense and he was so adept at stripping the ball from opposing players that he shattered the school's fumble records. Hendricks once blocked a quick kick, caught the ball before it hit the ground and nearly scored a touchdown. He was such a good athlete that Hendricks played linebacker in the NFL and was named one of the seven players at that position on the league's 75th anniversary team.

Penn State's Joe Paterno and USC's John McKay, who had

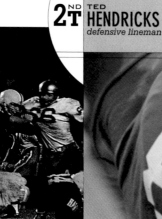

2ND T #89 | 6'8" | 220
TED HENDRICKS
defensive lineman

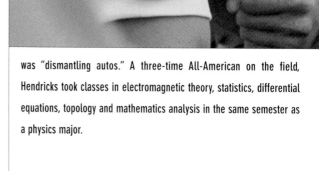

O. J. Simpson in the Trojan backfield at the time, had no qualms about avoiding Hendricks's side of the field at all costs. Paterno once ran 14 straight plays opposite Hendricks while McKay violated a Vince Lombardi axiom in the process of running away from Hendricks.

"I'd remembered what Vince Lombardi always said — 'run at the other team's strength,' " said McKay. "Well, we ran one of our first plays at Ted Hendricks and we found out he was there all right, so we didn't try to test him much more."

Hendricks no doubt figured as much. At Miami, he listed "solving mathematical problems" as one of his hobbies and said his chief hobby was "dismantling autos." A three-time All-American on the field, Hendricks took classes in electromagnetic theory, statistics, differential equations, topology and mathematics analysis in the same semester as a physics major.

"I remember one of the toughest defenses I ever faced was in my first year, 1980, when we played our arch rival Pittsburgh. They had Ricky Jackson and Hugh Green on opposite ends. They were as good an individual tandem as I can ever remember seeing. They were explosive like Lawrence Taylor. They were too quick and elusive for most tackles and too powerful for most backs and tight ends."
— TODD BLACKLEDGE former ABC Sports announcer and Penn State quarterback

Hugh Green ended up at the University of Pittsburgh by accident and one game into his career Notre Dame must have felt like the victim of one.

Green, who is considered by some the greatest defensive lineman ever at the collegiate level, was headed to Southern Mississippi when Pitt coaches discovered him on game film they were reviewing of another player. Then, in the 1977 season-opener against defending national champion Notre Dame, Green provided the Fighting Irish with a highlight reel. The freshman had 11 tackles, two quarterback sacks and blocked a punt. The only accidents involving Green after that involved running backs and quarterbacks unable to avoid him. At 6-feet-2-inches and 222 pounds, Green was the kind of athlete who could have played just about anywhere on the field. Green ran a 4.5 40-yard dash and had enough natural strength that he rarely lifted weights.

Jimmy Johnson, then coaching at the University of Miami, had seen enough of Green by his junior season that he didn't care to see any more — at least in college. "Whatever you ask him to do on the football field, he'll do it better than anybody has ever done it before," said Johnson. "You can build your entire defense around him. Heck, you can build your entire team around him. If Hugh Green is on your football team, you're automatically one of the finest in the country."

Green was a three-time consensus All-American and as a senior won the Lombardi, Maxwell and Walter Camp Awards in addition to finishing second to South Carolina's George Rogers in the 1980 Heisman Trophy voting. But the best perspective on Green's talent might have been provided by voting for Pitt's All-Time Team in 1978. Green made the team easily. He was a sophomore.

#99	6'2"	222

HUGH
GREEN 1ST
defensive lineman

HUGH GREEN

40   30   20   10   G

Size, speed, quickness and strength: Alan Page was a unique package with all the tools for greatness. Though he stood 6-feet-5-inches, Page weighed only 238 pounds. But his quickness and speed, unusual for a defensive lineman of any size, complemented Ara Parseghian's defensive attack.

"Our whole philosophy was based on speed, quickness and agility," says Parseghian. "In fact, we took some guys who had been in the offensive backfield and moved them to the defensive line for their quickness.

"I don't know that it was inherent intelligence, but we did have an understanding of the game."

And the rest of the country had an understanding of the Notre Dame defense in 1966. The Irish won the national title thanks to a punishing defense led by Page and fellow All-American Jim Lynch that allowed an average of just 3.8 points a game and had six shutouts.

"People used to call Alan crafty," said Gary Danielson. "He took such pride in his ability and he seemed to have such a vision of where he wanted to go that he almost became unblockable. I heard stories about his ability to time the snap count, that he would study stances and how opposing players would block him.

"He was the first modern inside lineman that changed that game and forced teams to double team him. Alan was one of the first guys to change blocking schemes because you were forced to double team him. You had to account for him on every play because he was so quick coming off the ball and he was absolutely determined."

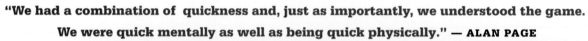

"We had a combination of quickness and, just as importantly, we understood the game. We were quick mentally as well as being quick physically." — ALAN PAGE

#75 | 6'5" | 238

2ND T ALAN **PAGE**
defensive lineman

> ## "Not mean enough? Not tough enough?
> I'd like to line up across from some of the people
> who say that and show them just how mean and tough I can be."
> — REGGIE WHITE

Normally, the kinds of things they were saying about Reggie White down around the University of Tennessee in 1982 aren't the kinds of things mentioned within hearing distance of a man 6-feet-5-inches and 270 pounds, especially when he can cover 40 yards in around 4.7 seconds.

After a brilliant sophomore season that included eight sacks, White stumbled — literally — through his junior season. Two bad ankles combined with too many expectations to create a season that disappointed everyone. But Reggie White soft? Not mean enough?

"Not mean enough? Not tough enough?" said White. "I'd like to line up across from some of the people who say that and show them just how mean and tough I can be."

A year later, White, who was ordained a Baptist minister at 17, did exactly that. The Minister of Defense, as he became known at Tennessee, finished his senior season with a school-record 15 sacks. For good measure, White also recovered a fumble, one of the many he caused, and picked off a pass.

Vols coach Johnny Majors called the performace "the most dominating" of any lineman on any team he had ever coached.

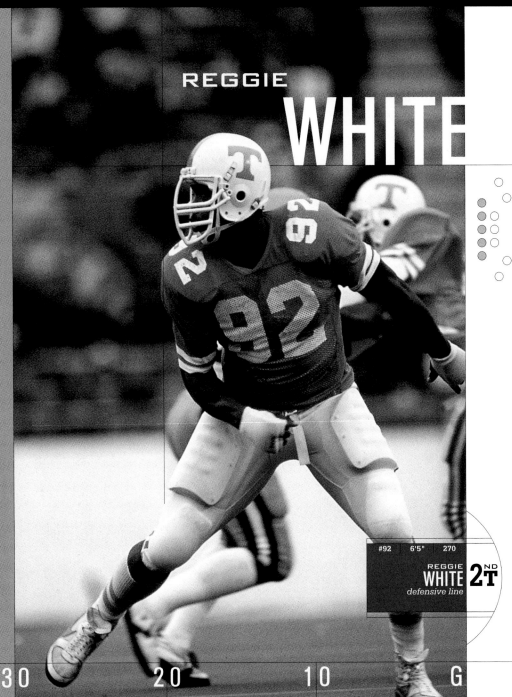

REGGIE WHITE

#92 6'5" 270
REGGIE WHITE 2ND T
defensive line

40 30 20 10 G

From Jerome Brown and Cortez Kennedy to Russell Maryland the evolution along the University of Miami's defensive line led to a combination of them all in Warren Sapp.

So it only made sense when Sapp won the Lombardi Award in 1994, something none of his predecessors had done. But that's not all he did. Sapp, who left Miami for the NFL after his junior season, had 10 1/2 sacks, broke up five passes, caused four fumbles and recovered three of them. And he controlled the middle of a Miami defense that led the nation.

Former Hurricane's Coach Dennis Erickson called Sapp "a combination of Russell and Cortez, but he's the fastest…He's the best defensive lineman I've ever coached."

For most 290-pounders speed is relative. In Sapp's case his 4.9 speed in the 40 was relatively amazing. But it was his quickness off the ball and down the line that could change the course of an entire game.

WARREN
SAPP

3RD 3T	#76	6'2"	290
	WARREN SAPP		
	defensive lineman		

"He was a guy that could intimidate, destroy, ruin a game."

— BOBBY BOWDEN
Florida State coach

G   30   40

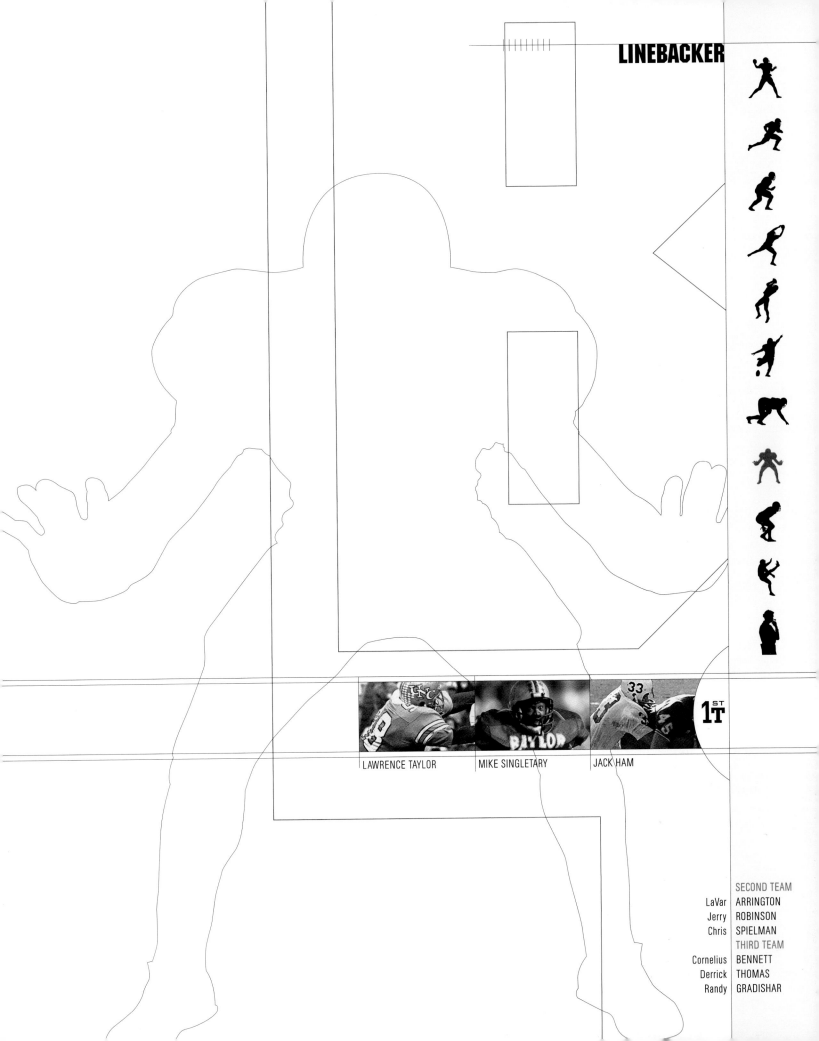

LINEBACKER

LAWRENCE TAYLOR

MIKE SINGLETARY

JACK HAM

1ST**T**

SECOND TEAM
LaVar ARRINGTON
Jerry ROBINSON
Chris SPIELMAN

THIRD TEAM
Cornelius BENNETT
Derrick THOMAS
Randy GRADISHAR

"The mold was broken by LT (Lawrence Taylor).
Nobody can claim to be better than him."

— JOHN SAUNDERS

#98	6'3"	237

1ST

LAWRENCE
TAYLOR
linebacker

LAWRENCE
TAYLOR

> "At first, I was just happy to
> be playing ball. After a while,
> I wasn't satisfied to just be
> playing ball with Carolina.
> I wanted to go out of Carolina
> as one of the best defensive
> players that ever played there.
> People remember Dee Hardison,
> Rod Broadway and
> Alan Caldwell off the 1977 team.
> Well, that was the way
> I wanted to be remembered."
>
> **— LAWRENCE TAYLOR**

Lawrence Taylor looked as if he'd been shot out of a cannon and into the middle of the 1979 college football season.

Until then, Taylor had been a bundle of talent wrapped inside a remarkable physical package. North Carolina coach Dick Crum had tried everything to get Taylor on the field. As a freshman, Taylor played primarily on special teams. In his sophomore season, Crum moved Taylor to nose guard and then inside linebacker. But it wasn't until Taylor moved to outside linebacker as a junior that the wraps came off.

"Taylor ushered in the modern era of pass rushers from the end or the linebacker positions," said Lee Grosscup. "The way people play those positions today was influenced by Taylor. He was in a world of his own with an ability to simply take over a game."

With a remarkable combination of size, speed, quickness and instinct, Taylor dominated. In 12 games as a senior, Taylor had 16 quarterback sacks and six other tackles for losses. In Carolina's only close games in the 11-1 season, Taylor secured victory. He recovered a fumble inside the Tar Heel 10-yard line in the fourth quarter of a 9-3 victory over Texas Tech. And he sacked Homer Jones in the final 30 seconds with Clemson on the North Carolina 1-yard line, trailing 24-19.

"After a while, I wasn't satisfied to just be playing ball with Carolina," said Taylor. "I wanted to go out of Carolina as one of the best defensive players that ever played there."

By the time Taylor got done at North Carolina and later in the NFL, few had left a more lasting impression.

"I know he played linebacker, but Lawrence Taylor was all over the place," said Brad Nessler. "I was in ACC country at the time and he was a phenomenal player."

40   30   20   10   G

MIKE
SINGLETARY

| #63 | 6'0" | 230 |

1ST

MIKE
SINGLETARY
linebacker

Man Mountain Mike

After making 31 tackles against Ohio State, Woody Hayes called him "unstoppable."

After Singletary had a Baylor record 33 tackles against Arkansas, Razorbacks coach Lou Holtz called him "the best middle linebacker I have ever coached against."

His career total of 662 tackles is 292 more than the second place total.

G   10   20   30   40

As a man of religious conviction, Mike Singletary no doubt accepts the strange way in which the world worked to land him on a football field.

Singletary was the son of a minister in the Sanctification Church, which prohibited sports. Then again, that was a minor irritation compared to the more pressing physical issues. As late as the seventh grade, the man who would become famous at Baylor University for breaking helmets stood 5-foot-5-inches and weighed 135 pounds.

"My father had to stop preaching in order for me to play football," said Singletary. "He thought it would cause problems in the church if he didn't. My brothers tried to sneak off and play when they were younger, but he'd catch them and give them a whipping. I didn't care. I'd go off anyway. I always thought I was meant to play football."

He was indeed.

Singletary was a star from the moment he walked onto campus at Baylor. He was the Southwest Conference "Newcomer of the Year" as a freshman and never looked back. The leadership skills that defined his career with the Chicago Bears were evident at an early age as well. Singletary was a three-year captain in college and over his last two seasons was widely considered the best linebacker of his era.

A two-time consensus All-American, Singletary rewrote the record book at the oldest school in Texas. After he made 30 tackles against Alabama as a senior, Bear Bryant said Singletary and Lee Roy Jordan, who played for Bryant, were the only two linebackers he had ever seen capable of making a tackle on every single running play.

In Singletary's case, he also might have been the only player capable of shattering a football helmet on every single play. Singletary hit so hard so often that he cracked or shattered 16 of his own helmets at Baylor. The team's equipment staff routinely kept three helmets fitted and prepared.

"Mike Singletary is the epitome of what a linebacker should be. He was the glue that held that (Baylor) defense together. He was what being a football player is all about. He didn't have the great size, height, or speed. But he was the guy who got to the ball the quickest the most often. If I was trying to build a team and I was the coach, I would try to get the other 10 to play the way Mike Singletary did."

— TERRY BOWDEN

Singletary has the top three spots for the most tackles in a season.

He was named Southwest Conference Defensive Player of the Year three straight seasons.

Singletary was named the best player in the Southwest as a junior and senior.

Singletary's 30 tackles against Alabama prompted Bear Bryant's comparison to Lee Roy Jordan.

40 30 20 10 G

They played linebacker at the same school for the same coach and had the same kind of impact on opposing college offenses.

But Jack Ham was then, and LaVar Arrington is now.

Ham won four Super Bowls rings and went on to a Hall of Fame career with the Pittsburgh Steelers. Arrington is the only linebacker at a school known for them to win the Butkus Award and he did it as a junior. Ham played linebacker for 12 seasons in the NFL by relying on guts, guile and intensity. He was 6-foot-1-inch, weighed 225 pounds and was not generally considered a nice guy on the field.

Arrington is 6-foot-3-inches and 250 pounds with sprinter speed, NBA jumping ability and a flair for the spectacular. He'll pick up the

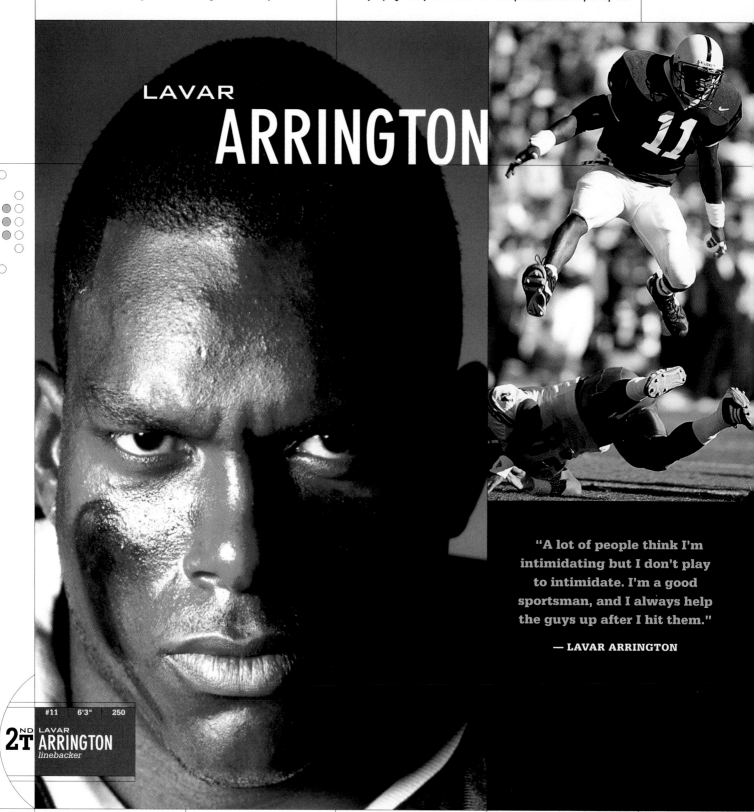

LAVAR ARRINGTON

"A lot of people think I'm intimidating but I don't play to intimidate. I'm a good sportsman, and I always help the guys up after I hit them."

— LAVAR ARRINGTON

#11 6'3" 250

2ND T **LAVAR ARRINGTON** *linebacker*

G 10 20 30 40

guys he knocks down. Ham played behind the Steel Curtain, Arrington played behind the No. 1 pick in the 2000 NFL Draft, Courtney Brown.

"A lot of people think I'm intimidating," says Arrington, "but I don't play to intimidate. I'm a good sportsman, and I always help the guys up after I hit them."

"Jack Ham was one of those guys with great instincts and bad intentions," said Tim Brandt. "I can't think of a better combination for a linebacker. I don't think size prohibits you from being a great player if you have those bad intentions. And Jack had them."

> **"Jack Ham was very good but LaVar Arrington is the best college linebacker of all time. Kryptonite won't stop him."**
> — BEANO COOK

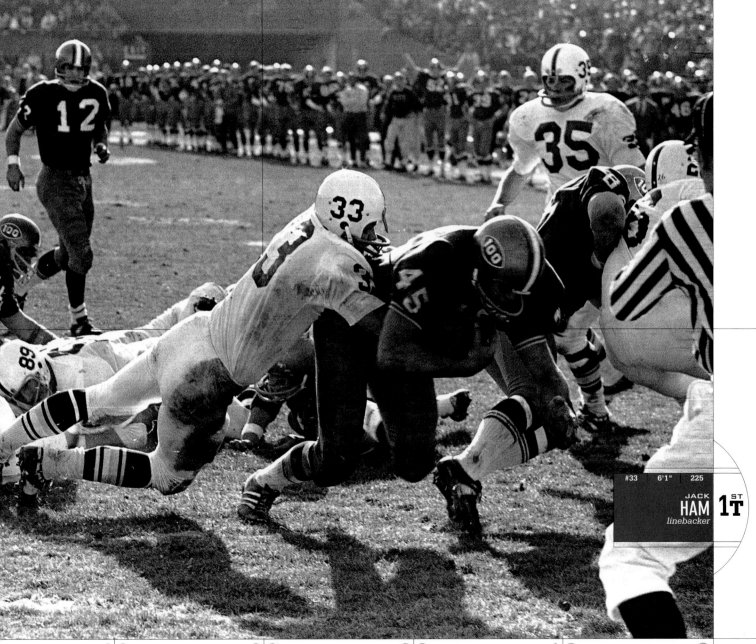

#33   6'1"   225
JACK HAM 1ST
linebacker

RANDY
GRADISHAR

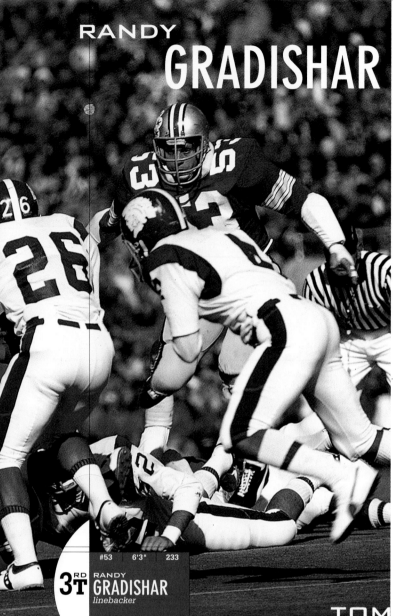

Randy Gradishar, just a freshman from a small Ohio high school, looked around the Ohio State football complex in search of the varsity. Woody Hayes liked to throw the freshmen against the varsity a week or two into practice, presumably to separate the young players' future from their past.

Gradishar sized up the veterans. Running back John Brockington, quarterback Rex Kern, All-America defensive back Jack Tatum. In 1969, all three were back after winning the national championship in 1968.

"I knew I played well in the scrimmage," says Gradishar. "From then on, I knew I belonged at Ohio State."

He also belonged to what has become a long line of great Buckeye linebackers. Gradishar, whom Hayes called "the best linebacker I ever coached at Ohio State," was a two-time All-American and still is considered one of the most complete middle linebackers ever to play college football. Indeed, Gradishar directed a 1973 Ohio State defense that had four shutouts and allowed just 64 points.

> "I knew I played well in the scrimmage. From then on, I knew I belonged at Ohio State."
> **—RANDY GRADISHAR**

	#53	6'3"	233
3RD T	RANDY **GRADISHAR** *linebacker*		

TOM COUSINEAU

	#36	6'3"	225
HONORABLE MENTION	TOM **COUSINEAU** *linebacker*		

From 1975 to 1978, Tom Cousineau was the definition of an Ohio State linebacker. He was in on 29 tackles in a 1978 game against Penn State, a school record matched by Chris Spielman, and set the Ohio State record for solo tackles in a game with 16 against SMU. In fact, six of the top 10 single-game tackle marks at Ohio State were set by Cousineau.

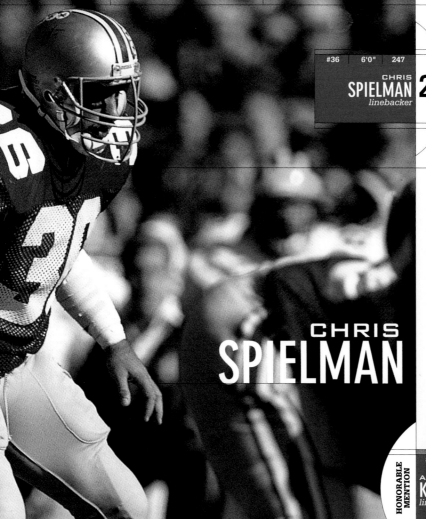

| #36 | 6'0" | 247 |

CHRIS
SPIELMAN **2ND**
linebacker

CHRIS SPIELMAN

Next came Spielman, a tenacious competitor who dominated his inside linebacker spot from the day he arrived in Columbus. He won the Lombardi Award as a senior and, like Gradishar, finished sixth in the Heisman Trophy voting.

"I roam the middle, look for stragglers, and when they get the ball I come up and mutilate them," said Spielman, "so they won't come up the middle again."

"Goodness, gracious, he is the best player I've ever coached," said former Buckeyes coach Earle Bruce. "I'm talking about a guy who loves the game, who has the most intensity of any player I've ever been around. When you're looking at the whole person, what kind of image he represents, Chris Spielman is college football personified."

| #45 | 6'4" | 255 |

HONORABLE MENTION

ANDY
KATZENMOYER
linebacker

ANDY KATZENMOYER

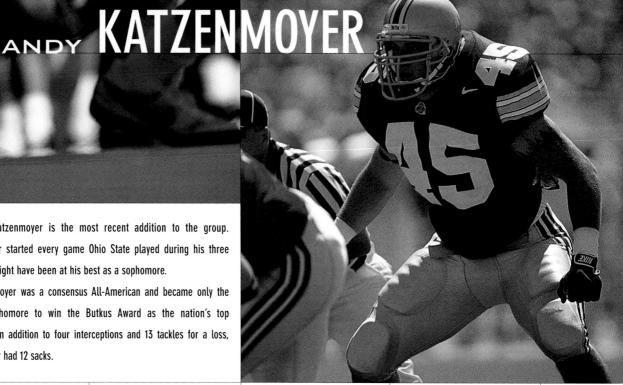

Andy Katzenmoyer is the most recent addition to the group. Katzenmoyer started every game Ohio State played during his three years and might have been at his best as a sophomore.

Katzenmoyer was a consensus All-American and became only the second sophomore to win the Butkus Award as the nation's top linebacker. In addition to four interceptions and 13 tackles for a loss, Katzenmoyer had 12 sacks.

40   30   20   10   G

DERRICK
THOMAS

JUNIOR YEAR **18** SACKS | SENIOR YEAR **27** SACKS

| #55 | 6'3" | 240 |

3TRD DERRICK
THOMAS
linebacker

10   20   30   40

Long before he took his place in Alabama history, Cornelius Bennett understood the significance of playing linebacker for the Crimson Tide. And just in case he didn't, former Alabama linebacker Emmanuel King made sure Bennett understood the responsibilities before him. It was a message Bennett passed on to Derrick Thomas who then delivered it to Keith McCants.

"There was Lee Roy Jordan in the '60s and after him guys like Woodrow Lowe and E. J. Junior," said Bennett. "I was compared to them and some people say I was better than they were. I knew people would come after me who would do better than I did. And that's good. Each of us set higher goals. Derrick broke my records for quarterback sacks. Some say Keith (McCants) was better than Derrick. I know someone will come along who will be better than Keith.

"But that's the way it should be. When I first came to the University of Alabama, Emmanuel King was a junior. When he left, he told me he was passing the tradition down the line to me. I told Derrick the same thing when I left and I'm sure he told Keith the same thing. We all tried to pass on what we learned to the next guy, tried to teach him all we had been taught and all we had learned on our own."

Though McCants would follow, the transition from Bennett to Thomas was as profound on the field as off. By his senior year, Bennett had established himself as one of Alabama's greatest players regardless of position. Then coach Ray Perkins, when asked if Bennett had reached his potential, responded, "If I were the coach of any team, college or pro, and had to put four linebackers out there, Bennett would be one that I'd choose."

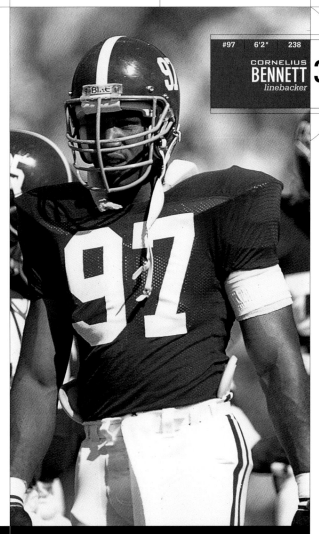

#97 | 6'2" | 238

CORNELIUS
BENNETT 3RD
linebacker

THOMAS **1988 BUTKUS AWARD**   BENNETT **1986 LOMBARDI AWARD**

Bennett won the Lombardi Award as the nation's top defensive lineman in 1986 and Thomas became the only Crimson Tide player to win the Butkus Award as the nation's outstanding linebacker in 1988. But when a major Alabama newspaper conducted a poll for the Alabama Team of the Decade in the 1980s, Thomas was named Defensive Player of the Decade and Bennett Player of the Decade.

Still, to understand Bennett's impact, consider what Thomas brought to Alabama. As a junior, he shattered the single-season record for quarterback sacks with 18. A year later, he had 27. Off the field, Thomas, whose father was killed in Vietnam, was a frequent visitor to the Tuscaloosa Veterans Administration Hospital and gave considerable time to the Fellowship of Christian Athletes' prison ministry and the Tuscaloosa Boys' and Girls' Club.

When Thomas was killed in a car accident in 2000, he was only a few hours short of his college degree, which he was studying to complete at the University of Missouri in Kansas City. Alabama presented Thomas's college degree to his grandmother, Annie Adams, to whom he promised to finish, at the 2000 graduation ceremony.

CORNELIUS
BENNETT

"I DON'T KNOW THAT I HAVE THE WORDS TO EXPRESS HOW IMPORTANT DERRICK HAS BEEN TO ALABAMA AND ITS TRADITION. WE'VE BEEN PLAYING FOOTBALL A LONG TIME HERE. WE'VE WON 12 NATIONAL CHAMPIONSHIPS AND I DON'T KNOW HOW MANY ALL-AMERICANS WE'VE HAD. BUT WE'VE ONLY HAD ONE BUTKUS AWARD WINNER AND THAT WAS DERRICK THOMAS."

— **MIKE DUBOSE Alabama head coach**

Throughout the history of college football hundreds of players, some of them among the best ever at their positions, have moved from one spot to another. Jack Tatum was a running back until Woody Hayes moved him to the defensive backfield. Ted Hendricks was a tight-end, Marcus Allen a defensive back, Lawrence Taylor a nose guard and even O. J. Simpson was thought to be a flanker at first.

Still, Jerry Robinson's transition from wide receiver to consensus All-American linebacker in the space of nine months — as a sophomore no less — might have been the most dramatic switch of all.

Robinson wasn't even a starting receiver his freshman season at UCLA. Then, during practices for the 1976 Rose Bowl, Bruins coach Terry Donahue decided to try Robinson at linebacker. By spring practice he was a projected starter at inside linebacker and by the end of his sophomore season Robinson was on his way to becoming the first three-time consensus All-American — at that time — since Doak Walker.

"His skill and competitiveness put him in a class by himself," said Donahue. "He's one of the most prominent players in the history of the Pac 10."

By current standards, Robinson was undersized at 6-foot-2-inches and 209 pounds. But when he left UCLA for the Philadelphia Eagles in 1979, Robinson had the school record for tackles and the top three spots in the single season tackle list.

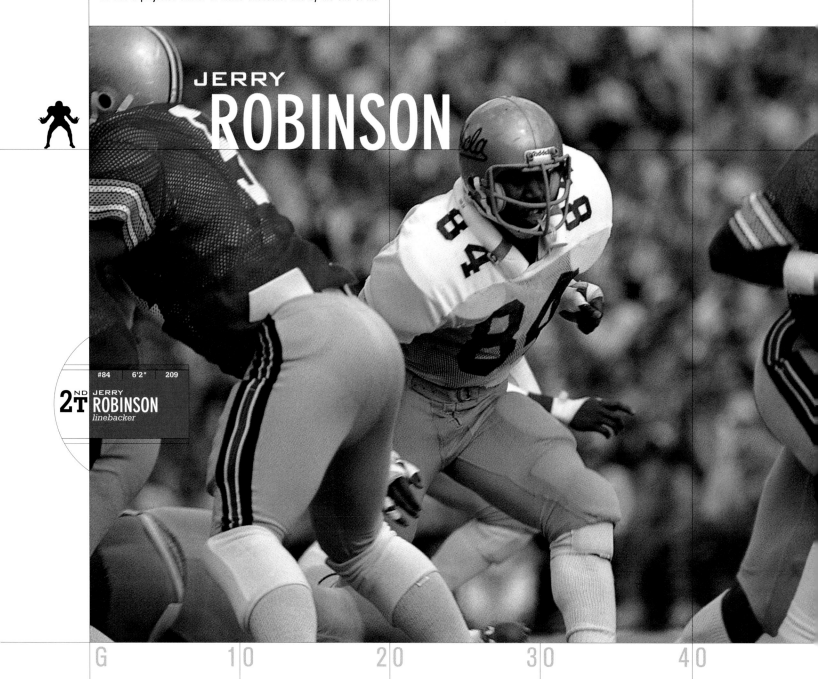

JERRY
ROBINSON

| #84 | 6'2" | 209 |

2ND T JERRY **ROBINSON**
linebacker

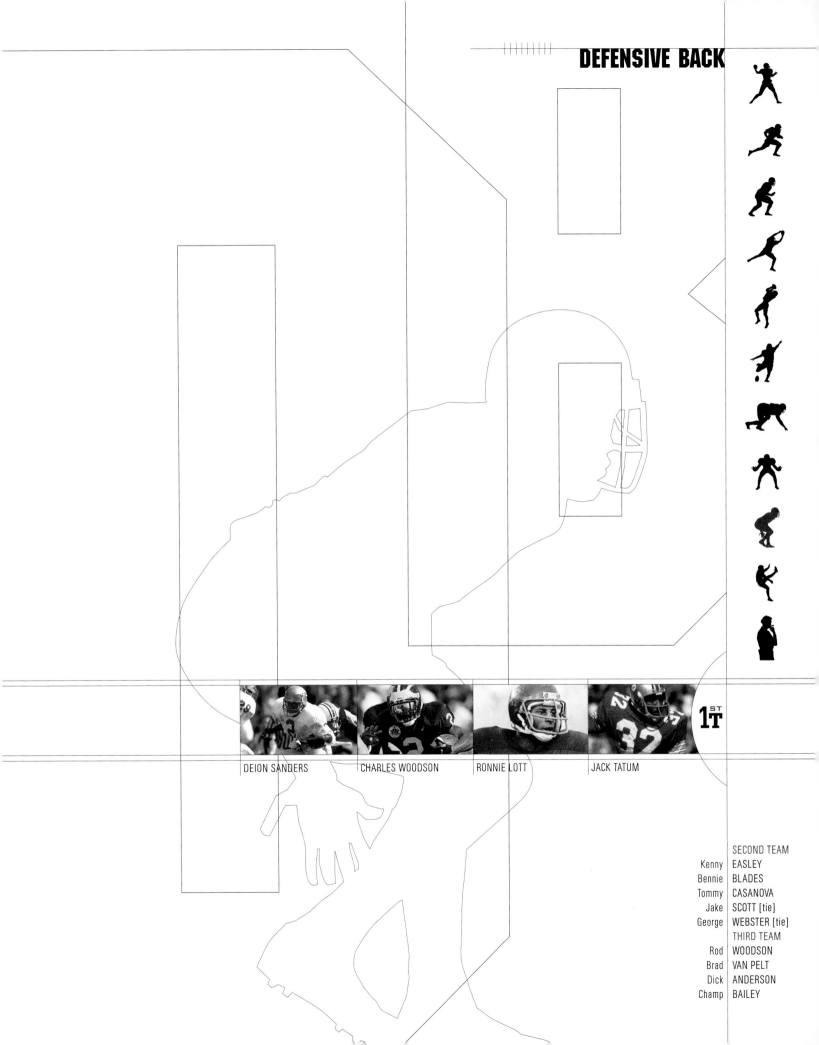

DEFENSIVE BACK

DEION SANDERS CHARLES WOODSON RONNIE LOTT JACK TATUM

1ST

SECOND TEAM
Kenny   EASLEY
Bennie   BLADES
Tommy   CASANOVA
Jake   SCOTT [tie]
George   WEBSTER [tie]
THIRD TEAM
Rod   WOODSON
Brad   VAN PELT
Dick   ANDERSON
Champ   BAILEY

E. MILLS
14

#2 | 6'1" | 195

1ST
1T

DEION
SANDERS
defensive back

Deion Sanders always seemed to know what others could only predict. When coaches looked at Sanders's speed and all-around athletic ability, they saw potential. Sanders, on the other hand, saw greatness — at that moment.

And he had plenty of history on his side by the time he left Florida State. A two-time consensus All-American, Sanders averaged more than 15 yards a punt return as a senior and finished his college career with 17 interceptions, three of those in bowl games. He scored six times off returns and converted four interceptions into touchdowns. But Sanders impacted games to a much greater degree than any baseline statistical analysis might suggest. Confident, fearless and forever mindful of the spotlight, Sanders enjoyed adding to the degree of difficulty on the field and off.

Consider:

○ "He came to his final regular season game against Florida in 1988 in a big strech limo wearing a tuxedo," said Terry Bowden. "If you lose that game, you set yourself up for humiliation. But they won (52-17) and he played great."

○ Sanders once played baseball in a Metro Conference Tournament game, ran to the track to help win a relay — still in his baseball pants — then returned to the diamond to get the game-winning hit in the second game of a doubleheader that won Florida State the 1987-88 Metro Conference All-Sports Trophy.

○ In 1987 Sanders played for a national championship in football — the Seminoles beat Nebraska in the Fiesta Bowl but wound up ranked No. 2 behind unbeaten Miami — and baseball — Florida State finished fifth in the College World Series.

○ In 1988, he ran a leg on the school's 400-meter relay team at the NCAA Track and Field Championships.

○ Sanders once ran a 4.21 40-yard dash at Florida State — in pads.

○ Sanders returned an interception 100 yards for a touchdown against Tulsa in 1985.

○ Sanders arrived at Florida State as a left-handed high school option quarterback. While wide receiver would have been a logical position, Sanders opted for defense. "Anybody can play wide receiver," he told coach Bobby Bowden. "I want to be special."

○ On Sept. 4, 1989, Sanders slugged a home run for the New York Yankees in a game at Seattle. Six days later, and just 5:31 into his first professional football game, Sanders returned a punt 68 yards for a touchdown for the Atlanta Falcons. The only other guy to go from the Yankees outfield to a professional football field was George Halas.

○ "He did things that were outrageous," says Terry Bowden, son of the FSU coach. "But he was the first guy on the practice field and the last guy off it. The guy comes to practice to practice and he comes to games to play. His teammates loved him. You are not talking about a prima donna. That's what makes him special, combining talent with those kinds of work habits."

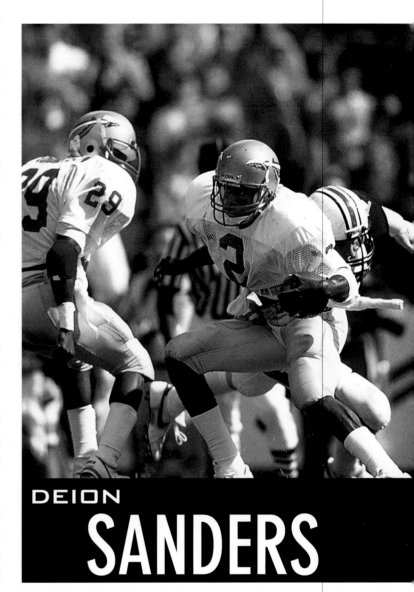

DEION
SANDERS

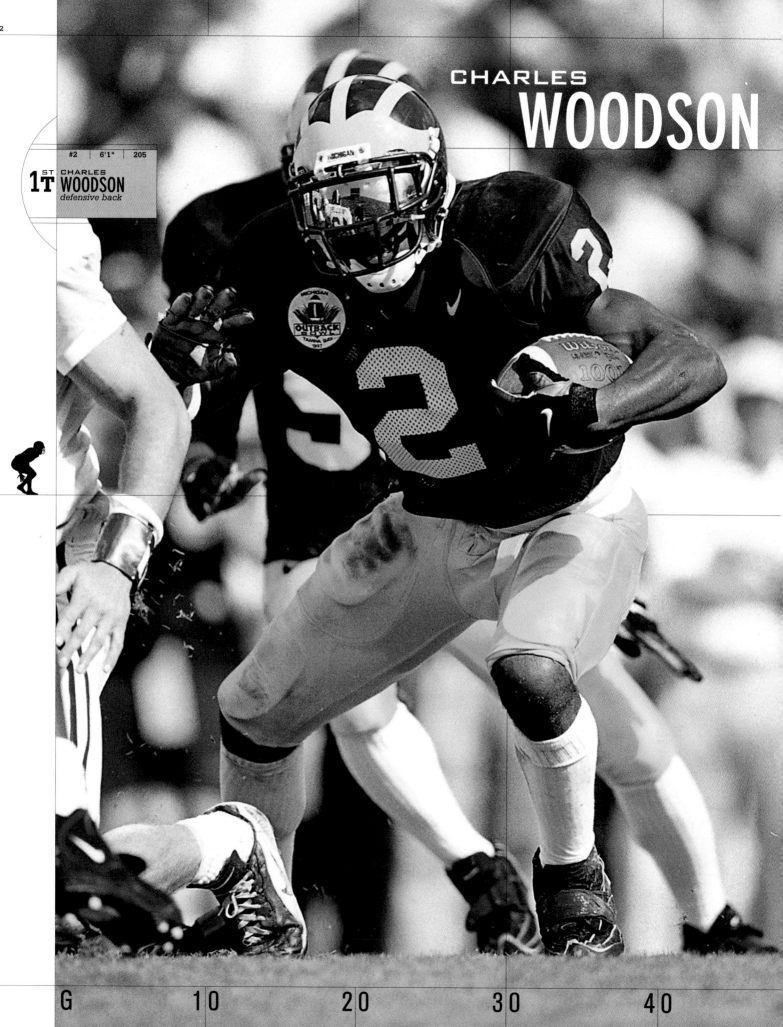

CHARLES
WOODSON

| #2 | 6'1" | 205 |

1st ST CHARLES
WOODSON
defensive back

G   10   20   30   40

Generally, cornerback is no place for the fragile, faint of heart or freshman. Charles Woodson had one of the three, but in his case being a freshman didn't matter. Not even at Michigan.

He started in his second game as a freshman and cemented his place in Michigan lore by shutting down Ohio State's All-America receiver, Terry Glenn, in a Wolverines victory. Of the six passes thrown to Glenn and caught that day, four were by the intended receiver and two by Woodson.

As a sophomore, Woodson moved to wide receiver when he wasn't leading the Michigan defense or returning punts. In the end, his presence proved as disruptive to opposing defenses as offenses. Woodson broke up a Michigan record 15 passes as a sophomore and picked off five more. By the end of his junior season, Woodson was a finalist for the Jim Thorpe Award, given to the nation's top defensive back, and the Biletnikoff Award, which goes to the country's best receiver.

Said Carr, "We believe if you aren't prepared, Charles is going to beat you."

> **"Our defense is simple. Woodson covers one half of the field and the other 10 of us take the other half."**
> **— MARCUS RAY**
> **Michigan strong safety**

But the kind of beating Woodson doled out was tantamount to brainwashing. When he moved into the slot on offense, or split wide on third down, every defender on the field knew Woodson was there. On defense, even coaches with accomplished quarterbacks would adjust their offenses to throw opposite Woodson.

"Our defense is simple," said Michigan strong safety Marcus Ray. "Woodson covers one half of the field and the other 10 of us take the other half."

Even his statistics belied the impact Woodson had on games. He won the Heisman Trophy as a junior, beating out Tennessee's Peyton Manning among others, on the strength of versatility and impact, not numbers. Although opposing teams rarely threw to his side, Woodson knocked down nine passes and intercepted eight in 1997. He returned a school record 44 punts, including a 78-yarder for a touchdown against Ohio State, but averaged less than 10 yards a return. The only two school records Woodson holds are for passes broken up in a season (15) and for a career (30).

But the sum of Woodson's parts appropriately added up to the Heisman Trophy, which was created for purpose of recognizing the nation's best player. Few have earned that designation more completely than Woodson did in 1997.

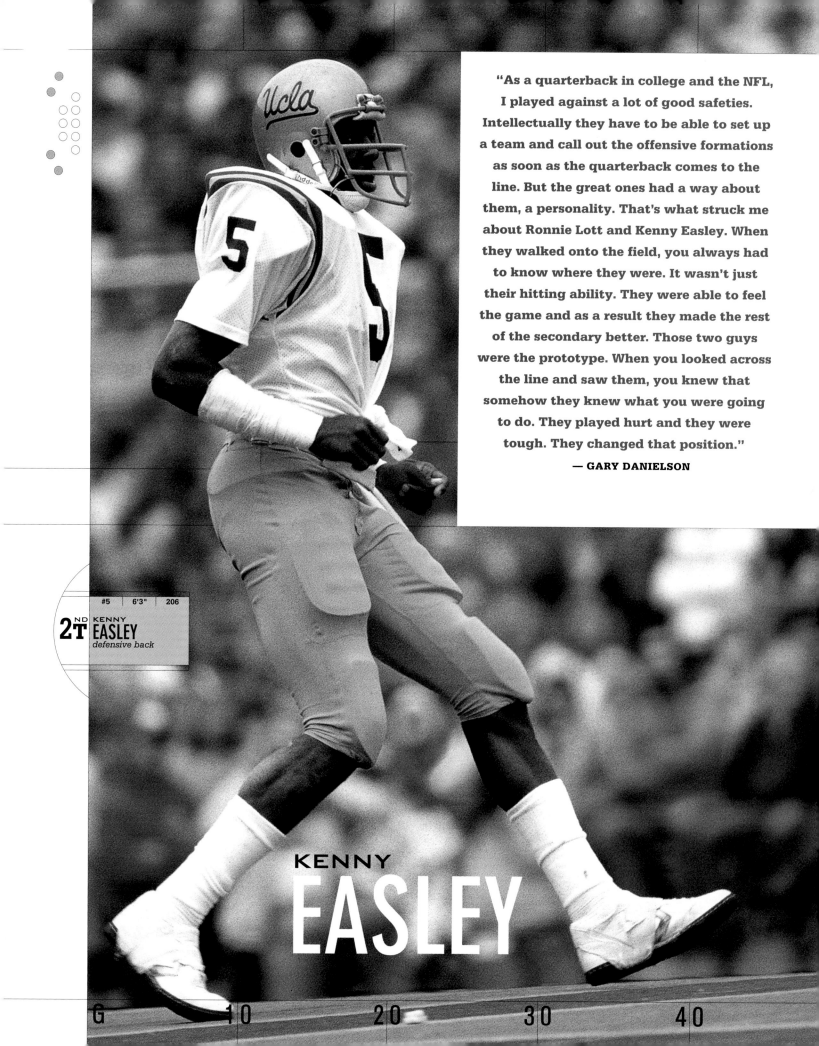

"As a quarterback in college and the NFL, I played against a lot of good safeties. Intellectually they have to be able to set up a team and call out the offensive formations as soon as the quarterback comes to the line. But the great ones had a way about them, a personality. That's what struck me about Ronnie Lott and Kenny Easley. When they walked onto the field, you always had to know where they were. It wasn't just their hitting ability. They were able to feel the game and as a result they made the rest of the secondary better. Those two guys were the prototype. When you looked across the line and saw them, you knew that somehow they knew what you were going to do. They played hurt and they were tough. They changed that position."

— GARY DANIELSON

2ND T | #5 | 6'3" | 206

KENNY
EASLEY
defensive back

KENNY
EASLEY

G   10   20   30   40

They spent most of their college careers lost in the shadows of one another, Ronnie Lott in the shade of a three-time consensus All-American and Kenny Easley in the specter of a USC team that went 28 games without a loss. Easley was the more naturally gifted and a great player from the moment he stepped onto the UCLA campus. He started the second game of his freshman season and was a consensus All-American by the end of his sophomore year. He also dabbled in basketball and as a sophomore once scored 25 points with 17 rebounds in a junior varsity game. Easley, said a Los Angeles writer, was "as much a free spirit as a free safety."

Across town, Lott worked to find his place in the rumble of one of the school's greatest runs. From midway through the 1978 season until late in the 1980 campaign, USC went 28 games without a loss. Meanwhile, Lott became a starter as a sophomore and proved to be a solid contributor. No one called him a free spirit. Between his junior and senior years, Lott described his summer to a local newspaper: "I'd work in a steel factory from seven to three, then I'd come back to USC and lift weights for a couple hours, and then attend classes in the evening. But it was all worth it. I try never to do things I later will regret."

Lott's Trojans beat UCLA three straight until 1980 when the Bruins returned the favor. But by the time Easley celebrated his first victory over USC, Lott had emerged from the shadows.

Both players were consensus All-Americans in 1980 and first round draft picks in 1981, Easley the No. 4 choice of Seattle and Lott the No. 8 selection by San Francisco. Lott became an All-Pro his first season, Easley in his second. Together they made 15 Pro Bowls in their first 17 seasons combined.

RONNIE

LOTT

| #42 | 6'0" | 203 |

RONNIE
LOTT 1ST
defensive back

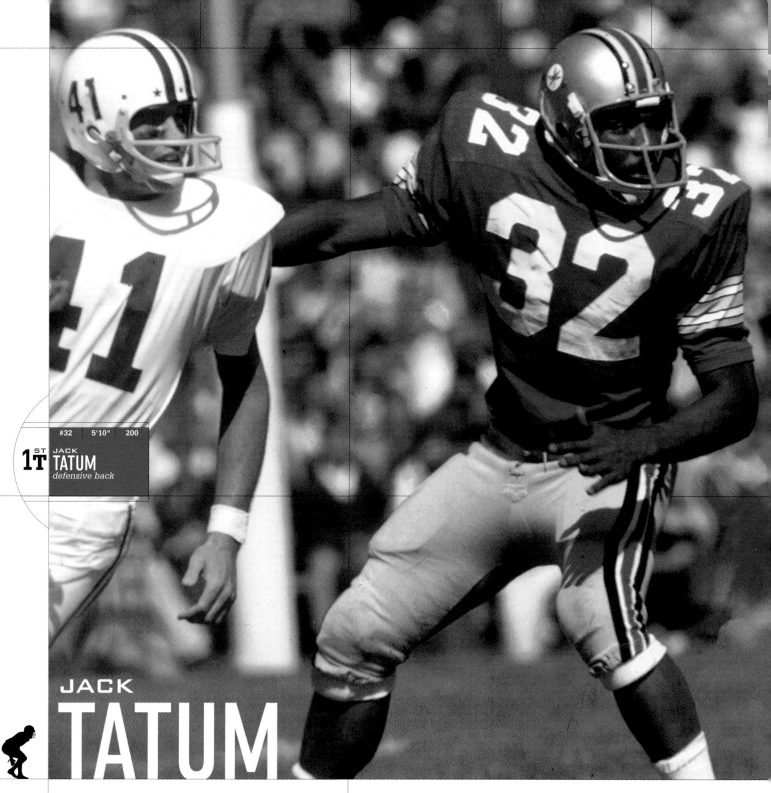

#32 | 5'10" | 200

1ST T JACK
TATUM
defensive back

JACK
TATUM

Ohio State coach Woody Hayes and one of his assistants, Lou Holtz, knew what they had in freshman running back Jack Tatum: An All-America defensive back.

Hayes moved Tatum across the line in the spring of his freshman season. By the fall of 1968, Tatum had won a starting spot and become one of the most intimidating defensive players in the country.

When Tatum shut down Leroy Keyes — Purdue's All-American running back — from the defensive backfield in 1968, the Associated Press named Tatum Back of the Week and Lineman of the Week. Said Holtz: "He's the greatest athlete I've ever coached. If he's not an All-American, there never was one."

Tatum was a two-time All-American and generally was considered the best defensive player at any position as a senior. Ohio State wasn't bad either, going 27-2 during Tatum's three-year roam of the Buckeyes defensive backfield.

"BARBARIC.

He played in an era in the Big Ten when no one passed much so he was basically a linebacker playing in the secondary. And Jack could change the tempo of a game with one of his hits. He had great timing on his hits, which is a skill in its own right. When you think of hitting in college, you think of Jack Tatum. Darryl Stingley and me were teammates at Purdue when I was a freshman. He was the greatest athlete I ever played with, college or pro. He could do everything. But Darryl and Jack always had it out for one another. Darryl would try to block him and Jack would take issue with that. Most other receivers in the Big Ten at that time were intimidated by Jack. But Darryl always went after him. He played slot receiver for us and when we played Ohio State, Jack was always lined up against him. Darryl would never back down and he never gave an inch. Who would have thought that could end up costing him his way of life?"

— GARY DANIELSON
when asked to describe Jack Tatum

Few players ever had a more fitting nickname than Bennie "Blaze" Blades.

The University of Miami defensive back had world class speed and Olympic aspirations by the time he left high school. Blades was so fast in fact, that he was invited to the 1984 Olympic trials in the 400 meters. As a high school senior, he had the fastest 400 meter time in the nation (46.5). When he dabbled in the sport at Miami, Blades teamed with his brother, Brian, and two other Miami football players to set the school record in the 400 meter relay (40.38). As a freshman, Blades ran a 33.67 300 meters indoors, the fastest in a decade, and turned a 10.19 100 meters. This as a full-time football player at a time when Jimmy Johnson had the Hurricanes at or near the top of the polls every year.

All of which made for some interesting practices with Brian one of the team's starting receivers.

"The only way to completely avoid him was to throw deep," said Johnson. "His great speed allowed him to get into position, his instincts and awareness let him anticipate the throw and his athletic ability allowed him to make the interception."

| #36 | 6'1" | 221 |

BENNIE
BLADES 2RDT
defensive back

BENNIE
BLADES

DICK
ANDERSON

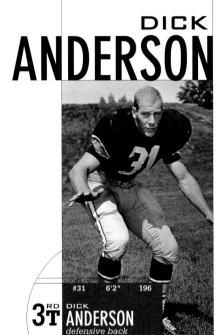

The infamous "No Name Defense" that powered the Miami Dolphins to the only unbeaten season in NFL history can trace half of its defensive backfield to the 1967 college football season.

Colorado's Dick Anderson and Georgia's Jake Scott, All-American defensive backs in a time that overwhelmingly favored the running game, roamed college backfields as they would the pros.'

Anderson left Colorado as the school's career leader with 14 interceptions, an impressive number for the era and the same number Deion Sanders had during the regular season at Florida State in the pass-happy game of the 1990s. Scott, a consensus All-American in 1968, had 16 career interceptions, including 10 as a junior.

DICK ANDERSON

14

INTERCEPTIONS

| #31 | 6'2" | 196 |

3RD
DICK
ANDERSON
defensive back

ROD
WOODSON

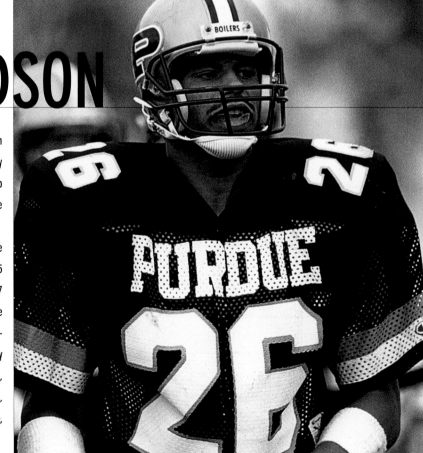

In the relative obscurity of West Lafayette, Indiana, Rod Woodson put together a four-year career that stands with any in the history of college football — on the field or off. And if he had any help at Purdue in those years, Woodson's All-Pro NFL career might have been expected.

Indeed, Woodson's last college game might be the best example of greatness operating in shadows of a poor team. In a dramatic 17-15 victory over in-state rival Indiana, Woodson was on the field for 137 plays, or more than 90 percent of the entire game. He made his college debut at running back that day and rushed for 93 yards, a team season-high, on 15 carries for a 6.2 yards per carry average. He caught three passes for 67 yards, had 10 tackles from his cornerback position, knocked down one pass, caused one fumble,

| #26 | 6'0" | 200 |

3RD
ROD
WOODSON
defensive back

Scott was so good in fact, that he skipped his senior year and played a season for the British Columbia Lions in the Canadian Football League before joining the Dolphins and Anderson in 1970.

Exceptionally hard hitters and rarely out of position, Anderson and Scott made up for any physical deficiencies with intellect.

"Jake Scott was an instinctive player," said Bob Griese, former Miami Dolphins All-Pro quarterback. "He had a knack for the ball. He understood tendencies like no one else. Dick Anderson was the same way. He was a long-legged guy and a good hitter. They both would gamble some if they had a hunch the ball was going somewhere specific. It made for some good practices. I was always trying to look them off while they were trying to pick me off."

JAKE SCOTT

16

INTERCEPTIONS

JAKE **SCOTT**

| #44 | 6'0" | 188 |

JAKE **SCOTT** 2ND T
defensive back

"I'll always wonder what I could have done in track, but I loved football and that's what I had to give up."

— ROD WOODSON

returned three punts for 30 yards and two kickoffs for 46 yards.

Off the field, Woodson was a three-time Big Ten champion in the hurtles. Running only the indoor season because of spring football commitments, Woodson set the Big Ten record (7.22 seconds) as a freshman, finished second as a sophomore in the NCAA Indoor Track and Field Championships and was named an All-American. His only outdoor attempts came in his freshman and senior seasons and both were spectacular.

Woodson had the third best time in the world for juniors (19 years old and under) and qualified for the 1984 Olympic Trials. As a senior, Woodson was named Athlete of the Meet in the Big Ten Indoor Championships by winning the 55-meter dash, finishing third in the 300-meters and winning the 55-meter hurdles.

Outdoors, Woodson broke Willie Gault's record in the 60-yard high hurdles (7.15) and qualified for the NCAA Outdoor Track and Field

Championships by running the 60-yard dash in 6.22 seconds, all around NFL scouting combine workouts.

"Even as a football player, he could have been number one or two in the world, a possible Olympic gold medal winner, if he was willing to pay the price and run during the outdoor season and in the summer programs," said Woodson's track coach, Mike Poehlein. "Some guys can coach 30 years and not coach that kind of talent. He's a very, very awesome natural talent."

"I'll always wonder what I could have done in track," says Woodson, "but I loved football and that's what I had to give up."

BRAD

VAN PELT

#10	6'5"	221

3RD**T** **BRAD**
VAN PELT
defensive back

In 1959 Duffy Daugherty created a defensive position he called "Rover," which called for a unique search and destroy mercenary who could attack from virtually anywhere on the field.

In most cases, the player would look like a defensive back. But he would have to hit like a linebacker, run like a safety and be strong enough to move up to the defensive line. He also had to be smart, unusually gifted athletically and instinctive.

What Daugherty didn't know in 1959 was that he created the perfect position for two players, first George Webster and then Brad Van Pelt, both of whom would transform the Rover skill set into All-Pro careers as linebackers in the NFL.

Of the two, Webster might have been the prototype. At 6-feet-4-inches and 218 pounds, he hit as hard and as often as any defensive player in the country in 1965 and 1966. And he did it with style. Though he was listed as a defensive back, Webster wore No. 90 and had a wide receiver's double-bar face mask with a horseshoe hook that came down over the helmet's bridge.

"That face mask was my trademark," said Webster. "Never thought about wearing anything else. It said I was a rugged dude. I liked that."

Webster didn't have to say anything to make that point and on the field rarely did. He was a defensive end as a sophomore and didn't move to Rover until his junior season.

It didn't matter. Like Van Pelt, Webster was born to play the position as evidenced by back-to-back consensus All-America seasons.

Still, In terms of all-around athletic ability, Van Pelt might have been even more gifted than Webster. He earned seven letters at Michigan State, three in football and two each in baseball and basketball. Like Webster, Van Pelt brought an unusual combination of speed and size — 6-feet-5-inches, 221 pounds — to the defensive backfield.

Indeed, Daugherty called Van Pelt "the best defensive player to attend Michigan State since George Webster."

He scored 16 points and had seven rebounds in a game against Iowa as a freshman for the Spartans basketball team. As a junior on the Michigan State baseball team, Van Pelt struck out 14 in a 1-0, 7-inning shutout against Illinois.

In 1972, he was a second team All-Big Ten pitcher in the spring and a consensus All-American defensive back in the fall.

Given Daugherty's invention and the two unique greats it inspired, it seems only fitting that Daugherty left Michigan State the same year Van Pelt headed to the NFL.

G   10   20   30   40

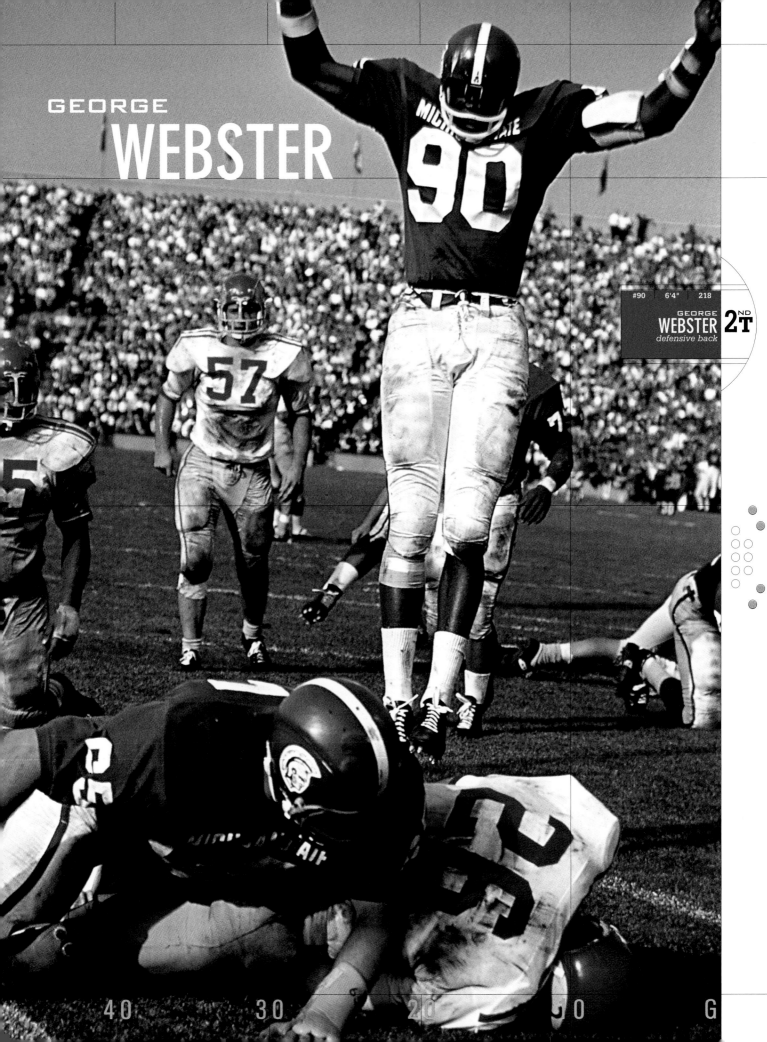

GEORGE
WEBSTER

#90 | 6'4" | 218

GEORGE
WEBSTER 2ND T
defensive back

40 30 20 10 G

#37 6'2" 202

2ND T TOMMY CASANOVA
defensive back

TOMMY
CASANOVA

If former LSU great Tommy Casanova was the first great multi-tasking defensive back in the two-platoon system, then Georgia's Champ Bailey is the latest.

In between, Deion Sanders, Rod Woodson and Charles Woodson improved upon Casanova's model until Bailey took it even a step further.

Casanova was an All-American cornerback who also returned punts and dabbled on offense. A three-time First Team All-Southeastern Conference selection, Casanova probably had enough ability to play both ways fulltime. As it was, he returned punts of 61 and 73 yards for touchdowns in one game against Mississippi and was considered a natural at tailback.

"He dominated games in college because of his coverage skills and intelligence back there," said Jim Lampley. "He made big plays game in, game out."

Bailey had the potential to dominate either side of the ball in any game. In his senior year at Georgia, Bailey won the Bronko Nagurski Award as college football's top defensive player and ranked among the nation's best wide receivers with three 100-yard games and more than 750 yards overall.

To put Bailey's two-way accomplishments into perspective, consider what Michigan's Charles Woodson did to win the 1997 Heisman. Though Woodson intercepted eight passes to Bailey's three and was a more feared and accomplished punt returner, the comparison stops there. Compared to Woodson's Heisman season, Bailey had more total plays, more than four times the number of receptions, more total tackles and more rushing attempts and yards in 1998.

As if he didn't do enough on the field, Bailey also became one of greatest long jumpers in school history. He jumped a school indoor record 25-10 3/4 to finish third in the SEC Indoor Track & Field Championships and finished second in the SEC Outdoor Championships. Bailey, just 6-1, also high jumped 6-8 3/4 for the Bulldogs as a freshman.

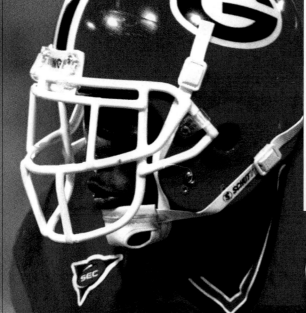

CHAMP
BAILEY

#4 6'1" 184

3RD T CHAMP BAILEY
defensive back

G 10 20 30 40

PUNTER

1STT

REGGIE ROBY

SECOND TEAM
Ray GUY
THIRD TEAM
Tom TUPA

"He has the strongest leg I've ever seen.
He's liable to kick one 80 yards, but it's also liable to go over the press box."

— HAYDEN FRY

Iowa coach Hayden Fry knew what he had in punter Reggie Roby long before Roby became one of the all-time best — college or professional. But he also knew Roby needed some guidance. "He has the strongest leg I've ever seen," said Fry of his freshman kicker. "He's liable to kick one 80 yards, but it's also liable to go over the press box."

Roby had averaged an impressive 43.7 yards per punt as a freshman but dropped off to 40.6 as a sophomore. Though he had thick, 28-inch thighs and near perfect mechanics, Roby lacked discipline. Fry wanted Roby to kick the ball into the corners and to sacrifice distance for height to allow coverage time to make a play. Roby preferred booming the ball straight down the field.

"I had such a bad sophomore year, Fry said if I was going to get noticed by the pros, I was going to have to boost my average," says Roby. "I did a lot of running, kicking and lifting that summer."

Fry did a little bit of lifting, too. He decided to platoon Roby with Tom Nichol, who was brought into the game for punts inside the opponent's 40-yard line. The net effect was an NCAA record 49.8 average that broke a record that had stood for 25 years. And it wasn't a fluke. Roby, doing virtually all the punting his senior season, averaged 48.1 yards a punt.

Roby rarely concentrated on the mechanics of his art. But anyone who saw him connect with a football never could forget the speed of his right leg slamming into the ball and following through so completely that Roby looked like he was doing the splits standing up.

"It's just like kicking those playground balls," he says. "I just drop the ball and kick it. Mostly, it's just flexibility and I have got a lot of that."

REGGIE ROBY

#7	6'2"	248

1ST
REGGIE ROBY
punter

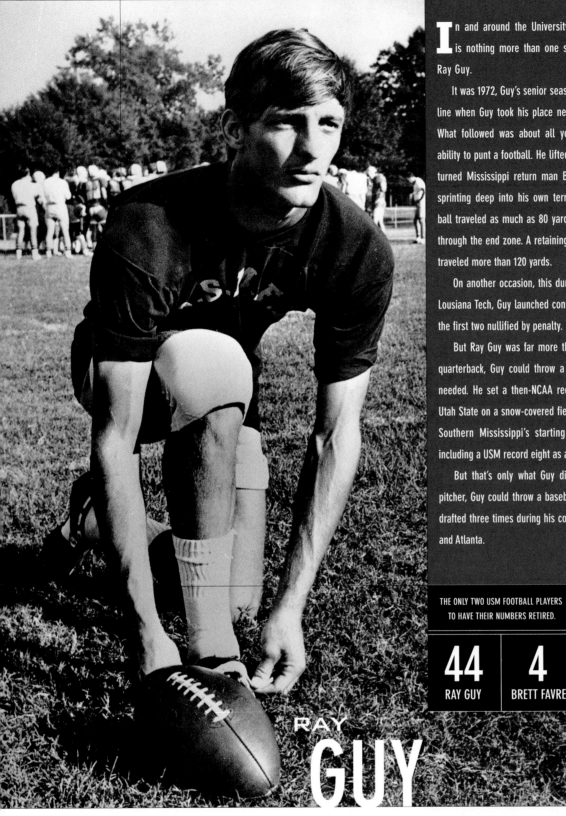

In and around the University of Southern Mississippi "The Kick" is nothing more than one story in a legion of them that define Ray Guy.

It was 1972, Guy's senior season. The ball rested on the USM 7-yard line when Guy took his place nearly five yards deep in the end zone. What followed was about all you needed to know about Ray Guy's ability to punt a football. He lifted a booming kick high into the sky that turned Mississippi return man Bill Malouf 180 degrees and had him sprinting deep into his own territory. Depending on the account, the ball traveled as much as 80 yards in the air before bouncing into and through the end zone. A retaining wall finally stopped the ball that had traveled more than 120 yards.

On another occasion, this during a 1971 homecoming game against Lousiana Tech, Guy launched consecutive punts of 67, 72 and 77 yards, the first two nullified by penalty.

But Ray Guy was far more than a punter. Though he never played quarterback, Guy could throw a football 70 yards and was on call if needed. He set a then-NCAA record with a 61-yard field goal against Utah State on a snow-covered field in Logan, Utah in 1972. He also was Southern Mississippi's starting safety, and intercepted 18 passes, including a USM record eight as a senior.

But that's only what Guy did on the football field. As a college pitcher, Guy could throw a baseball nearly 100 miles per hour. He was drafted three times during his college career by Cincinnati, Kansas City and Atlanta.

THE ONLY TWO USM FOOTBALL PLAYERS TO HAVE THEIR NUMBERS RETIRED.

44	**4**
RAY GUY	BRETT FAVRE

#44	6'3"	195

RAY GUY **2ND**
punter

RAY
GUY

"I saw Guy boom a 93-yard punt that actually traveled 115 yards. I saw him kick a 61-yard field goal in a snowstorm. I saw him, playing safety, hit an opponent so hard they had to stop the game to pick the guy's teeth out of the grass. He was an all-state basketball player in high school. He dabbled in baseball at USM and once threw a no-hitter six weeks after knee surgery. Scouts routinely clocked his fastball at nearly 100 miles per hour." — RICK CLEVELAND, *Jackson (MS) Clarion Ledger*

40 30 20 10 G

College football recruiters had seen enough of Todd Sauerbrun's right leg in high school that most of them didn't even care whether or not he could punt the ball too. Sauerbrun drilled a New York state high school record 62-yard field goal at Ward Melville High on Long Island and hit the crossbar on a 75-yard attempt.

But when Sauerbrun decided on West Virginia, he also decided he would become the team's punter. Despite adding up to 300 punts a day to his kicking practices, Sauerbrun didn't launch his first college punt until the final game of the 1991 season against Syracuse.

"We knew he could punt, too," says West Virginia's special teams coach at the time, Dave McMichael. "We saw him nailing the ball in practice every day. Then, against Syracuse, the kid comes in and nearly kicks the ball off the freakin' roof at the Carrier Dome."

For Sauerbrun, the ceiling disappeared after that. As a senior, 54 of his 67 kickoffs went into or out of the end zone for touchbacks.

> "I've never seen somebody kick the ball as far as he (did). When we played against him, we had our guy 50 yards behind the line of scrimmage and it still went way over his head."
>
> —TOMMIE FRAZIER,
> former Nebraska quarterback

DEFINING GAME

WEST VIRGINIA vs. NEBRASKA	**1994**	CONSECUTIVE PUNTS

90 YRDS	**71** YRDS	**64** YRDS	**54** YRDS	**54** YRDS	**53** YRDS	**52** YRDS	**52** YRDS	**51** YRDS

SINGLE SEASON **UWA RECORD**		CAREER **NCAA RECORD**
32 NUMBER OF PUNTS MORE THAN 50 YARDS	**48.4** AVERAGE YARDS PER PUNT	**46.3** AVERAGE YARDS PER PUNT

HONORABLE MENTION

#16	185	6'0"

TODD
SAUERBRUN
punter

TODD **SAUERBRUN**

3**RD** T

TOM
TUPA
punter

#19	6'4"	220

Tom Tupa deserved better when he took over as Ohio State's starting quarterback prior to the 1987 season. As the team's punter since his freshman year, Tupa was All-Big Ten as a sophomore and junior. He was even better as a senior averaging 47 yards and becoming the consensus All-America punter.

But before Tupa could turn a similar trick at quarterback his two top receivers — Cris Carter and Nate Harris — were ruled ineligible. Tupa still managed to throw for 1,786 yards and he completed more than 55 percent of his passes in 1987.

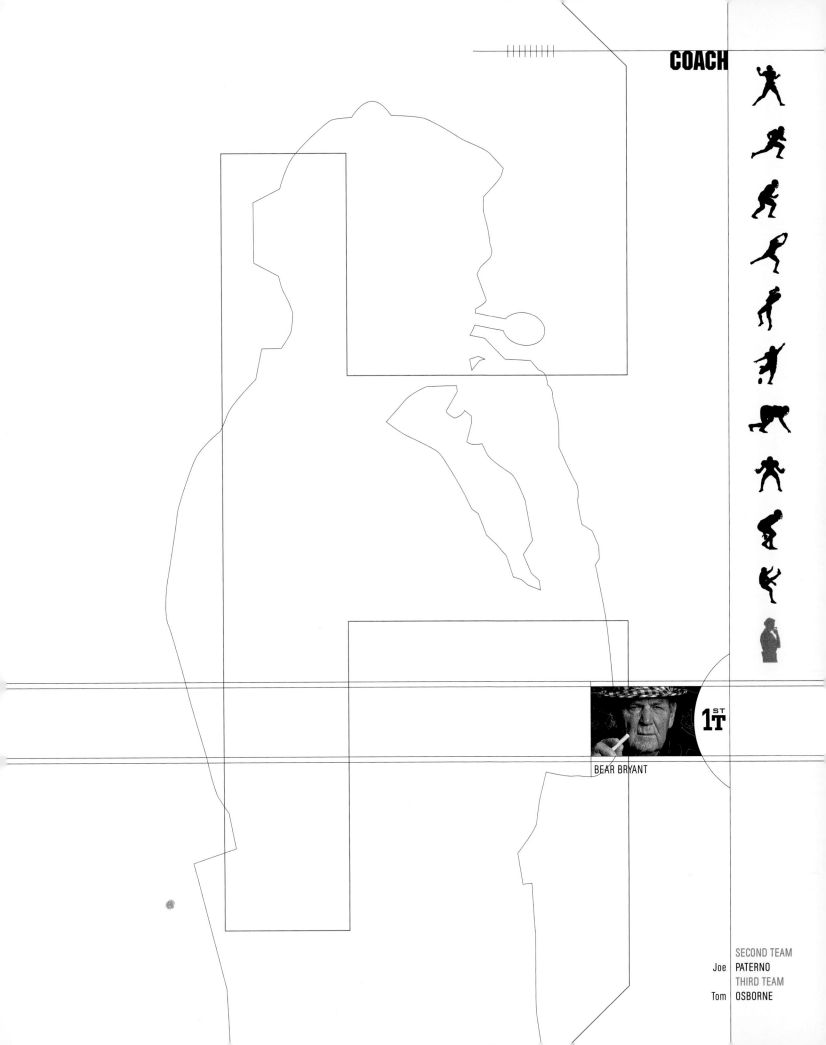

COACH

BEAR BRYANT

1ST T

SECOND TEAM
Joe PATERNO
THIRD TEAM
Tom OSBORNE

Just about anyone who did anything around college football the last half of the 20th century had a Bear Bryant story.

And they're still telling 'em.

More than 16 years after his death in 1983, two new books — one in 1999 and another in 2000 — were published about Bryant and the way he coached football. One detailed the brutality of Bryant's preseason camp at Texas A&M and the other detailed 323 of Bryant's quotes, one of which became the title: "I Ain't Never Been Nothing But a Winner."

From 1933 to 1939, Bryant was a player and then assistant coach on Alabama teams that went a combined 52-8-5. Bryant left for Vanderbilt in 1940 and eventually built the program at Kentucky and turned around Texas A&M. But it was at Alabama that Bryant became an icon. His teams won six national champions and 13 Southeastern Conference titles in 25 years. He never had a losing season at Alabama and three times his teams went undefeated.

"Bear Bryant was someone who had a massive ego, someone who thought football was the most important thing to the world," said Jim Lampley. "He wanted you to cater to his majesty in a gentle way. He saw and knew everything about what went on on the field. I've never

PAUL BRYANT

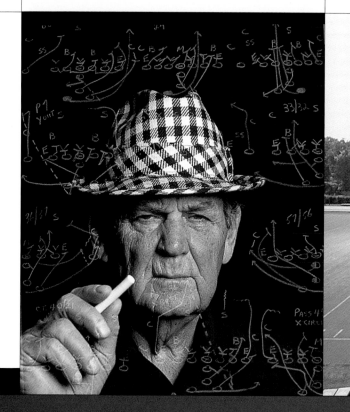

HOW A MAN BECAME A **BEAR**

By 1965, Paul "Bear" Bryant had long become a legend in Alabama. His team had won two straight national championships and would go undefeated in 1966. Talk of Bryant running for governor could be heard in just about every corner of the state.

Prior to the 1966 season, Bryant agreed to a wide ranging and lengthy autobiographical first-person series for *Sports Illustrated*. In the first installment of the five-part series, Bryant detailed the origin of his nickname. Though he had no doubt told the story before, it was the first time he provided all the details in print.

"I was always a big kid, and I remember one summer we walked in from the farm to Mr. Smith's picture theater in Fordyce. Drucilla Smith, who was a good-looking little gal, was standing by this poster that showed a picture of a bear and a guy offering a dollar a minute to anyone who would wrestle that bear. Mr. Smith was out front, and he was all excited because the man that was going to do the wrestling hadn't showed up.

"Somebody said to me, 'Why don't you go in there?' and I sorta glanced at Drucilla Smith and said, 'For a dollar a minute I'd do anything.' You know, big-dogging it. This was in summer, because I was chopping cotton for 50 cents a day at the time and I felt I'd wrestle King Kong for a dollar a minute.

seen anything like it. I remember I would go to practice with him and he would take me up to that tower. I would think he was just there listening to me and thinking about nothing else. Then, we would come down and he would tell an assistant, 'Hey, you need to do this.' And he would tell another assistant, 'Hey, you need to do that. I saw that.' It was amazing how much he saw and took in."

"All-around in terms of strategy, motivation and charisma, Bear had it," said Bill Flemming. "Through it all, Bear had no arrogance."

When Alabama played USC, the biggest Hollywood stars at the time, including his friend John Wayne, could be found around Bryant.

Some of them, Wayne included, would fly into Tuscaloosa for Alabama games. Late in his career, even opposing players sought out Bryant.

"We played Alabama up at our place (Penn State) one year and lost," said Todd Blackledge. "It was a signature win for Bear Bryant and even though we lost I remember shaking his hand after the game. We had lost and I was disappointed, but at the same time I was honored that I got to say hello to him. I knew after that game why he was recognized as one of the all-time greats. Now I played for one of the all-time greats in Joe Paterno, but I knew I had to make sure to say hello to Bear Bryant."

PAUL "BEAR"
BRYANT **1**ST
coach

"The theater was a little old thin room, and the seats went downhill. Well, they brought this bear out and it was the scrawniest thing my friends had seen, but to me it looked 30 feet tall. I must have wanted that money real bad. Anyway, I knew one thing about wrestling. I knew if you got hold of somebody and kept your body away from him, he'd have a hard time breaking your hold. That was what I was going to do. Keep that bear from rolling over on me.

"Well, the man made his speech about this big, ferocious thing and introduced me, and about the time the bear reared up I charged him and in a second had him down and there we lay. Finally the man began pushing at me, telling me to let him up, but I wasn't ready to do that because time was flying by. He

wanted action. But I just lay there.

"Finally the bear worked loose, and I got him again, and he got loose again, and now he was getting pretty mad, and when I looked up his muzzle was off. I felt this burning on the back of my neck, and when I reached to touch it I got a hand full of blood. When I saw that, I jumped off that stage and nearly killed myself getting behind those seats to hide.

"After a while I went around to get my money, but the man with the bear had flown the coop. All I got out of the whole thing was a nickname."

A half century ago 23-year-old Joe Paterno arrived at Penn State for an assistant coaching job.

He's still there.

The 2000 college football season marked Paterno's 50th season in essentially the same job at the same place. He took over the head coaching duties in 1966 and has never experienced a losing season. Under Paterno, the Nittany Lions have won two national championships and nearly 80 percent of their games.

"My first year as head coach, we lost to four good football teams (Michigan State, Georgia Tech, UCLA, Syracuse)," said Paterno. "I was having my doubts and then we opened up with Navy my second year and we lost (23-22). We were terrible. I came home and made some changes. The next week we beat Miami down there, 17-8 and from there on in we had a lot of luck and success. After we beat Miami, I felt that, maybe, I knew a little bit about the game."

Since then, nearly everyone has learned a little about the game

JOE
PATERNO

from Paterno. A man of character and integrity, Paterno is the only college football coach ever named Sportsman of the Year by *Sports Illustrated*. His teams have one of the highest graduation rates in major college football and Paterno has contributed as much to higher education at Penn State as he has to the football program.

"It's unbelievable how he still has the energy and will to coach," said Frank Broyles. "He deserves the most credit for being able to evolve throughout the decades. For all the experiences he has had and all the athletes he has coached, I rate him the No. 1 statesman in

college football. Bobby Bowden and Joe are the only two who have been able to go through the cycles and keep the same enthusiasm."

Todd Blackledge won the Davey O'Brien Award as the nation's top quarterback in 1982 when he led Penn State to the national championship.

"He has a great passion for what he's doing," said Blackledge. "He loves being a teacher. He realizes that people change. But he's always been flexible whether it was with strategy or dealing with the changing attitudes of players. He had a great vision about what he wanted to do as a coach and he's still doing it. At a time when most guys his age are chilling out on some golf course, Joe is still grinding it

out and loving every minute."

Paterno has had five unbeaten seasons and went into the 2000 season just six victories short of Bear Bryant's Division I record of 323 career wins.

"To understand Joe Paterno you have to understand his background," said Keith Jackson. "What's his background? Well, in Brooklyn where he grew up Vince Lombardi was an assistant coach at his high school. Joe went on to become a pretty fair quarterback at Brown and had just under a 4.0 average as an English literature major. But he loved football and everyone saw this in him. He didn't even have a driver's license when he arrived at Penn Sate. Joe road buses to

2ND T JOE PATERNO coach

G 10 20 30 40

recruit. Now that's passion. Guys like Joe Paterno are extraordinary people as far as I'm concerned. They are the foundation of the whole thing. There is a vibrancy that runs through these people."

"I have been blessed," says Paterno. "I am very thankful that anybody can work 50 years at something he loves. I have never missed a day of practice because of health. I get up in the morning excited. It is hard for me to believe that it has been 50 years."

BOBBY
BOWDEN
coach
HONORABLE MENTION

BOBBY
BOWDEN

College football has produced some great coaches who have in turn produced great seasons, but it's likely none of them ever had a year like Bobby Bowden did in 1999.

Bowden won his second national championship, had his first unbeaten season, beat his son Tommy's Clemson team for his 300th career victory and celebrated his 50th wedding anniversary. He also extended several records and Florida State finished the 1990s with 109 victories, the most ever in any decade in NCAA history.

"He's the same guy now as he was when he was 30," said Terry Bowden. "Other than being wiser, he has not waffled in his philosophical views, his spiritual philosophy or his moral philosophy. He has a very consistent personality. He doesn't get too low with the lows or too high with the highs."

On the football field, lows have always been relative for Bowden. Heading into the 2000 season, Bowden had two losing seasons in 34 years, none since 1976. He has recorded a record 13 straight 10-win seasons and 13 straight top four finishes in the Associated Press poll. He has won more bowls than Bear Bryant and has a higher post-season winning percentage than Joe Paterno.

"To me his greatest strength is that he can change with times," said Terry. "Bobby Bowden has been on the front end of every trend and he's been smart enough not to be on the back end of any of them. He became a head coach in the '50s. And now I sit and watch him relate to young people when he's 70 years old."

40 30 20 10 G

Barry Switzer had skipped the event for years until 1998. That's when the National Football Foundation and College Football Hall of Fame decided it was time for Tom Osborne, Switzer's rival at Nebraska for 16 years, to become a member.

In the 1970s and 1980s, the Oklahoma-Nebraska battles rivaled any in college football history. Switzer's Sooners won 12 of 17 during his tenure, but by the time Osborne retired the score had been evened, 13-13.

"I always enjoyed the games we played, but I always had the horses to compete against Tom," said Switzer upon Osborne's retirement. "I'm sure a lot of other coaches didn't like going up against him. The thing I always enjoyed about playing Tom's teams is that the game always had national consequences. I remember those games, but not because of the success we had. It's because both teams always represented their states well and had a tremendous pride. The games were always competitive but at the end, whether you won or lost, you knew you could walk off the field with your head held up high. A lot of that had to do with Tom."

Steady, consistent, confident and calm, Tom Osborne did the impossible at Nebraska — he followed a legend in Bob Devaney by becoming one himself. In 25 seasons, Osborne's Nebraska teams won 255 games and lost just 49. And they were never more dominant than in Osborne's final seven seasons when Nebraska won six conference championships and three national titles. Over his final five seasons, the Cornhuskers were 60-3.

"Tom Osborne was a tactician of a mold similar to Bud Wilkinson," said Frank Broyles. "Wilkinson was a math genius with a military background. He was into outnumbering or outflanking you. That's what Osborne did with the option."

But it was the way Osborne created and then responded to his success that impressed those in the coaching fraternity.

"I don't know if there has ever been a better representative for college football than Tom Osborne," said Florida State's Bobby Bowden. "And he was a winner. It's hard for me to even think of Nebraska without Tom Osborne."

HONORABLE MENTION

BARRY
SWITZER
coach

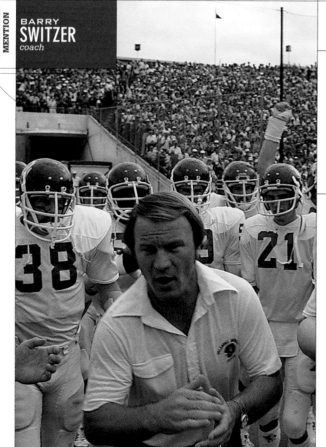

BARRY
SWITZER

He was the fire to Tom Osborne's ice during 16 seasons at Oklahoma and for Barry Switzer the heat was fine.

Like Darrell Royal and some of the other great southern coaches of his era, Switzer was a self-made man who sculpted a brilliant career out of courage, brains, desire and not much else. It was Switzer who talked Oklahoma coach Chuck Fairbanks into switching from the I formation to the Wishbone after Switzer spent hundreds of hours studying the formation on his own. And ultimately it was Switzer who used the Wishbone to make Oklahoma a national power for nearly two decades.

G   10   20   30   40

TOM
OSBORNE

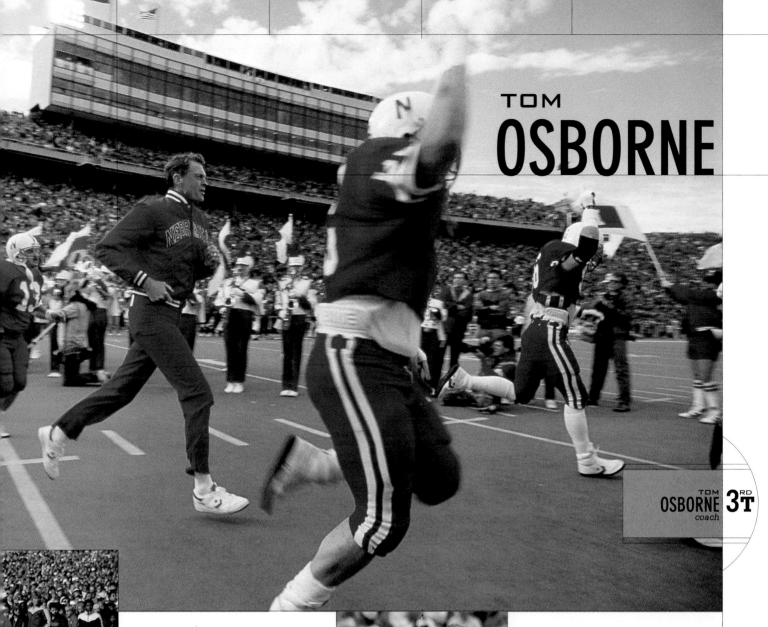

Like Royal and Woody Hayes, Switzer's approach was born from personal experience. In a 1984 interview with local television sports director, Al Eschbach, Switzer painted the background of one of football's great coaching careers.

"If people saw where I grew up they could see my insecurity," said Switzer. "That's what it is, insecurity. I grew up there in the country, a bootlegger's son, paranoid with an inferiority complex. Girls' fathers and mothers wouldn't let them date me because my father was the county bootlegger. Just think about the psychological impact that has on someone.

"When we grew up we were like anyone else in that part of the country. We didn't have running water, we didn't have electricity until I was in the ninth grade. We had no heat other than the butane and two fireplaces. I didn't get a telephone until I got to college.

"So I've tried to take advantage of the opportunities…My upbringing had a lot to do with my drive."

The Sooners won 83.7 percent of their games under Switzer and outscored opponents by an average of 32.1 to 12.8 over 16 years.

"Barry Switzer," said Keith Jackson, "was a great college football coach."

No one sat on the fence with Wayne Woodrow Hayes. Even in Columbus, where Hayes turned Ohio State into a national football power, nearly everyone seemed to have an opinion. And Woody Hayes probably wouldn't have wanted it any other way.

On the field, Hayes ruled with an efficiency, precision and authority that mirrored his military experience. His offense, dubbed "three yards and a cloud of dust," was an extension of everything Hayes admired — strength, power, courage and consistency. His Buckeyes would run the ball all afternoon and dare anyone to stop them. It was man-to-man combat with a winner and a loser on every play. It was fearless football directed by a fearless leader.

But Hayes was far more than a football coach. He could speak in depth about virtually any subject and particularly military history. His beliefs on issues of individual integrity, courage and the meaning of manhood in America were fundamental and thoroughly consistent. He demanded his players graduate, quietly devoted hundreds of hours to visits with veterans and would rise at any hour of the day or night if asked to visit a hospital. Few were more in demand as a public

speaker than Hayes, particularly after he retired in 1979 after 28 seasons. And even fewer, particularly in the coaching fraternity, ever touched as many as deeply as Hayes.

When he died in 1987, it was former president Richard Nixon who stood up at the First Community Church in Columbus and delivered a eulogy.

WOODY
HAYES

HONORABLE MENTION

WOODY
HAYES
coach

G   10   20   30   40

BO
SCHEMBECHLER
coach

BO
SCHEMBECHLER

STUDENT TEACHER

Football brought them together and fate secured the connection. Bo Schembechler was 18 years old the first time he met Woody Hayes. Schembechler was a freshman football player at Miami of Ohio and Hayes was the head coach. Over the next 40 years, Schembechler would play for Hayes, coach under him and then against him in an annual Ohio State–Michigan series Schembechler called the "Ten Year War."

It was the play of Schembechler and the other players at Miami of Ohio who helped Hayes impress the folks at Ohio State. And it was something Hayes not only understood, but something he never forgot. Schembechler earned his master's degree in education at Ohio State in 1952 while working as a graduate assistant coach to Hayes. He later spent five years as a full-time assistant to Hayes before taking the head coaching job at Miami of Ohio in 1963 and then Michigan in 1969.

"No question in my mind he was the greatest coach the (Big Ten) conference has ever had," said Schembechler, whom many consider to own that distinction. "He set the tone. If you violated the rules, sooner or later you had to face the Old Man."

Of the 10 meetings between Schembechler and Hayes, Michigan won five, Ohio State four and they tied once. During that period, Michigan and Ohio State shared six Big Ten titles, won two each outright and split 10 Rose Bowl appearances.

"NO QUESTION IN MY MIND HE WAS THE GREATEST COACH THE (BIG TEN) CONFERENCE HAS EVER HAD. HE SET THE TONE. IF YOU VIOLATED THE RULES, SOONER OR LATER YOU HAD TO FACE THE OLD MAN." — BO SCHEMBECHLER

Earle Bruce, the man who followed Hayes at Ohio State, was a player under Hayes when a severe knee injury appeared to drive him off the team and out of an education. Hayes sent his long-time assistant, Harry Strobel, out onto the campus with a simple directive: Return Earle Bruce to the campus on full scholarship.

In those days, recalled Bruce, "you lost your scholarship at other institutions with an injury. But Woody cared about people at the top and the bottom of the roster — he cared that they got their degrees."

Overall, Hayes ranks sixth on the all-time coaching victories list (238) with Schembechler right behind him in seventh (234). In the Big Ten, Hayes and Schembechler are Nos. 1-2 with 205 and 194 victories respectively.

"I thought that competition — as intense as it was — actually brought us closer together," said Schembechler at a memorial for Hayes inside Ohio Stadium less than a week after his death in 1987. "There's something about when you know you are competing against the best."

DARRELL
ROYAL

One of the transforming eras in college football ended on a December night in 1976 in Austin, Texas.

Darrell Royal walked across the field and embraced Arkansas coaching legend Frank Broyles after a 29-12 Longhorns' victory.

Royal, the Texas icon, and Broyles, who cut a similar figure at Arkansas, walked off the field and announced their retirements, each leaving fingerprints all over the history of the sport.

Given his path, Royal's affection for country-western music seems appropriate. But not even a country song could capture the winding road and twisted circumstances that conspired to deposit Royal at the University of Texas in 1956 at the age of 32.

Like others of his generation, Royal lived a lifetime by his 30th birthday. When he was 12, his family left Oklahoma and the dust bowl to pick fruit in California. A year later Royal grabbed his baseball glove and headed back home to Oklahoma to live with his grandmother.

Weighing not much more than 150 pounds, Royal worked his way onto the University of Oklahoma football team after high school. He still holds the Sooners' career interceptions mark. On offense, Royal made some All-America teams as a quarterback in 1949 and led Oklahoma to 11 straight victories.

"I remember my first year at Oklahoma," said Royal, "we started working out in the middle of what had to be the hottest summer ever. It was right after the war, all the boys were returning from the service.

"They must have run 200 candidates through that camp. I didn't care if they ran a thousand through. A lot of them couldn't stand the heat, literally. I knew I could defeat the majority of them just by staying."

By the mid 1950s, that kind of passion and toughness defined Royal, if not his teams. Paul "Bear" Bryant and Royal had become such close friends that Bryant, coaching bitter rival Texas A&M at the time, recommended Royal for the head job at Texas. Royal had coached 30 games winning 17.

But in 20 years at Texas, Royal's teams won 11 Southwestern Conference titles, three national championships (two consensus) and once ran off 30 straight victories. But it was the way Royal handled himself that ultimately made him as famous in Texas as his friend, President Lyndon Johnson.

"Darrell Royal was almost embarrassed that he was the star of the state of Texas," says Jim Lampley. "When you went to dinner with him, normally gathered around would be a crowd of two country singers, a business man, a lawyer and a professor. You always talked about things other than football. He took a great interest in what others were doing."

And he never forgot them. After Texas beat Bryant's Alabama team in the 1973 Cotton Bowl, Royal helped Bryant install the Wishbone offense at Alabama.

"One reason I like to be around Country and Western entertainers," Royal said in a 1973 interview, "is that they don't give a damn about your rank and smell."

In Texas, very few rank with Darrell Royal.

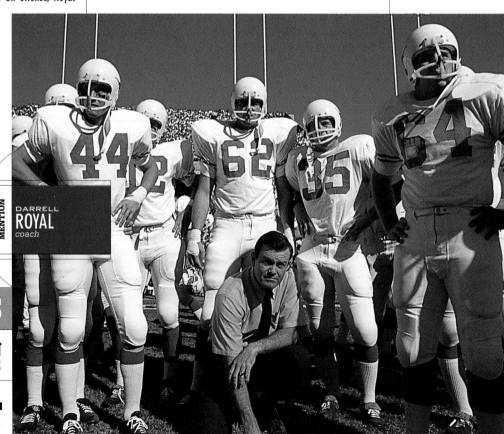

HONORABLE MENTION

DARRELL
ROYAL
coach

IN 20 YEARS

11 SOUTHWESTERN CONFERENCE TITLES

3 NATIONAL CHAMPIONSHIPS

G   10   20   30   40